Righteous by promise

NEW STUDIES IN BIBLICAL THEOLOGY 45

Series editor: D. A. Carson

Righteous by promise

A BIBLICAL THEOLOGY
OF CIRCUMCISION

Karl Deenick

APOLLOS

INTERVARSITY PRESS
DOWNERS GROVE, ILLINOIS 60515

APOLLOS
(an imprint of Inter-Varsity Press, England)
36 Causton Street, London SW1P 4ST, England
Website: www.ivpbooks.com
Email: ivp@ivpbooks.com

InterVarsity Press, USA
P.O. Box 1400, Downers Grove
IL 60515, USA
Website: www.ivpress.com
Email: email@ivpress.com

Inter-Varsity Press, England, publishes Christian books that are true to the Bible and that communicate the gospel, develop discipleship and strengthen the church for its mission in the world.

IVP originated within the Inter-Varsity Fellowship, now the Universities and Colleges Christian Fellowship, a student movement connecting Christian Unions in universities and colleges throughout Great Britain, and a member movement of the International Fellowship of Evangelical Students. That historic association is maintained, and all senior IVP staff and committee members subscribe to the UCCF Basis of Faith. Website: www.uccf.org.uk.

InterVarsity Press®, USA, is the book-publishing division of InterVarsity Christian Fellowship/ USA® and a member movement of the International Fellowship of Evangelical Students. Website: www.intervarsity.org.

Unless otherwise noted, Scripture quotations are taken from The ESV® Bible (The Holy Bible, English Standard Version®), published by HarperCollins Publishers, © 2001 by Crossway. Used by permission. All rights reserved.

Quotations marked NETS are taken from A New English Translation of the Septuagint, © 2007 by the International Organization for Septuagint and Cognate Studies, Inc. Used by permission of Oxford University Press. All rights reserved.

First published 2018

Set in Monotype Times New Roman
Typeset in Great Britain by CRB Associates, Potterhanworth, Lincolnshire

UK ISBN: 978-1-78359-601-0 (print)
UK ISBN: 978-1-78359-602-7 (digital)

US ISBN: 978-0-8308-2646-9 (print)
US ISBN: 978-0-8308-7415-6 (digital)

British Library Cataloguing-in-Publication Data
A catalogue record for this book is available from the British Library.

Library of Congress Cataloging-in-Publication Data
A catalog record for this book is available from the Library of Congress.

For Mum and Dad, who taught me the gospel:

*'And they were both righteous before God, walking blamelessly
in all the commandments and righteous requirements of the Lord.'
(Luke 1:6, my tr.)*

Contents

Series preface

New Studies in Biblical Theology is a series of monographs that
address key issues in the discipline of biblical theology. Contributions
to the series focus on one or more of three areas: (1) the nature and
status of biblical theology, including its relations with other disciplines
(e.g. historical theology, exegesis, systematic theology, historical
criticism, narrative theology); (2) the articulation and exposition of
the structure of thought of a particular biblical writer or corpus; and
(3) the delineation of a biblical theme across all or part of the biblical
corpora.

Above all, these monographs are creative attempts to help thinking
Christians understand their Bibles better. The series aims simultaneously to instruct and to edify, to interact with the current literature,
and to point the way ahead. In God's universe, mind and heart should
not be divorced: in this series we will try not to separate what God
has joined together. While the notes interact with the best of scholarly
literature, the text is uncluttered with untransliterated Greek and
Hebrew, and tries to avoid too much technical jargon. The volumes
are written within the framework of confessional evangelicalism, but
there is always an attempt at thoughtful engagement with the sweep
of the relevant literature.

Circumcision is one of those topics that is either largely ignored
by Christian theologians, or, as has been the case in recent years, it
becomes the very centre of controversy among New Testament
scholars over the nature of the 'problem' that Paul addresses in, say,
Galatians. What has been lacking is a rich biblical theology of
circumcision – and this lacuna is what Karl Deenick carefully fills
in. Focusing on the themes of righteousness and faith with reference
to circumcision, Dr Deenick arrives at nuanced definitions of
both physical circumcision and circumcision of the heart. His study
sheds fresh light not only on many Old Testament passages, but also
on Romans 2 – 4, much of Galatians, Philippians 3, Colossians 2,
and Acts 7 and 15. Better yet, it suggests an integrating line of

development across the canon, a line that intertwines with other biblical-theological themes.

D. A. Carson
Trinity Evangelical Divinity School

Author's preface

It is hard to believe that it is seven years since I started working on this most curious of biblical topics, here and there amid a host of other, frequently more pressing obligations. And yet curious as it is and irregular as it has been, nevertheless through it I have been graciously and richly blessed by God. I have often found myself (to borrow the words of John Piper) transported into the very vestibule of heaven and unexpectedly moved, sometimes even to tears, as God has shown me the glory of Christ. I have often marvelled as I caught glimpses of God's skill in weaving the message of his Christ into the fabric of his people's history recorded in the Bible. For that gift and for that gospel I remain eternally grateful to him.

Yet over seven years one builds up a debt to many others as well. Thanks must also go to Peter Adam and Lindsay Wilson who guided me through the project that formed the foundation for this book. Both have been so kind, helpful and encouraging. They have made what follows much better than it could have been had I been left to my own devices. I am especially indebted to Peter, who has been not only a study supervisor but a ministry mentor and friend.

Others at Ridley College also deserve thanks for their feedback and support. Not least my fellow postgraduate students and a number of the faculty, especially Mike Bird who went beyond the call of duty by reading over the New Testament chapters for me. I am indebted to my uncle, David Runia, for his translations of the two Latin quotes from Rupert Tuitiensis. I have modified them, and any problems with the final forms are entirely my own. In addition, his helpful advice on combining academic work with the busyness of a full-time job was what finally enabled me to make significant headway with this project. That I ever finished is due to his wisdom. So too Mikey Lynch, a colleague and friend in ministry down here in 'Tassie', kindly offered assistance in various ways throughout the project. His help, genuine interest and support have been invaluable, not only for this, but for many other things besides. A small army of people from Inter-Varsity

Press and other places have also helped to get this book to print. I am immensely appreciative of their work, expertise and patient help.

I am deeply indebted also to the long-suffering people of the Branch Christian Church where I pastor. They have supported me and have given me the time to complete this. They have been tremendously kind and loving and are truly God's gift to me. Special thanks must go to my leadership team for their generosity and support, and also to my growth group who are my second family and who have regularly sustained me through their love.

I am also grateful to Philip Duce of Inter-Varsity Press and Don Carson for the opportunity of publishing in the NSBT series. It is a great pleasure to be able to contribute to a series I have very much appreciated in my ministry. This work also owes a great deal to Don Carson in another way. It was his example of godly scholarship that inspired me and persuaded me to pursue a calling I was determined to leave behind. His book, *The Difficult Doctrine of the Love of God*, blew my mind and changed the way I read the Bible. I hope my exegesis in what follows is as careful and subservient to the text as his.

However, my greatest debt, humanly speaking, belongs to those who have travelled with me for much longer than this project has existed. My brother and sisters – Jono, Elissa and Tanya – and their families too have been and are a constant source of love, counsel and support. I would be lost without them. But no one deserves as much gratitude as my mum and dad. Nothing could repay the debt I owe them. But as a small token of appreciation this book is dedicated to them, because although they have made no contribution to the scholarly debates that follow, they taught me the gospel that underpins it all. And that, I think, is a much greater contribution by far.

My sincere prayer is that as you read this book it would be that same gospel of the glory of God in the face of Christ that shines most brightly of all.

Karl Deenick
Launceston, Tasmania

Abbreviations

1Q28a	*Rule of the Congregation* (Dead Sea Scrolls)
1Q28b	*Rule of the Blessings* (Dead Sea Scrolls)
1QHᵃ	*Thanksgiving Hymns* (Dead Sea Scrolls)
1QpHab	*Pesher Habakkuk* (Dead Sea Scrolls)
1QS	*Rule of the Community* (Dead Sea Scrolls)
4Q434	*Barkhi Nafshi* (Dead Sea Scrolls)
4Q458	*Narrative A* (Dead Sea Scrolls)
11Q5	*Psalms Scroll* (Dead Sea Scrolls)
11Q19	*Temple Scroll* (Dead Sea Scrolls)
א*	Codex Sinaiticus (original reading)
A	Codex Alexandrinus
B	Codex Vaticanus
AB	Anchor Bible
AIL	Ancient Israel and Its Literature
Ant.	*Jewish Antiquities* (Josephus)
AOTC	Apollos Old Testament Commentary
APOT	*The Apocrypha and Pseudepigrapha of the Old Testament*, ed. Robert H. Charles, 2 vols., Oxford: Clarendon, 1913
AUS	American University Studies
Barn.	*Epistle of Barnabas*
BBR	*Bulletin for Biblical Research*
BDAG	W. Bauer, F. W. Danker, W. F. Arndt, and F. W. Gingrich, *Greek-English Lexicon of the New Testament and Other Early Christian Literature*, 3rd edn, Chicago: University of Chicago Press, 2000
BECNT	Baker Exegetical Commentary on the New Testament
Bib	*Biblica*
BNTC	Black's New Testament Commentaries
BSac	*Bibliotheca sacra*
b. Shabb.	*Babylonian Talmud Shabbat*

BST	The Bible Speaks Today
BZ	*Biblische Zeitschrift*
BZAW	Beihefte zur Zeitschrift für die alttestamentliche Wissenschaft
CBET	Contributions to Biblical Exegesis and Theology
CC	Continental Commentaries
CCGNT	Classic Commentaries on the Greek New Testament
CD	*Damascus Document* (Dead Sea Scrolls)
Clem.	*Epistles of Clement*
ConcC	Concordia Commentary
Conf.	*On the Confusion of Tongues* (Philo)
CTJ	*Calvin Theological Journal*
Decal.	*On the Decalogue* (Philo)
Did.	*Didache*
DOTP	*Dictionary of the Old Testament: Pentateuch*, ed. T. Desmond Alexander and David W. Baker, Downers Grove: InterVarsity Press; Leicester: Inter-Varsity Press, 2003
DSS	Dead Sea Scrolls
*EBC*²	*Expositor's Bible Commentary*, ed. T. Longman III and D. E. Garland, rev. edn, 13 vols., Grand Rapids: Zondervan, 2006–12
EDNT	*Exegetical Dictionary of the New Testament*, ed. Horst Balz and Gerhard Schneider, 3 vols., Grand Rapids: Eerdmans, 1990–3
EGGNT	Exegetical Guide to the Greek New Testament
ESV	English Standard Version
Exod. Rab.	*Exodus Rabbah*
ExpTim	*Expository Times*
FOTL	Forms of Old Testament Literature
fr.	fragment
Gen. Rab.	*Genesis Rabbah*
HCSB	Holman Christian Standard Bible
Herm. *Sim.*	Shepherd of Hermas, *Similitude*
HeyJ	*Heythrop Journal*
HS	*Hebrew Studies*
IBC	Interpretation: A Bible Commentary for Teaching and Preaching
ICC	International Critical Commentary
Ign. *Eph.*	*To the Ephesians* (Ignatius)
Ios.	*On the Life of Joseph* (Philo)

ITC	International Theological Commentary
JAOS	*Journal of the American Oriental Society*
JBL	*Journal of Biblical Literature*
JPSTC	Jewish Publication Society Torah Commentary
JSNT	*Journal for the Study of the New Testament*
JSNTSup	Journal for the Study of the New Testament: Supplement Series
JSOT	*Journal for the Study of the Old Testament*
JSOTSup	Journal for the Study of the Old Testament: Supplement Series
Jub.	*Jubilees*
LCC	Library of Christian Classics
LHBOTS	The Library of Hebrew Bible/Old Testament Studies
lit.	literally
LNTS	The Library of New Testament Studies
LS	*Louvain Studies*
LSJ	Henry George Liddell, Robert Scott, Henry Stuart Jones, *A Greek-English Lexicon*, 9th edn with revised supplement, Oxford: Clarendon, 1996
LXX	Septuagint
Migr.	*On the Migration of Abraham* (Philo)
MT	Masoretic Text
NAC	New American Commentary
NACSBT	New American Commentary Studies in Bible and Theology
NCB	New Century Bible
NCBC	New Cambridge Bible Commentary
NDBT	*New Dictionary of Biblical Theology*, ed. T. D. Alexander and B. S. Rosner, Leicester: Inter-Varsity Press; Downers Grove: InterVarsity Press, 2000
NET	New English Translation
NETS	New English Translation of the Septuagint
NICNT	New International Commentary on the New Testament
NICOT	New International Commentary on the Old Testament
NIDNTT	*New International Dictionary of New Testament Theology*, ed. Colin Brown, 4 vols., Grand Rapids: Zondervan, 1975–8
NIDOTTE	*New International Dictionary of Old Testament Theology and Exegesis*, ed. Willem A. Van Gemeren, 5 vols., Grand Rapids: Zondervan, 1997

NIGTC	New International Greek Testament Commentary
NIV	New International Version
NIVAC	New International Version Application Commentary
NLCNT	New London Commentary on the New Testament
NovT	*Novum Testamentum*
NovTSup	Supplements to Novum Testamentum
NSBT	New Studies in Biblical Theology
NT	New Testament
NTL	New Testament Library
NTS	*New Testament Studies*
OT	Old Testament
OTL	Old Testament Library
P^{46}	Papyrus 46
PBM	Paternoster Biblical Monographs
PL	Patrologia Latina, ed. J.-P. Migne, 217 vols., Paris, 1844–64
PNTC	Pillar New Testament Commentary
Post.	*On the Posterity of Cain* (Philo)
Pss Sol.	*Psalms of Solomon*
RB	*Revue biblique*
RTR	*Reformed Theological Review*
SBJT	*Southern Baptist Journal of Theology*
SBLDS	Society of Biblical Literature Dissertation Series
SBLMS	Society of Biblical Literature Monograph Series
SNTSMS	Society for New Testament Studies Manuscript Series
SNTW	Studies of the New Testament and Its World
SP	Sacra Pagina
Spec.	*On the Special Laws* (Philo)
TANZ	Texte und Arbeiten zum neutestamentlichen Zeitalter
T. Ash.	*Testament of Asher*
T. Benj.	*Testament of Benjamin*
TDNT	*Theological Dictionary of the New Testament*, ed. Gerhard Kittel and Gerhard Friedrich, tr. Geoffrey W. Bromiley, 10 vols., Grand Rapids: Eerdmans, 1964–76
TDOT	*Theological Dictionary of the Old Testament*, ed. G. Johannes Botterweck and Helmer Ringgren, tr. John T. Willis et al., 8 vols., Grand Rapids: Eerdmans, 1974–2006
Tg. Ket.	*Targum of the Writings*
Tg. Ps.-J.	*Targum Pseudo-Jonathan*

ABBREVIATIONS

Them	*Themelios*
THOTC	Two Horizons Old Testament Commentary
T. Jud.	*Testament of Judah*
T. Levi	*Testament of Levi*
TOTC	Tyndale Old Testament Commentaries
tr.	translation, translated by
TynBul	*Tyndale Bulletin*
VT	*Vetus Testamentum*
VTSup	Supplements to Vetus Testamentum
WBC	Word Biblical Commentary
WTJ	*Westminster Theological Journal*
WUNT	Wissenschaftliche Untersuchungen zum Neuen Testament
ZECNT	Zondervan Exegetical Commentary on the New Testament

Chapter One

Introduction

More than once I have been asked what on earth it was that led me to study and write on circumcision. Why *that* topic? At what point did that begin to seem like a good idea? But actually, the reason is surprisingly simple. Because although circumcision is of foundational importance in the OT and is central to many of the debates in the NT on the nature of the gospel, and while it is often remarked upon in passing by biblical scholars and theologians, it still remains curiously neglected. Very little detailed work has been done on establishing a biblical theology of circumcision.[1] Bernat's observation of the state of play of circumcision in the OT is true more broadly:

> Despite the importance attributed to circumcision in the Hebrew Bible, the topic has not been accorded sufficient attention in the scholarship . . . Studies of circumcision have been more narrowly focussed, on individual biblical passages or topics, while attempts at synthesis tend toward summary, appearing as entries in encyclopedias, excurses in commentaries, chapters of larger works, and brief notices in survey literature . . .[2]

What longer treatments of circumcision do exist are either too broadly focused or too narrowly focused, both in the questions they ask and the texts and sources they use.[3]

---

[1] By 'biblical theology' here I understand an attempt to trace a theme through the biblical canon in order to present a coherent understanding (or theology) of that theme and its development within the context of the whole biblical narrative. See Carson 2000: 89–101.

[2] Bernat 2009: 1–2. Curiously, Bernat attempts to fill this 'lacuna' by considering circumcision only within the Priestly material.

[3] Livesey 2010 studies intertestamental literature, Josephus, Philo and Paul; Cohen 2005, circumcision and gender within the history of Judaism; Thiessen 2011, circumcision and identity in the Bible but also in wider Jewish and Christian writings; Berkley 2000, circumcision of the heart in Rom. 2. Blaschke's work (1998) is by far the most comprehensive, yet his purpose is to survey widely and to summarize, rather than to establish a synthesis of the biblical material. The most *biblically* comprehensive study is that of Schreiner (1983) in an unpublished dissertation. Schreiner studies circumcision in the OT, intertestamental Judaism and in Paul, but his focus is on Paul's view

1

This lack of detailed work on a biblical theology of circumcision is surprising given the place circumcision holds in both Testaments: it is connected with some of the most foundational covenant passages in the OT (e.g. Gen. 15, 17), it occurs repeatedly in the OT in connection with the future hope for Israel (Lev. 26; Deut. 30), it forms the background for some of the most hotly contested writings of the apostle Paul where he defends the gospel against misunderstandings of circumcision (e.g. Rom. 2 – 4; Galatians; Phil. 3), and it is the occasion of one of the earliest church councils (e.g. Acts 15) because circumcision was in danger of overshadowing the gospel. But not only is circumcision a biblically important topic; it is a theologically important topic as well. It is often considered central to the argument for whether to baptize infants or not. And, more recently, it has played a leading role in the debates surrounding the New Perspective on Paul and the question of righteousness.

Nevertheless, despite the lack of detailed work, the unspoken assumption often seems to be that the meaning of circumcision is relatively well understood. In fact, on closer inspection, the issues are much more complicated than one might have expected.

Defining the problem

In seeking to establish a biblical theology of circumcision, the two facets on which this book focuses are the key biblical concepts of righteousness and faith. Part of the motivation for that comes from Paul's remark that Abraham 'received the sign of circumcision as a seal of the righteousness that he had by faith while he was still uncircumcised' (Rom. 4:11).[4] Paul's connection of circumcision with the ideas of righteousness and faith is not limited to this particular verse. The three are also clearly connected in Romans 2 – 4, Galatians and Philippians 3. Moreover, in other places circumcision is linked with related concepts like cleansing (John 7:22–23; Acts 15:1–11), reconciliation (Eph. 2:11–22), forgiveness (Col. 2:6–23) and the receipt of the Holy Spirit (Acts 10:45; 15:1–11).

However, Romans 4:11 connects the ideas in a way that opens up the subject and some of its inherent complexities. Furthermore, it also highlights Paul's biblical-theological sensitivity with respect to the meaning of circumcision in so far as it relates to righteousness and

(note 3 *cont.*) of circumcision and his shift away from demanding physical circumcision, rather than on establishing a biblical theology.

[4] Unless otherwise indicated, Bible quotations are taken from the ESV.

faith. Paul's claim in Romans 4:11 is not first of all anchored in what his opponents thought about circumcision but in how circumcision worked in the OT. Circumcision was given to *Abraham* as a 'seal of the righteousness that he had by faith'. In Paul's mind at least, circumcision was intended to mean something to Abraham. Paul is not making a claim about what became apparent about circumcision later, but about what circumcision already meant from the very beginning. It was intended to communicate something to Abraham about righteousness and faith. That raises the possibility of finding those two themes of righteousness and faith woven into the very fabric of circumcision both in the OT and the NT.

Yet circumcision in the OT presents a somewhat different and apparently more complex picture. Circumcision and uncircumcision are related to Yahweh's covenant with Abraham and to the promise of land and descendants (Gen. 17; Josh. 5). It is used as a slur (Judg. 14:3; 15:8; 1 Sam. 14:6; 17:26, 36; 31:4; 2 Sam. 1:20; 1 Chr. 10:4). It is used as a metaphor to describe the inadequacies of the heart (Lev. 26:41; Deut. 10:16; 30:6; Jer. 4:4; 9:25–26; Ezek. 44:7, 9), ears (Jer. 6:10) and lips (Exod. 6:12, 30) and even fruit trees (Lev. 19:23). It is linked with blood and possibly sacrifice (Exod. 4:24–26), uncleanness (Isa. 52:1), with those who are judged by God (Ezek. 28:10; 31:18; 32:19–32; Hab. 2:16), with obedience and love for God (Lev. 26:40–42; Deut. 10:16; 30:6), and with pride and the sin of Adam (Ezek. 28:1–10). The diverse portrayal of circumcision within the OT does not immediately suggest that righteousness and faith lie at the very heart of its meaning. Moreover, it is not at all obvious why *circumcision* is a sign of righteousness by faith. Why not something else? Why not something more visible? And why not something in which both men and women can share?

Nevertheless, it is clear that Paul believed there was some connection between circumcision, righteousness and faith. And the existence of numerous letters and speeches in the early church seeking to clarify the connection between the three (e.g. Acts 7; 15; Rom. 2 – 4; Galatians; Phil. 3) suggests that others thought there was a connection too, even if they misunderstood it.

The nature of the righteousness portrayed by circumcision

Another apparent problem in understanding circumcision is that contemporary scholarship understands the nature of the righteousness signified by circumcision quite differently between the two Testaments. In the OT the metaphor of circumcision of the heart is generally understood as relating to some kind of moral transformation, while in the NT circumcision is bound up with arguments about justification, which has been understood within Protestant circles, until more recently at least, as a forensic, legal category. So too the extent of the moral transformation envisaged by circumcision of the heart is uncertain: is it merely repentance, or is it a wholesale transformation into a perfect person?

So, with respect to the OT, circumcision of the heart is often understood *subjectively* as referring to a change in a person's character. For example, Merrill writes regarding Deuteronomy 30, 'circumcision of the heart . . . speaks of internal identification with [the Lord] in what might be called regeneration in Christian theology'.[5] While Meade notes that circumcision of the heart refers to 'the internal transformation which will devote the people to a loyal love of Yahweh'.[6]

In contrast, the nature of the righteousness that circumcision was intended to confirm has also been understood *objectively*; most commonly as the imputation of a right standing before God. For example, Murray explains the purpose of Abraham's circumcision was to indicate to believers that 'the righteousness which was imputed to Abraham will be imputed to them also'.[7] Stott says that Abraham 'received circumcision as a visible sign and seal of the justification which was already his'.[8] Similarly, Cranfield believes that circumcision was the 'outward and visible attestation of the *status* of righteousness which he already possessed'.[9]

In recent times, of course, the notion of imputed righteousness has been challenged by N. T. Wright and others.[10] Wright rejects the idea that 'Jesus "obeyed the law" and so obtained "righteousness" which could be reckoned to those who believe in him.'[11] Instead, for Wright, righteousness refers to 'covenant status'.[12] Interestingly, Wright sees

---

[5] Merrill 1994: 388. See also J. M. Hamilton 2006: 162.
[6] Meade 2014: 77.
[7] Murray 1967: 1:139.
[8] Stott 1994: 129.
[9] Cranfield 2004: 236 (emphasis mine).
[10] The so-called New Perspective is a very 'broad church'. Nevertheless, it is useful to see how two of its major proponents, N. T. Wright and James Dunn, seek to integrate faith, righteousness and circumcision.
[11] Wright 2009: 205.
[12] E.g. ibid. 128, 195.

as crucial to understanding Paul passages such as Genesis 15 and 17, and Deuteronomy 27 – 30.[13] The former are, of course, part of the Abraham/covenant/circumcision narrative, while Deuteronomy 30 is one of the central passages pertaining to circumcision of the heart. In other words, although Wright travels in a distinctly different direction on the understanding of righteousness, he does so in order to ground that concept more squarely in the Abrahamic covenant. That unavoidably brings within its compass the matter of circumcision.

Wright contends that calling circumcision a sign of 'righteousness by faith' is simply another way of saying 'sign of the covenant'.[14] That is, Paul means that circumcision was 'a sign and seal of the covenant status he had by faith while in uncircumcision'.[15] The covenant to which Paul is referring is not 'the promise that his sins would be forgiven and that he would go to heaven when he died',[16] but rather it involved worldwide blessing, that 'whereas the whole world had been cursed through Adam and Eve, through the human pride which led to Babel, the creator God would now bring blessing to that same world'.[17] Wright still maintains that God's purpose in establishing his covenant with Abraham was to 'create a worldwide family whose sins were forgiven'.[18] Nevertheless, the point is that for Wright righteousness is about covenant membership.

James Dunn, another major proponent of the New Perspective, also sees circumcision as vital to understanding Paul's notion of justification. According to Dunn, Abraham's circumcision was a sign of his being 'accepted by God'.[19] However, for Dunn the primary background is first-century Judaism. He writes:

> In sociological terms, circumcision functioned as a primary and effective identity and boundary marker, particularly for Jewish minorities in the cities of the diaspora. It was not the only such marker, but because circumcision was such a distinctive feature within a Hellenistic environment, because it had been so integrally tied into the covenant from the first, and because it had become such a test-case for national loyalty for all who regarded themselves

---

[13] For instance, ibid. 15–16, 48, 74–75.
[14] Ibid. 77.
[15] Ibid. 195; also Wright 2002: 494–495.
[16] Wright 2009: 194.
[17] Ibid. 78.
[18] Ibid. 196.
[19] Dunn 1988: 1:232.

as heirs of the Maccabean inheritance, it was bound to be *the* mark of the covenant people for most Jews of Paul's time.[20]

For Dunn, first-century Judaism understood circumcision as *the* boundary marker of who was in the covenant and who was not. He understands Paul's doctrine of justification to be trying to demolish that view. Dunn's view of circumcision as a boundary marker stands opposed to the more typical Reformation view that saw the fundamental issue with circumcision in Paul's day as being bound up with 'meritorious works' and 'self-achieved salvation'.[21] Nevertheless, Dunn agrees that understanding circumcision is crucial to understanding Paul.

But both the traditional view and the New Perspective view (represented here by Wright and Dunn) give short shrift to the broader understanding of circumcision that the OT presents. In applying circumcision spiritually, the OT writers appear to look almost universally to a transformation of the heart – people will love God with all their heart. The connection is with radical spiritual surgery rather than with land, descendants, imputed righteousness or even covenant status. Indeed, the degree of emphasis on the moral/ethical side of (metaphorical) circumcision seems to suggest that it *primarily* has a moral/ethical reference in the OT, at least after Genesis. Thus although Wright has tried hard to reconcile Paul's view of circumcision in Romans 4:11 with Genesis, he does not seem to have given sufficient attention to the connection with the view of circumcision given by the OT more broadly. Similarly, Dunn's view is more concerned with first-century Judaism than with the OT background. He judiciously constructs a first-century view of circumcision, but makes little attempt to construct a broader biblical view – the point of view from which Paul argues. Finally, those who along traditional lines have understood Paul to be talking about imputed righteousness seem to be speaking in categories quite different from those used by the OT writers. None of these views seem to show a particular regard for integrating the various strands of biblical thought with sensitivity to their position in the unfolding of redemptive history, even though they may purport to do precisely that.

Nevertheless, many writers still pick up on the apparent double reference of circumcision to 'righteousness' and heart transformation.

---

[20] Dunn 2008: 162–163 (emphasis his).
[21] Ibid. 154.

For instance, Calvin suggests that '[f]or the Jews, circumcision was the symbol by which they were admonished that whatever comes forth from man's seed, that is, the whole nature of mankind, is corrupt and needs pruning.' But he also suggests that circumcision was 'a seal by which they are more certainly assured that their faith . . . is accounted to them as righteousness by God'.[22] Likewise, Harstad notes of the circumcision in Joshua 5 that '[God] is placing on them the seal of righteousness that he has credited to them through faith'. Yet he goes on to affirm that '[t]rue circumcision is the work of God in the heart in which he creates spiritual life.'[23] While Barker, writing of circumcision of the heart in Deuteronomy, contends, 'This action on Israel's heart and the obedience which flows from that corresponds to what the New Testament calls justification and sanctification.'[24] Yet Barker does little to prove that link, concerned as he is with Deuteronomy more than biblical theology as a whole.

A number then are willing to ascribe both meanings to circumcision. But few have given detailed attention to how the two relate. Some simply overlook the fact that the OT writers do not mention justification. Thus Reymond maintains that justification 'is not simply a Pauline perception . . . being read back into the Old Testament', and that 'already in the Old Testament times the import of the rite began to be transferred metaphorically into the spiritual realm, and it came to be understood as conveying symbolically the removal of sin's defilement through salvation . . .'.[25]

Nevertheless, while he can amass considerable evidence for the OT testimony to the idea of the removal of sin's defilement, by which he appears to mean heart transformation,[26] when it comes to the imputation of righteousness he refers only to Romans 4:11.[27]

Moreover, even if one presses back to Genesis 15, as is sometimes suggested,[28] where faith and righteousness are mentioned, the covenant itself is again bound up with the promise of land, not the promise of righteousness. Although Paul in his argument in Romans 4:1–11 has clearly pointed to the primacy of Genesis 15, where Abraham is counted righteous, it is one thing to say that Abraham

---

[22] Calvin 2006: 4.14.21.
[23] Harstad 2004: 226–227.
[24] Barker 2004: 178.
[25] Reymond 2002: 937, n. 50.
[26] Ibid. 719.
[27] Ibid. 952.
[28] E.g. Harstad 2004: 226.

was righteous before he was circumcised and hence circumcision did not make him righteous; it is quite another to say that circumcision was a *sign* and a *seal* of righteousness when the original context seems to be more interested in land and descendants. Moreover, establishing that connection between Genesis 15 and 17 solves only one half of the problem: it does nothing to explain the later use of circumcision as a metaphor for radical spiritual heart surgery.

Perhaps one of the most influential contributions to the understanding of circumcision has been that of Meredith Kline.[29] For Kline the connection between circumcision and righteousness lies in the notion that circumcision is about justification through ordeal. Justification comes through sharing in the circumcision-death/judgment of Christ in our place. Yet he also recognizes that circumcision moves beyond justification. He writes:

> Paul traces this wider import of circumcision beyond justification so as to include regeneration and sanctification. The appropriate expression and inevitable accompaniment of our judicial circumcision-death in Christ is the death of the old man, our dying to the dominion of sin. Paul interprets the circumcision-putting off as such a spiritual transformation . . . The element of subjective, spiritual-moral qualification thus occupies a place in the Pauline doctrine of circumcision as a derivative from the rite's prior meaning as a sign of the objective curse of the covenant.[30]

Thus Kline understands the 'circumcision-death' idea as central, but the 'spiritual-moral' as derivative, so that transformation is the necessary consequence of circumcision as judgment. But Kline does not really elaborate on how that is so.[31] Moreover, Kline's emphasis on circumcision as a sign of judgment does not appear to do full justice to the view of the later OT writers, who seem to view circumcision primarily in ethical terms, not judicial ones. They put the stress almost universally on spiritual transformation and the need for some kind of radical spiritual surgery. In fact, it is striking, in the light of Kline's view, that the notion of judgment seems almost totally absent from the later use of circumcision within the OT. The later OT writers do not appear to look ahead so much to Yahweh's taking on himself

[29] See esp. Kline 1968 and the slight revision in Kline 2006: 312–318.
[30] Kline 1968: 47. See also Kline 2006: 316–317.
[31] To be fair to Kline, that is largely because it is not the primary focus of his work.

the 'oath-curse' as they envisage a time when Yahweh will create a new people who love him with all their heart. Those ideas seem quite distinct. Kline's analysis seems almost to map a straight line from Genesis 15 and 17 to Colossians 2 (a passage that contains some notion of judgment in connection with circumcision) but with very little reference to what lies between.[32] In contrast, the aim here is to try to map out how the meaning of circumcision unfolded within the contours of redemptive-history.

Circumcision and faith

So the relationship between circumcision and righteousness is complex. But so too is the relationship between circumcision and faith. Within the NT, for instance, circumcision is considered both a threat to faith and a seal of righteousness by faith. Even within Romans, Paul displays the duality presented by circumcision. Although in chapter 4 circumcision is a seal of Abraham's righteousness by faith, in chapter 2 circumcision is of value only 'if you obey the law' (Rom. 2:25). So too in 1 Corinthians 7:19 Paul considers circumcision a matter of indifference, yet what *really* matters is 'keeping the commandments of God'; while in Galatians, circumcision stands totally opposed to faith: 'I testify again to every man who accepts circumcision that he is obligated to keep the whole law' (Gal. 5:3). On the basis of which Lightfoot makes an extraordinary claim that appears almost totally at odds with Paul's view of circumcision in Romans 4:

> Circumcision is the seal of the law. He who willingly and deliberately undergoes circumcision, enters upon a compact to fulfil the law. To fulfil it therefore he is bound, and he cannot plead the grace of Christ; for he has entered on another mode of justification.[33]

And yet in the same letter Paul contrasts the law with the promise to Abraham (Gal. 3:16–18), the promise to Abraham that was signified by circumcision!

Similar tensions can be found when one considers the views regarding Genesis 17. The circumcision episode there is introduced with these words:

---

[32] E.g. Kline 1968: 46; 2006: 316–317.
[33] Lightfoot 1874: 203.

When Abram was ninety-nine years old the LORD appeared to Abram and said to him, 'I am God Almighty; walk before me, and be blameless, that I may make my covenant between me and you, and may multiply you greatly.' (Gen. 17:1–2)

Williamson argues that Abraham's walking before Yahweh and being blameless are the grounds for the covenant to be 'given'. In fact, Williamson goes to great lengths to show that the prologue of the covenant in Genesis 17 constituted a divine test Abraham had to pass in order for the covenant to be established. He writes:

> the ethical obligation imposed here upon Abraham should be understood as the moral prerequisite for a divine–human relationship. Abraham is expected to emulate Noah's ethical perfection, prior to the perpetual covenant that God would make with him and with his 'seed'. On such a prerequisite the establishment of God's eternal covenant with Abraham and his 'seed' was dependent.[34]

Milgrom leaves us in no doubt, writing:

> That God's covenant with Abraham was one of pure grace is totally refuted by the P source itself: . . . 'Walk before me and be blameless and I will make a covenant between me and you' (Gen 17:1b–2a). Therefore, the covenant with Abraham is conditioned on Abraham's blameless behaviour, not on God's grace . . . Thus the Abrahamic covenant is not one of grace; it is not even unconditional . . . [it is] clearly conditioned on Abraham's moral rectitude.[35]

Yet some are tempted to read into 'blameless' little more than the idea of faith. Thus Hamilton opts for something like 'transparent or candid'.[36] Or, as Williamson writes, 'The idea is not one of sinless perfection or moral faultlessness – such would be an impossible goal . . . Rather, the idea here seems to be . . . being totally dedicated to God.'[37] Similarly, Westermann concludes that what God is calling Abraham to do is 'to live his life before God in such a way that every single step is made with reference to God and every day experiences

---

[34] Williamson 2000: 176.
[35] Milgrom 2001: 2340.
[36] V. P. Hamilton 1990: 461.
[37] Williamson 2007: 87; 2000: 246, n. 105.

him close at hand. This is not meant to be some sort of lofty demand; it is something quite natural.'[38] In contrast, Wenham rejects Westermann's idea that blamelessness is something quite natural, writing that 'Abraham is expected to emulate Noah's moral perfection.'[39] It is an 'extreme demand'. Though curiously, in the end, that means little more than that they were 'devout and pious throughout their lives'. For Gunkel, to be blameless is to be 'ethically and cultically blameless' or 'innocent'. He translates it as 'perfect'. Yet though it is 'lofty and rare', a few like Noah and Enoch possessed it.[40]

The same tension exists again when the views regarding the meaning of circumcision of the heart are considered. Christensen writes, 'The promise that "YHWH will circumcise your heart" means that God himself will remove whatever prevents the people from choosing to follow God's teachings.'[41] Sarna sees circumcision of the heart, ears and lips as representing 'dedication and commitment to God'.[42] For McConville, circumcision of the heart is a 'new thing' intended to 'deal effectively with Israel's sinful disposition'.[43] But in each case, the notion of heart circumcision seems to be less than the picture that Deuteronomy paints.

The context of Deuteronomy 10 shows the extent of what is envisaged by circumcision of the heart. Moses tells the people:

> And now, Israel, what does the LORD your God require of you, but to fear the LORD your God, to walk in *all* his ways, to love him, to serve the LORD your God with *all* your heart and with *all* your soul, and to keep the commandments and statutes of the LORD, which I am commanding you today for your good? . . . Circumcise therefore the foreskin of your heart, and be no longer stubborn . . . You shall therefore love the LORD your God and keep his charge, his statutes, his rules, and his commandments *always* . . . You shall therefore keep the *whole* commandment that I command you today . . . (Deut. 10:12 – 11:8, emphases mine)

Similarly, the circumcision of the heart envisaged in Deuteronomy 30:6 is one in which the people will 'love the LORD your God with *all*

---

[38] Westermann 1995: 259.
[39] Wenham 1994: 20.
[40] Gunkel 1997: 143, 263.
[41] Christensen 2002: 739.
[42] Sarna 1989: 387.
[43] McConville 2002: 427.

your heart and with *all* your soul'. In short, the obedience connected with circumcision of the heart appears to be total.

All that, however, is not to say that no attempts at a solution have been made. Kline, for example, resolves the tension of obedience and faith through his notion of the oath-curse function of circumcision. Kline's view is that circumcision was an oath-curse by which the person swore their allegiance to God under the threat of death, symbolized by the 'cutting off' of circumcision.[44] The one who was disobedient to the covenant would be cut off, while the one who was obedient to the covenant would be blessed. The problem is that humanity's sinful nature would seem to leave no option other than condemnation.[45] Yet although for Kline circumcision is a law covenant – blessing requires obedience – it is a 'redemptive law covenant', by which he means that a person may be disobedient and yet be saved by the 'divine Redeemer-Substitute', who suffers the curse on that person's behalf.[46] It is appropriating this promise of a divine Redeemer-Substitute, inherent in circumcision, that resolves the tension between faith and obedience. Thus for Kline, circumcision

> conveyed the threat of being cut off from God and life for the one who, disclaiming the grace of the covenant and thus breaking it, would undergo in himself the judgement due to Adam's fallen race. But circumcision also presented the promise of the Cross, inviting the circumcised to identify by faith with Christ, to undergo the judgment of God in him, and so find in his circumcision-judgment the way to the Father, to justification and life. *Because Paul perceived this gospel option as one specific aspect of the generic judgment significance of circumcision he could interpret it as a seal of the righteousness of faith which Abraham had, yet being uncircumcised* (Rom. 4:11).[47]

But the same problem as raised above with respect to Kline's view applies here as well: the notion of judgment seems absent from many of the later references to circumcision by the OT writers.

Horton has attempted to resolve the apparent tension in the meaning of circumcision by suggesting that its meaning is modified by its connection with the covenant it ratifies. He writes:

---

[44] Kline 1968: 42–43.
[45] Ibid. 48.
[46] Ibid. 48–49.
[47] Kline 2006: 316 (emphasis mine).

If it is the sign and seal of justification – the cutting away of sin rather than the cutting off of the sinner – then it functions as God's gracious promise to provide a substitute. This is how it functioned in the covenant of grace that God made with Abraham, Isaac, and Jacob. However, in terms of the *national* covenant (Sinaitic), circumcision obligated the one circumcised to personal fulfilment of all stipulations.[48]

For Horton this is what Paul means when he says, 'I testify again to every man who accepts circumcision that he is obligated to keep the whole law' (Gal. 5:3).[49] Yet while a convenient solution, it is not at all clear that the faith aspect of circumcision can be so easily separated from the Mosaic covenant, nor that the obedience aspect of circumcision can be so easily separated from the Abrahamic covenant. For instance, Horton's view seems to overlook the obligations placed on Abraham at the very outset: to be blameless before God (Gen. 17:1–2).

Wright solves the problem, in a sense, by redefining faith and righteousness. According to Wright, circumcision was a sign and seal of 'faith-demarcated righteousness'. It was an 'advance signpost' of the 'proper mark of covenant membership' that is heart-circumcision or faith.[50] Such faith-demarcated covenant membership finds its fulfilment in 'the Messiah's faithfulness, in which his people share through their own *pistis*'.[51] That is, Jesus fulfils Israel's vocation of 'faithfulness' and people share in that through their faith. In a way, because Wright has redefined righteousness as covenant status, faith/*pistis* must then be redefined to do double duty for both faith and faithfulness. But it remains to be seen whether, in the context of circumcision, such a redefinition of those terms is valid. Irrespective, it is apparent that Wright sees the two ideas of faith and faithfulness as intimately bound up with the definition of circumcision.

In short, both in the NT and the OT, circumcision is connected both with obedience and faith in ways that are not immediately reconcilable, just as circumcision was connected with justification but also the notion of inner transformation.

---

[48] Horton 2011: 789 (emphasis his).
[49] Ibid.
[50] Wright 2013: 362–363, 1175; 1993: 167.
[51] Wright 2013: 847, 989–991.

The way ahead

The purpose of this brief tour has been to highlight the range of ways the biblical material presents circumcision in relation to the two key concepts of righteousness and faith, and also to see some of the ways that scholars have understood circumcision, and, more particularly, circumcision in relationship to righteousness and faith. In the chapters that follow I hope to show that the notions of righteousness and faith are neither peripheral to the significance of circumcision, nor is their connection with circumcision a NT invention; rather, they are central to both the NT understanding and the developing OT understanding of the significance of circumcision. Along the way, we will not consider every reference to circumcision in the OT and NT; rather, we will consider those references which help to demonstrate that faith and righteousness are woven into the fabric of circumcision. The purpose being not to demonstrate that every reference to circumcision pertains directly to those themes, but to show that those themes are really and coherently presented throughout both Testaments.

Chapter 2 examines the institution of circumcision in Genesis 17, tracing the language of that passage through Genesis and the rest of the OT. Chapter 3 considers other references to circumcision within the OT, both physical and metaphorical: the major references to circumcision in Leviticus 26, Deuteronomy 10 and 30, and Joshua 5, together with a number of other OT passages. Chapter 4 traces the concepts found in connection with circumcision in the OT into the NT in order to assess whether the NT writers construed circumcision in primarily the same way as the OT writers. It also briefly explores how some of those same themes were understood within the broader NT milieu. Chapters 5 and 6 then explore the two most significant NT circumcision passages. Chapter 5 focuses on Paul's argument in Romans 2 – 4, where he seeks to explain the relationship between circumcision, righteousness and faith. Chapter 6 examines Paul's argument in Galatians, where he explains how the coming of the 'seed of Abraham' has brought circumcision to an end in favour of the righteousness by faith which comes through that seed. Finally, chapter 7 draws all the strands together and suggests how we should understand circumcision and its connection with righteousness and faith.

Chapter Two

Circumcision in Genesis:
the sign of the promise
established

The first reference to circumcision (*mwl, mll, mûlâ*) or uncircumcision/
foreskin (*'rl, 'ārēl, 'ārlâ*) in the Bible is at the institution of the covenant
of circumcision in Genesis 17. God promises that he will make
Abraham 'the father of a multitude of nations', that his name will no
longer be Abram but Abraham,[1] that kings will come from him, that
God will be God to Abraham and to his offspring, and that God will
give to Abraham and his offspring the land of Canaan for an
'everlasting possession' (Gen. 17:4–8). Transparently, the covenant
seems to be about land, descendants and a relationship with God
and seems to have very little connection to either righteousness or
faith. Moreover, the chief obligation laid upon Abraham, which is
circumcision itself, appears to have little to do with faith. In fact,
Genesis 17:1–2 seems to present a condition of some kind in order
for the covenant to be established: 'I am God Almighty, walk before
me and be blameless, and I will give my covenant between me and
you and I will multiply you exceedingly' (my tr.)

The covenant seems to require from Abraham what sounds like a
very thoroughgoing obedience: he must be 'blameless'. And yet God
has already established a covenant with Abraham in Genesis 15, a
covenant that looked to be established on the basis of Abraham's
faith, which was counted by God as righteousness (Gen. 15:6). What
is the connection between the covenant event in Genesis 15 and the
one in Genesis 17? The fact that both chapters refer to a covenant,
and the covenant (or covenants) involves the same two parties,
suggests that the covenant sign of Genesis 17 may be connected in
some way with the faith and righteousness mentioned as the precursor
to the covenant ceremony of Genesis 15. That in turn suggests
there may be a connection between circumcision, righteousness

---

[1] For the sake of simplicity, I will always use the name Abraham.

15

and faith, which extends right back to the original institution of circumcision.

This chapter will explore the nature of those connections together with the nature of the obligations laid on Abraham in Genesis 17, and will seek to show that righteousness and faith have been part of the fabric of circumcision from the very beginning. We begin with the introductory words of Genesis 17:1–2, which raise three important questions that will help frame our investigation. First, what does Yahweh mean when he says he will 'give' Abraham his covenant? Second, what is the relationship between the command to 'walk before me and be blameless' and giving the covenant? Third, what does it mean to 'walk before me and be blameless'?

The sign of a new covenant or an existing one?

That Yahweh says he will 'give' his covenant to Abraham is certainly one of the most curious aspects of the institution of circumcision. In chapter 12 Yahweh called Abraham out of Ur of the Chaldeans and promised he would bless him, give him the land of Canaan, and that through him all nations of the earth would be blessed. In chapter 15 Yahweh confirmed that promise with a covenant. What then does it mean in Genesis 17 that Yahweh will 'give' Abraham his covenant? Establishing the nature of the relationship between Genesis 15 and 17 is crucial for this project, since the relationship between the two covenant events will reveal how the circumcision of Genesis 17 relates, if at all, to the righteousness and faith of Genesis 15.

Various reasons for this peculiarity have been offered. Some suggest different authors. So according to Coats, Genesis 17 is P's reworking of the earlier tradition in Genesis 15.[2] Wenham and others solve the riddle by viewing Genesis 17 as a confirmation of the Genesis 15 covenant[3] or as 'two sides of the one transaction'.[4] Similarly, Cotter suggests that while Genesis 12 and 15 focus on God's promises to Abraham, Genesis 17 introduces the requirement of an 'active response from Abraham' by way of circumcision.[5] In contrast, McComiskey sees two distinct covenants: the first, in Genesis 15, is a 'promissory' covenant, while the circumcision covenant is an 'administrative'

---

[2] Coats 1983: 136. Our interest here is in the final form of the text.
[3] Wenham 1994: 20.
[4] Kidner 1967: 139.
[5] Cotter 2003: 109.

one,[6] such that the circumcision covenant 'administers' an aspect of the human response to the divine promise. Williamson also solves the problem by viewing Genesis 17 as a separate covenant, though the Genesis 17 covenant 'encompasses' the one in Genesis 15, both broadening and narrowing it.[7] Dumbrell's view is the opposite, though with the same effect: they are the same covenant but Genesis 17 'operated as a consolidation of the Abrahamic covenant and as an extension of its detail'.[8]

The suggestions are almost endless. In part, the answer is bound up in the meaning of *ntn* (give) and to some extent also *hēqîm* (establish). While God promises only to 'give' his covenant to Abraham once in Genesis 17, on three other occasions he promises to 'establish' his covenant with Abraham and with his 'offspring', or more literally 'seed' (*zera'*), after him (vv. 7, 19, 21).

In the case of both words, numerous word studies have sought to establish the meaning in one direction or another.[9] For those like Wenham who see Genesis 17 as a reconfirmation of the Genesis 15 covenant, *ntn* and *hēqîm* mean nothing other than 'confirm', whereas for Williamson, *ntn* and *hēqîm* refer to the formation of a new covenant.[10] Yet many of the studies fail to grant sufficient weight to the meaning of the two words *in this chapter*. As Williamson argues with respect to *hēqîm*, 'Fixing the precise nuance must therefore be determined by the function of Genesis 17 within its literary context. It cannot be established by linguistics alone.'[11] The way to proceed then is to examine the meaning of both words in connection with *běrît* (covenant) more broadly but also to examine their particular use and nuance within Genesis 17. We will consider the meaning of *hēqîm* in Genesis 17 much later in this chapter. We begin, however, with the meaning of *ntn*.[12]

'I will give'

A look more broadly at how *ntn* is used in connection with *běrît* actually yields surprisingly little fruit. *Ntn* is used in connection with

[6] McComiskey 1985: 146–150.
[7] Williamson 2000: 189.
[8] Dumbrell 2009: 74.
[9] One of the most extensive is the recent effort by Gentry and Wellum 2012. See particularly pp. 247–299 and the appendix which examines every use of *běrît* in the OT.
[10] Williamson 2000: 195–206.
[11] Ibid. 198–199.
[12] Gentry and Wellum (2012: 266) propose that *ntn* is merely an example of 'natural stylistic variation' and is used as 'a substitute for *hēqîm*'. But that gives scant regard to how the two words are used in this chapter.

bĕrît only in Genesis 9:12, 17:2 and Numbers 25:12.[13] In Genesis 9:12 Yahweh tells Noah, 'This is the sign of the covenant which I am giving [*ntn*], between me and you and every living thing which is with you, for all generations . . .' (my tr.). It is not immediately apparent here whether the 'giving' refers specifically to the covenant or to the sign of the covenant. But Wenham helpfully points out that a comparison with the relative clause in 9:17, where *hēqîm* is used in the place of *ntn*, suggests that what is being given is the covenant.[14]

In Numbers 25:12 a covenant is 'given' (*ntn*) to Phinehas the priest. Williamson suggests that the covenant with Phinehas may be a covenant in its own right.[15] Yet it seems to make more sense to view this as bound up with a more general covenant with the Levites. That covenant is referred to several times later in the OT (Neh. 13:29; Jer. 33:17–22; Mal. 2:1–9).[16] Although the arrangement with the priests is not described as a covenant when it is introduced (Exod. 28 – 29; Lev. 8 – 9), it can hardly be overlooked that the arrangement is introduced in the context of the Mosaic covenant, and the hereditary priesthood is given to Aaron by a statute within that covenant (Exod. 29:9). The author of Hebrews certainly argues that the priesthood and the Mosaic covenant are so intertwined that there cannot be a change of the priesthood without a change of the law (Heb. 7:12). Thus God is not establishing a new covenant with Phinehas but rather specifying more particularly that the existing covenant will be worked out through his particular line of descendants. It is another way of saying, 'What I promised to Aaron, I am now giving to you.' Such an understanding of *ntn*, however, is not possible in Genesis 17 since the covenant already belonged to Abraham.

A look at how *ntn* is used within Genesis 17 itself and more broadly in the patriarchal narratives, however, begins to shed some light on what is meant by Yahweh's 'giving' Abraham his covenant. After calling Abraham in chapter 12, God promises multiple times to 'give' things to Abraham. In every instance where God speaks to Abraham and the word *ntn* is used (excluding Gen. 17) the object is the land (12:7; 13:15, 17; 15:7–18), and Yahweh is either promising to give it to Abraham directly or to his 'seed'. On another occasion Abraham

---

[13] Wenham 1994: 20.

[14] Wenham 1987: 195.

[15] Williamson 2000: 200.

[16] That some kind of covenant relationship exists between Yahweh and the Levites before Num. 25 is demonstrated by the reference to a 'covenant of salt' in Num. 18:15 (Williamson 2003: 152).

asks what God can possibly 'give' him since God has not 'given' him an heir (Gen. 15:2–3).

Similarly, in chapter 17, *ntn* is used several times in addition to verse 2. Twice Yahweh promises to 'give' Abraham to be the father of many nations (17:5–6); once to 'give' him and his 'seed' the land (17:8); once to 'give' to Abraham a son through Sarah (17:16); and once to 'give' Ishmael to be a great nation (17:20). In each case, God's giving pertains not to the *creation* or *confirmation* of the covenant, but to the realization of *what was promised*. Thus Dumbrell understands *ntn* to be about 'setting the covenant in operation'. He writes, 'The content of the revelation is about to be set in train in the form of activated promises.'[17] It would seem that while the covenant enshrines, codifies and guarantees what God will do and give, those things are yet to be given.

This is further supported by the fact that the 'giving' of the covenant in 17:2 is almost certainly in the future. Although the Hebrew imperfect can refer to the past, present or future, the context here makes clear that what is spoken of is specifically future. The 'giving' of the covenant is linked with Yahweh's 'multiplying' Abraham. Yahweh says, 'I will *give* you my covenant and I will *multiply* you exceedingly' (Gen. 17:2, my tr.).

Multiplying Abraham exceedingly is clearly in the future, not the present. At this stage Abraham has only one child. His only other child, Isaac, is yet to be conceived. Since both 'give' and 'multiply' are in the imperfect, it makes sense to take them as both referring to the future, rather than taking 'multiplying' as referring to the future and 'giving' as referring to the present. Moreover, all the other things Yahweh says in chapter 17 he will 'give' Abraham, where the imperfect is used, are also things he will receive in the future and not at that present moment (17:6, 8, 16, 20).

We have then a tentative answer to what it means that Yahweh will 'give' his covenant to Abraham: Yahweh was speaking of giving to Abraham not the promise itself, but *what was promised*. As we examine other references to circumcision throughout the rest of the OT and the NT that view will be seen to be more and more likely.

A condition for fulfilment?

Our next question then is the relationship between Yahweh's 'giving' what was promised and the command to Abraham to 'walk before

---

[17] Dumbrell 2009: 73; also Keil and Delitzsch 1996: 1:143; Williamson 2000: 204–205.

me and be blameless'. The nature of that relationship is disputed. Alexander rightly points out that 'generally in the verbal sequence imperative + cohortative "the second clause expresses a purpose or result"'.[18] Thus he offers the translation 'I am God Almighty; walk before me, and be blameless *so that* I may make my covenant between me and you, and multiply you exceedingly.' So Alexander contends, 'it is evident that certain conditions are placed upon Abraham which must be fulfilled before the covenant is made'.[19] Yet other authors draw different conclusions.

Hamilton, noting that the structure of 'imperative(s) followed by imperfects (with *waw* consecutive)' is the same as in 12:1–2, concludes similarly that the imperfects express intention. Yet he understands that 'God's command for Abraham to walk blamelessly is but a means to an end'.[20] In other words, the means by which God will accomplish what he has promised is *through* Abraham's walking blamelessly before him, though that clearly is dependent on Abraham's cooperation. So too Kaiser, following Rogers, believes that the cohortatives emphasize 'intentionality rather than obligation', yet the call to 'walk before me and be blameless' is not a condition, but rather an 'invitation to receive the gift of promise by faith'.[21] However, Rogers can still write, 'it cannot be denied that a certain conditional element is present'.[22] Moreover, in all the examples that Rogers cites to support his notion of intentionality, there is in each at least some sense of the events being consecutive. That is, the syntactically later event is subsequent also in time and dependent in some way on the first having taken place. So Abraham must first go to the land and it will be there that God will bless him (12:1–2). Joseph must bring his father, his brothers and their households to Pharaoh before Pharaoh can give them the best of the land of Egypt (45:18). Jacob must name his wages before Laban is able to give those wages to him (30:28). Jacob must first return to the land of his kindred before (or where) Yahweh will do him good

[18] Alexander 1983: 19, quoting Lambdin 1973: 119.

[19] Alexander 1983: 19. Alexander believes that the condition to 'walk before Yahweh and be blameless' is met in Genesis 22 when Abraham nearly sacrifices Isaac (Alexander 2012: 179–80; also Williamson 2000: 246). However, as we will see, there are good reasons to believe that expression envisages something much more comprehensive and ongoing, and that the condition is ultimately met not by Abraham but by his 'seed'.

[20] V. P. Hamilton 1990: 463.

[21] Kaiser 1978: 93.

[22] Rogers 1970: 252.

(32:9). Esau's hunting in the field requires him first to take his bow and his quiver (27:3).[23]

Whether the stress is on the condition or on Yahweh's intention is hardly material. What is clear is that the precursor of 'giving the covenant' is 'blamelessness'. The latter must be a reality before the former takes place. Taken in concert with the definition of *ntn* above, the most straightforward reading of this passage is that 'walking before Yahweh' and being 'blameless' is the prerequisite for Abraham's receiving the *content* of what God had promised. That relationship will also be confirmed in the following chapters. Crucially, in contrast to Alexander and Williamson, blamelessness was not the prerequisite for the promise being made or for it being confirmed as a covenant; rather, blamelessness is the prerequisite for receiving what was promised. God had already made his promise to Abraham and had confirmed that promise with an oath. Yet the fulfilment awaited the realization of both 'blamelessness' and 'walking before Yahweh'. Recognizing that, however, does not allow us to determine whether blamelessness is properly a condition or simply a means to an end, as Hamilton suggests. In large measure, the answer to that turns on how we understand the terms 'blameless' and 'walking before Yahweh'. We will consider those ideas in turn.

'Be blameless'

At its most basic *tāmîm* means 'complete' or 'whole'. On a handful of occasions it simply refers to the whole of something, such as the whole tail of a peace offering, or a whole day (Lev. 3:9; 23:15; 25:30; Josh. 10:13; Ezek. 15:5; Prov. 1:12). Yet it is clear from other examples that it has a more substantial meaning. For example, the world and the future can be divided into the blameless and the wicked (e.g. Ps. 37:18–20). Similarly, a number of proverbs also speak of blessing for the blameless and disaster for the wicked (Prov. 2:21; 11:5, 20; 28:10, 18). So while *tāmîm* can simply refer to something being whole or complete, our interest here is in what *tāmîm* means in the moral/religious sphere or what constitutes wholeness or completeness in relationship to God and in terms of human relationship with God.

Several scholars argue that 'wholeness' in the moral/religious sphere is understood in terms of the sincerity of one's allegiance to God, or

---

[23] The other examples that Rogers (ibid. 252–253) mentions (1 Sam. 14:12; 28:22; 2 Sam. 14:7) all presuppose consecation of some kind, if not purpose.

in terms of faith. Often that is in contrast to what might be called 'perfect obedience'. For example, Kedar-Kopfstein writes, 'It suggests neither sinless nor particularistic obedience to a specific legal system ... The word group *tmm* denotes conduct that is right, benign, upstanding, and just, whether expressed in a single act or in a general way of life.'[24]

With respect to Genesis 17, Kline contends that God's command to Abraham to be blameless 'matches that used in ancient covenants of grant for the basic obligation to display integrity in allegiance and fidelity in service, the kind of conduct that would meet with the royal approval and reward'.[25]

The point is also frequently made that only a few chapters earlier in Genesis 6:9 Noah has been described as 'whole' and 'walking before Yahweh'. So Williamson argues:

> The idea is not one of sinless perfection or moral faultlessness – such would be an impossible goal, and as readers we already know from Noah's description back in Genesis 6 that what God was demanding of Abraham here is possible. Rather, the idea here seems to be being whole or complete; being totally dedicated to God.[26]

Yet a survey of the use of *tāmîm* through the rest of the OT suggests that the requirement of 'wholeness' means more than simply integrity or even faith. It refers to absolute personal holiness, though the lack of that holiness is accounted for in the interim through sacrifice.

There are admittedly a number of passages where *tāmîm* simply seems to mean 'genuine'. In Judges 9:16 and 19 it appears to mean little more than acting in 'good faith'. In a similar vein, in Amos 5:10 Yahweh refers to the hatred the wicked have for the person who 'speaks the truth [*tāmîm*]'. Nevertheless, the two occurrences in Judges are referring primarily to human relationships, while the one in Amos still represents an absolute standard though in a limited sphere (i.e. truth). Our interest is in what *tāmîm* means in the moral/religious

---

[24] Kedar-Kopfstein 2006: 707.

[25] Kline 2006: 310. Weinfeld (1970: 185–186) notes the remarkable parallel in an Assyrian grant of Ashurbanipal: 'Balṭya ... whose heart is devoted (lit. is whole) to his master, served me (lit. stood before me) with truthfulness, acted perfectly (lit. walked in perfection [*ittalaku šalmiš*]) in my palace, grew up with a good name and kept the charge of my kingship.'

[26] Williamson 2007: 87.

sphere, in relation to God. Furthermore, these few uses that seem to mean little more than 'genuine' are significantly outweighed by the uses that depict something more absolute – more than sincere but imperfect obedience.

For instance, several times *tāmîm* is used to refer to God's attributes or actions: God's work is 'perfect' (Deut. 32:4); his way is 'perfect' (2 Sam. 22:31; Ps. 18:30); his law is 'perfect' (Ps. 19:7); he is 'perfect in knowledge' (Job 37:16); he shows himself 'blameless' (2 Sam. 22:26; Ps. 18:25). Astonishingly, in Job 36:4, Elihu claims that his words are true because he is 'perfect in knowledge'. Although Elihu's claim is pompous and exaggerated,[27] the logic of his statement reveals his understanding of *tāmîm*: he believes that the truth of his words is guaranteed by his 'perfect' knowledge. In Ezekiel 28:14 the king of Tyre is pictured (perhaps sarcastically)[28] in an Edenic state. In that state, Yahweh says:

> You were blameless [*tāmîm*] in your ways
> from the day you were created,
> till unrighteousness was found in you.
> (Ezek. 28:15)

Using *tāmîm* to describe the pre-fall condition suggests that ultimately 'wholeness' describes a life totally without sin, as in the Garden of Eden.[29]

Within the Pentateuch, Deuteronomy 18:13 is the only other occasion besides Genesis 17:1 where the *command* to be blameless is found.[30] Moses says to the people that when they come into the land, they should not follow the detestable practices of the nations but 'you shall be blameless [*tāmîm*] before the LORD your God' (Deut. 18:13). Admittedly, either notion of blamelessness could fit here – absolute perfection or genuine commitment. As with Genesis 17:1, the meaning must be decided by an understanding of how *tāmîm* was perceived more broadly.

Perhaps the most astonishing use of *tāmîm* comes at the end of Joshua, where Joshua having gathered the people commands them to 'fear Yahweh and serve him in blamelessness [*tāmîm*] and in truth and

[27] Wilson 2015: 173.
[28] Duguid 1999: 345.
[29] Even if the language being used here is allegorical or sarcastic it still gives us a picture of what *tāmîm* means. For more on this passage see the next chapter.
[30] Hahn 2009: 114.

turn aside from the gods which your fathers served beyond the river and in Egypt and serve Yahweh' (Josh. 24:14, my tr.).

What is surprising is that after the people commit to serving Yahweh (Josh. 24:16–18), Joshua replies, 'You are not able to serve the LORD, for he is a holy God. He is a jealous God; he will not forgive your transgressions or your sins' (Josh. 24:19). Butler notes that 'Joshua's answer is perhaps the most shocking statement in the Old Testament. He denies that the people can do that which he has spent the entire chapter trying to get them to do.'[31] Once again we find the call to wholeness, yet Joshua portrays it as an impossible wholeness. Yet the mistake for Israel was to think that the impossibility of attaining the standard meant that they should simply give up. On the contrary, as we will see from further investigation of the Abrahamic promises, the point is that despite the inevitable failure, the people were to pursue a righteousness from God while living in the hope of the Abrahamic promise – the hope that God would finally bring about the conditions such that his people could live for him in wholeness and truth.

Numerous psalms bring together the notions of walking and being whole, as in Genesis 17:1 (Pss 15:2; 84:11; 101:2, 6; 119:1, 80). Psalm 15:1 asks a significant question:

> O LORD, who shall sojourn in your tent?
> Who shall dwell on your holy hill?

The answer to which is, 'the one who walks blamelessly [*hôlēk tāmîm*] and who does what is righteous, and who speaks the truth in his heart' (Ps. 15:2, my tr.). In Psalm 101 David speaks of his thoroughgoing commitment to 'blamelessness':

> I will ponder the way that is blameless [*tāmîm*].
>   Oh when will you come to me?
> I will walk with integrity of heart ['*ethallēk bĕtom-lĕbābî*]
>   within my house;
> I will not set before my eyes
>   anything that is worthless.
> I hate the work of those who fall away;
>   it shall not cling to me.
> A perverse heart shall be far from me;
>   I will know nothing of evil . . .

---

[31] Butler 2014: 2:323.

I will look with favour on the faithful in the land,
    that they may dwell with me;
he who walks in the way that is blameless [*tāmîm*]
    shall minister to me.

No one who practises deceit
    shall dwell in my house;
no one who utters lies
    shall continue before my eyes.

Morning by morning I will destroy
    all the wicked in the land,
cutting off all the evildoers
    from the city of the LORD.

(Ps. 101:2–8)

David's language is polarizing: 'I will know *nothing* of evil . . . *No one* who practises deceit . . . *no one* who utters lies . . . I will destroy *all* the wicked . . . cutting off *all* the evildoers'. Whether David viewed the standard of blamelessness as achievable or not is largely irrelevant. What is clear from David's language is that he understood that blamelessness brooked no imperfection – it was more than trust. Moreover, his desire was not simply a blameless past, but a blameless character. In other words, the notion of blamelessness is not merely concerned with past deeds and the question 'What has this person done?' But with the broader question 'What kind of person *is* this?'

Psalm 119 also brings together the language of walking with blamelessness:

Blessed are those whose way is blameless
    [*tĕmîmê-dārek*];
those who walk in the law of Yahweh
    [*hahōlĕkîm bĕtôrat yhwh*].
(Ps. 119:1, my tr.)

Yet the next few verses demonstrate that while the psalmist desires to walk in the law of Yahweh and to have blameless ways, he is not quite there: 'Oh that my ways may be steadfast in keeping your statutes!' (Ps. 119:5). More telling is verse 80, in which he specifically prays for blamelessness:

> May my heart be blameless [*tāmîm*] in your statutes
> that I may not be ashamed.
>
> (my tr.)

Psalm 119 pushes us again to a high view of blamelessness, yet it is a blamelessness that somehow comes from God – it can be prayed for. How that blamelessness comes will become clear in this and subsequent chapters.

Kedar-Kopfstein summarizes the situation well when he observes that 'the root *tmm* conveys the notion of completeness, a *totality without any diminution*'.[32] Indeed, that definition highlights that even if one were to take *tāmîm* to refer to sincerity or integrity, the standard for those characteristics is absolute. How sincere is *wholly* sincere? What degree of integrity is *sufficient* integrity? Wholeness means whole in every respect in one's relationship with Yahweh, *without diminution*. Thus it includes integrity and sincerity, but it represents the perfection of those qualities, best exemplified in God himself. We will see later in chapter 4 that the NT presents the same high standard when it uses the language of 'perfection' and 'blamelessness'. For the moment, however, we simply note that 'blameless' or 'perfect' is a suitable translation of *tāmîm* that conveys the standard to which God was calling Abraham.

Blamelessness and sacrifice

Given the apparent unattainability of blamelessness, what is striking is that the OT does not attempt to diminish that standard to make it more accessible, but rather maintains that standard by introducing the notion of sacrifice. Of the 91 uses of *tāmîm* in the OT, 51 refer to the offering up of animals that are 'without blemish'.[33] In other words, the most significant use of blamelessness language is found in the sacrificial system.

Kiuchi argues that 'wholeness' in the sacrificial system refers to 'wholeheartedness and a willingness to forgo all earthly desires'. He notes that blamelessness does not refer to 'moral perfection' and that 'it lies not in trying to observe the Lord's commandments *as much as possible*, but in laying bare the heart and becoming completely honest

---

[32] Kedar-Kopfstein 2006: 702 (emphasis mine).
[33] Exod. 12:5; 29:1; Lev. 1:3, 10; 3:1, 6; 4:3, 23, 28, 32; 5:15, 18; 6:6; 9:2–3; 14:10 (twice); 22:19, 21; 23:12, 18; Num. 6:14 (three times); 19:2; 28:3, 9, 11, 19, 31; 29:2, 8, 13, 17, 20, 23, 26, 29, 32, 36; Ezek. 43:22, 23 (twice), 25; 45:18, 23; 46:4 (twice), 6 (twice), 13.

before the Lord, without which any apparently pious endeavour is hypocritical'.[34] Furthermore, he argues by referring to the 'whole-heartedness' of Noah and Abraham that such a requirement is attainable. Their wholeness consisted in their 'sacrificial character'. Yet, as we have seen, *tāmîm* in the moral/religious realm has more to do with the perfections of God than it does with the kind of openness, transparency or wholeheartedness Kiuchi suggests.

It would seem that the point of offering a perfect/whole animal is in order to atone for the imperfection of the offerer. Taking the life of the animal is, in some way at least, intended to portray the necessity of a life being taken on account of the imperfection of the one bringing the offering (Lev. 17:11). Hence the one bringing the sacrifice would lay their hands on the head of the animal before it is sacrificed and the offering would be accepted '*for him* to make atonement *for him*' (Lev. 1:4, emphases mine). Indeed, arguably the imperfection of the offerer is the *raison d'être* of the entire sacrificial system. That is, the *physical* wholeness/perfection of the animal represents the *moral/religious* wholeness/blamelessness/perfection required, but not found in the offerer.

The predominance of blamelessness language in the sacrificial system is suggestive for how we understand the blamelessness of Noah and Abraham. In the recorded histories of both Noah and Abraham, the description of Noah as *tāmîm* and the command to Abraham to be *tāmîm* are foundational in describing their relationship to God. For an ancient Israelite reading the Torah, the very next use of *tāmîm* was to be found in early Exodus in the sacrificial regulations. From then on in the Pentateuch it refers repeatedly to animals 'without blemish' with only five exceptions.[35] This overwhelming use of *tāmîm* within the sacrificial legislation would seem to function almost as a commentary on the meaning of *tāmîm* within the Genesis narrative.[36] But it was not merely a textual commentary; it was a commentary that was lived out. The whole way of life of God's people was a kind of commentary on the text of Genesis. They could hardly be expected not to read Genesis 6:9 and 17:1 through the lens of their daily practice. Like the Israelites

[34] Kiuchi 2007: 63–65 (emphasis his).
[35] It is used to refer to the 'whole' of something (Lev. 3:9; 23:15; 25:30); in the call to be 'blameless' (Deut. 18:13); and to refer to God's works (Deut. 32:4).
[36] Von Rad (1972: 126) also explains *tāmîm* from its association with the sacrificial system but rejects its ethical significance; while Kedar-Kopfstein (2006: 707) rejects Eichrodt's suggestion that the use of *tāmîm* to describe moral conduct must have arisen from the sacrificial system. Yet, as we will see, the moral and sacrificial content of *tāmîm* is confirmed by the way the NT and Qumran authors reflect on the language.

who could be both not *tāmîm* by virtue of their sin, but at the same time *tāmîm* on account of God's mercy through sacrifice, in the same way Noah and Abraham could be both not *tāmîm* on account of their sins, which are plainly evident in the Genesis narrative, but they could also, presumably, be described as *tāmîm* on account of God's mercy. Thus the sacrificial system, in its symbolism at least, appears designed to resolve the impossibility of 'blamelessness', but it does so without diluting the demand to be blameless.

That also helps to make sense of the later use of *tāmîm* language in the Psalms and Proverbs. Any claim, commitment or call to a blameless life must be held within the context of a sacrificial system which declared that, through the sacrifice of a 'whole' substitute, blamelessness was available to people who did not deserve it on the basis of their own life. While such a connection between the moral meaning of *tāmîm* and the sacrificial system may at this point seem somewhat speculative, we will see in chapter 4 that it is supported by the way both the NT and the Qumran material use the language of blamelessness.

In contrast, Jewish interpretation has often understood blamelessness in Genesis 17 not chiefly in ethical terms but in physical terms. Abraham's blemish was his foreskin, and thus circumcision itself makes Abraham 'whole'. *Targum Pseudo-Jonathan* records:

And Yahweh appeared to Abram and said to him, 'I am El Shaddai. Serve before me and be whole in your flesh and I will give my covenant between my word and between you and I will multiply you very much.' And because Abram was not circumcised, he was not able to stand and he bent down upon his face. (*Tg. Ps.-J.* 17.1–3, my tr.)

Commenting on Genesis 17, *Gen. Rab.* 46.4 asserts:

This may be illustrated by a noble lady whom the king commanded, 'Walk before me.' She walked before him and her face went pale, for, thought she, who knows but that some defect may have been found in me? Said the king to her, 'Thou hast no defect, but that the nail of thy little finger is slightly too long; pare it and the defect will be gone.' Similarly, God said to Abraham, 'Thou hast no other defect but this foreskin: remove it and the defect will be gone.' Hence, walk before me, and be thou whole.[37]

---

[37] Freedman and Simon 1939: 1:391.

Yet, as we have seen, in the ethical/religious sphere blamelessness/ wholeness is bound up with the perfections of God himself, and the sacrificial cult foreshadowed provision for the lack of moral/ethical wholeness of individuals through a 'whole' substitute. Moreover, the fact that Noah was blameless before circumcision was instituted supports the idea that blamelessness/wholeness is not found in circumcision.[38] Nevertheless, although in *Genesis Rabbah* the blemish is considered to be physical rather than ethical/moral, it is still significant that blamelessness is understood as being *entirely without defect*, in line with what has been argued above.

We left unanswered earlier the question as to whether blamelessness was for Abraham a condition or a means to an end. We are yet to discover a definitive answer to that question. However, either way, apart from God's provision of a 'whole' substitute, it is an impossibly high call: a call to the moral standards of God himself. The necessary condition for Abraham and those with him to live in the presence of God is not merely faith, but a character that possesses the same perfections as God himself. The issue is not simply a spotless record – past sins being covered – but more significantly, that the possibility of ongoing sin is ruled out by the blameless character of the one living before Yahweh. Yet despite the impossible nature of the call, God's provision of a 'whole' substitute suggests that faith in that provision opens the door to possessing blamelessness, which would otherwise be impossible.

Blamelessness and righteousness

Before we move on to consider the phrase 'walk before me', there is one other important observation to make regarding blamelessness. That is, that the concept of 'blamelessness' (*tāmîm*) is also connected with 'righteousness' (*ṣaddîq*). The two are connected throughout the OT, but also in Genesis in particular. Moreover, as we will see, Yahweh's call to Abraham to 'walk before' him and 'be blameless' cannot be separated from the righteousness God reckoned to Abraham's account in Genesis 15 on the basis of his faith.

On a number of occasions throughout the OT, blamelessness and righteousness appear together. In Deuteronomy 32:4 God is

> the Rock, his work is perfect [*tāmîm*],
> for all his ways are justice.

[38] Rabbinic Midrash would argue that circumcision was already present. This is best exemplified by the view that Noah's son Shem was born circumcised (*Gen. Rab.* 26.3).

A God of faithfulness and without iniquity,
just [*ṣaddîq*] and upright is he.

That is, God's 'perfect' works flow from his 'righteousness', uprightness and absence of iniquity. Job describes himself as 'righteous'
(*ṣaddîq*) and 'blameless' (*tāmîm*; Job 12:4). In Psalm 15:2 the person
who can ascend the hill of Yahweh is 'the one who walks blamelessly
[*hôlēk tāmîm*] and who does what is righteous [*ṣedeq*]' (my tr.). In
Proverbs 11:5 the 'righteousness of the blameless [*ṣidqat tāmîm*] makes
his way upright' (my tr.). In these examples, the two words function
almost as synonyms.

Similarly, the cognates of *tāmîm*, *tōm* and *tām*, are occasionally
connected with *ṣaddîq*. For example, in Psalm 7:8, 'Judge me, Yahweh,
according to my righteousness and my blamelessness [*kĕṣidqî
ûkĕtummî*]' (my tr.). Proverbs 20:7 refers to 'the righteous who walks
in his blamelessness [*mithallēk bĕtummô ṣaddîq*]' (my tr.). In Job 9:20
the verb *ṣaddîq* is parallel with *tām*: 'though I am righteous [*ṣdq*], my
mouth will condemn me; though I am blameless [*tām*], he will declare
me guilty' (my tr.). Again the two function almost as synonyms.

In Genesis 20:4 Abimelech declares that he is 'innocent' (*ṣaddîq*)
of the crime of sleeping with Abraham's wife. He then goes on to
protest that '[i]n the integrity of my heart [*bĕtom-lĕbābî*] and the
innocence of my hands I have done this' (Gen. 20:5). To which God
replies, 'Yes, I know that you have done this in the integrity of your
heart [*bĕtom-lĕbābĕkā*], and it was I who kept you from sinning against
me' (Gen. 20:6).

Perhaps most significant for our purposes, though, is that even
before Abraham is called to be blameless in Genesis 17:1, the two
notions of blamelessness and righteousness have been connected in
the person of Noah: 'Noah was a righteous [*ṣaddîq*] man; he was
blameless [*tāmîm*] in his generation' (Gen. 6:9, my tr.). The parallelism
between the first two clauses suggests that the phrase 'he was blameless
in his generation' is explanatory of the first, 'Noah was a righteous
man.'[39] As above, the ideas of blamelessness and righteousness appear
virtually synonymous. Moreover, these two terms have not been placed
together in passing but function as a key description of Noah, who
himself is a central character in the early chapters of Genesis. From
a literary standpoint, the fact that 'righteousness' and 'blamelessness'

---

[39] Wenham (1987: 169) notes that most commentators, following the accents, see the
two clauses as in apposition.

have been so significantly drawn together in the person of Noah suggests that for the reader of Genesis, 17:1 may easily be rephrased as 'walk before me and be righteous'.[40]

Yet between Genesis 6 and 17 is the account of Genesis 15:6, where Abraham is 'reckoned' (*ḥšb*) as righteous on account of his trust in Yahweh. The semantic connection between *ṣaddîq* and *tāmîm* suggests that Genesis 6:9, 15:6 and 17:1 all work together to make a statement about the nature of blamelessness/righteousness. Most peculiarly, it would appear that in Genesis 17:1 Abraham is called to be blameless/righteous when he already is blameless/righteous. The solution to that puzzle would seem to lie in the verb *ḥšb* ('to reckon'; Gen. 15:6). Abraham was reckoned by Yahweh to have what he did not yet in fact possess. He was counted righteous/blameless on account of his faith. This was ratified when Yahweh confirmed his promise to Abraham with a covenant. But the receipt of what was promised in the covenant awaited the realization of Abraham's blamelessness. Moreover, the realization of Abraham's blamelessness must lie with God. In Genesis 15 Yahweh had taken sole responsibility for the fulfilment of his promises to Abraham by being the sole party to the covenant to pass between the sacrificial animals (albeit in the form of a smoking fire pot and flaming torch).[41] Thus if blamelessness is required before the complete fulfilment of what was promised, then that must lie in the hand of God also.

Although there is some disagreement as to whether Genesis 15 and 17 represent one covenant or two, the same result holds in either case, since the connection proposed here is between the notions of righteousness and blamelessness rather than simply covenant-making. Nevertheless, if the two chapters do represent one covenant, as I have argued, then the case is significantly strengthened. Circumcision then becomes the sign of the Genesis 15 covenant that has been established on the basis of Abraham's by-faith-righteousness, rather than circumcision being the sign of another (related) covenant.

The question was raised above whether blamelessness was for Abraham a condition or a means to an end. The connection between

---

[40] That also suggests that 'blamelessness' is not equivalent to 'integrity' or 'faith'.

[41] Smoke and fire are generally noted as symbolic of the presence of God (e.g. Exod. 13:21; 19:18; 20:18; see Wenham 1987: 332). Regardless of whether Gen. 15 constitutes an oath of self-imprecation (e.g. Kline 2006: 295–297; Gentry and Wellum 2012: 250–258; cf. Hasel 1981; V. P. Hamilton 1990: 430–434), the fact that the smoking fire pot and flaming torch representing Yahweh pass alone between the animals suggests that the covenant is unilateral (V. P. Hamilton 1990: 436–437; cf. Wenham 1987: 332–333).

blamelessness and righteousness in Genesis 15 and 17 begins to point to the fact that it is a condition, but that the fulfilment is found ultimately in Yahweh.[42] Abraham, for his part, is called to trust in Yahweh and his provision. We have already caught a glimpse of that provision in the 'whole' substitute of the sacrificial system. The manner of Yahweh's provision becomes clearer still as we investigate the other component of his call to Abraham.

'Walk before me'

The other component of Yahweh's call to Abraham is to 'walk before me' (*hithallēk lĕpānay*). *Hlk* occurs in the OT over 1,500 times. Most commonly it refers to walking in a non-metaphorical sense; but it also occurs hundreds of times as a metaphor for life, and particularly, a life lived in either obedience or disobedience.[43]

Like *tāmîm*, references to 'walking with' Yahweh are found prior to Genesis 17. In Genesis 5:22 and 24 we are given a glimpse of Enoch, who 'walked with God [*wayyithallēk ḥănôk 'et-hā'ĕlōhîm*]' (Gen. 5:24, my tr.; cf. 5:22). The description of Enoch walking with God is clearly significant since he alone in a long list of people is not said to die; instead, he simply 'was not' because 'God took him'. Similarly, we are told that 'Noah was a righteous man; blameless in all his ways. Noah walked with God [*'et-hā'ĕlōhîm hithallek-nōaḥ*]' (Gen. 6:9, my tr.). This description of Noah's character is also significant since it is on account of his righteousness that Yahweh saves him through the ark (Gen. 7:1). Both these references, however, are to walking *with* God. The command in Genesis 17:1 is to 'walk *before* me'. Sailhamer sees 'walking with God' and 'walking before God' as synonymous and meaning to fulfil one's covenant obligations, by which he means, 'simple obedience to God's commands and trust in his provision'.[44] While Hamilton sees in 'walking with' a greater intimacy and in 'walking before' the notions of 'obedience and subordination'.[45] However, it is unlikely that the different prepositions are significant.[46] Given the connection of 'walking with/before God' in Genesis with three very significant figures, it seems sensible to suppose that even if they are not identical, they are intimately related.

---

[42] Similarly, Gentry and Wellum 2012: 279, 294.
[43] See Merrill 1997; Helfmeyer 1978. For examples see n. 51 below.
[44] Sailhamer 1992: 118–119, 124.
[45] V. P. Hamilton 1990: 258.
[46] Wenham 1994: 20.

There are a few other references outside Genesis to 'walking with' Yahweh. For instance, in Malachi 2:5–6 in reference to the covenant Yahweh made with Levi:

> My covenant with him was one of life and peace, and I gave them to him. It was a covenant of fear, and he feared me. He stood in awe of my name. True instruction was in his mouth, and no wrong was found on his lips. He walked with me [*hālak 'ittî*] in peace and uprightness, and he turned many from iniquity.

In Micah 6:8 'walking with God' is modified by humility. Micah says:

> and what does the LORD require of you
> but to do justice, and to love kindness,
> and to walk humbly with your God
> [*wĕhaṣnēa' leket 'im-'ĕlōhêkā*]?
>   (Mic. 6:8)

Significantly, the expression 'walk with me' is also used numerous times in Leviticus 26. We will consider Leviticus 26 in much more detail in the next chapter. But there, 'walk with me' is modified by 'hostility': if the people walk contrary to Yahweh (lit., 'walk with me in hostility [*waḥălaktem 'immî bĕqerî*]'), then he will walk contrary to them (Lev. 26:21, 23–24, 27–28, 40–41). Remarkably, the remedy to that situation is to humble their uncircumcised hearts (Lev. 26:41).

Nevertheless, our primary interest is in the phrase 'walking before'. Again, it will be useful to follow through the remainder of the OT occurrences of this phrase where Yahweh appears as the object of the preposition 'before'. Apart from the command in Genesis 17:1, the phrase appears only in Genesis in 24:40 and 48:15. In Genesis 24:40 Abraham's servant quotes Abraham's words to Laban: 'Yahweh, before whom I have walked ['*ăšer-hithallaktî lĕpānāyw*], will send his angel with you and he will prosper your way' (my tr.). Abraham appears to be claiming to have done precisely what God had asked of him in Genesis 17:1 (in terms of walking, at least). In Genesis 48:15 Jacob blesses Joseph by saying, 'The God before whom my fathers Abraham and Isaac walked [*hithallĕkû 'ăbōtay lĕpānāyw*] . . .'. Again Jacob says that Abraham and Isaac *did* walk before God.

The next reference to someone walking before Yahweh occurs in the books of Samuel. Speaking to the high priest Eli, Yahweh recounts how he promised that Eli's house and the house of his father (i.e. Aaron),[47] would 'walk before me for ever' (*yithallĕkû lĕpānay 'ad-'ôlām*; 1 Sam. 2:30, my tr.). The phrase here refers to the work of the priesthood and to their service before Yahweh in the temple. This language is then picked up a few verses later in a significant promise. Yahweh says that Eli and his house will no longer walk before him and that in their place

> I will establish for myself a faithful priest, who will do all that is in my heart and soul, and I will build for him a faithful house, and my anointed one will walk before me all the days [*wĕhthallēk lipnê-mĕšîḥî kol-hayyāmîm*]. (1 Sam. 2:35, my tr.)

This translation repoints *lipnê* (walk before) to *lĕpānay* (walk before me) and takes *mĕšîḥî* (my anointed) as the subject of *wĕhthallēk* (he will walk).[48] This brings the verse into line with verse 30, where Yahweh has already described the priests as walking 'before *me*'. What 1 Samuel 2:35 envisages is the eventual demise of the Aaronic priesthood and its replacement with another 'anointed one'/messiah. But the definitive quality of that messiah who will walk before Yahweh is faithfulness (*'mn*) – it will be someone who will 'do all that is in my heart and soul'. As the books of Samuel unfold, it becomes apparent that such a figure will come ultimately from the line of David.[49]

It is unsurprising to find then that all but one of the subsequent references to 'walking before me' occur in instances where the king is being addressed, and often specifically in connection with the Davidic covenant. Moreover, in each case the character of their walk before Yahweh is described with terms such as 'faithfulness', 'obedience' and 'righteousness'. For instance, in 1 Kings 2:2–4 we have these words from David to Solomon:

> I am about to go the way of all the earth. Be strong, and show yourself a man, and keep the charge of the LORD your God, walking in his ways and keeping his statutes, his commandments, his rules, and his testimonies, as it is written in the Law of Moses, that you may prosper in all that you do and wherever you turn,

---

[47] Deenick 2011: 328–329.
[48] I have argued extensively for this translation in Deenick 2011.
[49] Ibid. 331–339.

that the LORD may establish his word that he spoke concerning me, saying, 'If your sons pay close attention to their way, to walk before me [*lāleket lĕpānay*] in faithfulness with all their heart and with all their soul, you shall not lack a man on the throne of Israel.' (1 Kgs 2:2–4)

Or Solomon's words to Yahweh:

You have shown great and steadfast love to your servant David my father, because he walked before you [*hālak lĕpānêkā*] in faithfulness, in righteousness, and in uprightness of heart towards you. And you have kept for him this great and steadfast love and have given him a son to sit on his throne this day. (1 Kgs 3:6)

The same sentiments are repeated in Solomon's prayer at the dedication of the temple (1 Kgs 8:23–25; also 2 Chr. 6:14–16) and in Yahweh's response (1 Kgs 9:4–7; also 2 Chr. 7:17–20). Hezekiah too claims to have 'walked before you [*hithallaktî lĕpānêkā*] in faithfulness and with a whole heart' (2 Kgs 20:3; also Isa. 38:3).

Beyond these references to the kings walking before God, twice the phrase is connected with deliverance from death. In Psalm 56:13 David writes:

For you have delivered my soul from death,
    yes, my feet from falling,
that I may walk before God [*lĕhithallēk lipnê 'ĕlōhîm*]
    in the light of life.

Or in Psalm 116:8–9:

For you have delivered my soul from death,
    my eyes from tears,
    my feet from stumbling;
I will walk before the LORD ['*ethallēk lipnê yhwh*]
    in the land of the living.

This last reference is the only occasion on which 'walking before Yahweh' is not specifically linked with the Davidic kingship.

Drawing these strands together, it seems that on its own 'walking before Yahweh' speaks first and foremost to privilege of relationship. In that light, God's call to Abraham to 'walk before me' looks like a call to intimacy with God and to a special kind of relationship.[50] But in addition, the notion of 'walking before Yahweh' is almost invariably described by some modifier. For instance, 'with integrity of heart', 'uprightness', 'doing all that I have commanded', 'with all their heart', 'in faithfulness' or 'in truth'. Yet a person may also walk before Yahweh 'in righteousness' or 'in blamelessness'. The presence of these modifiers suggests that people may walk before Yahweh with a whole heart, or they may not; they may walk before him and be blameless or they may walk before him in an inappropriate way.[51] That militates against the suggestions of some that blamelessness is the *fruit* of walking before Yahweh. Thus Sailhamer translates, 'Walk before me and you will be blameless.'[52] Instead, the evidence from the rest of the OT suggests that the phrase 'walk before me' on its own speaks only of privilege. Yet when put together with the call to be blameless, it is seen as a relationship governed by certain requirements – blamelessness and righteousness.

However, most significant of all is the connection we have seen between 'walking before Yahweh' and the Davidic kingship, and even to the Davidic kingship as a replacement for the priesthood. In that setting, 'walking before' Yahweh 'blamelessly' becomes a *condition* for the permanence of the Davidic kingship and for the fulfilment of all God's promises to David. 1 Kings 2:4 is typical: '*If* your sons pay close attention to their way, to walk before me [*lāleket lĕpānay*] in faithfulness with all their heart and with all their soul, you shall not lack a man on the throne of Israel' (1 Kgs 2:4, emphasis mine).

The kingship is also connected specifically with the language of blamelessness. The most significant example is the psalm that also occurs at the end of the books of Samuel. There David maintains:

[50] Gentry and Wellum (2012: 259–260; following Walton 1994: 72–73) suggest that the primary meaning of 'walking before God' is to 'serve as his emissary or diplomatic representative'. Still, in the end, they arrive at a similar point though with a slightly different emphasis: for Abraham to be a 'diplomatic representative' means that 'when the world looks at Abram they will see what it is like to have a right relationship to God and to be what God intended for humanity'.

[51] The same is true of the expression 'to walk' more generally. That expression is often used in the psalms with a modifier of some kind to denote a relationship of fidelity to Yahweh. A person can walk 'blamelessly' (Ps. 15:2; cf. 26:1, 11; 84:11; 101:2, 6), 'in my integrity' (Ps. 26:1, 11), 'in your faithfulness' (Ps. 26:3), 'according to his law' (Ps. 78:10; cf. 119:1), in Yahweh's 'ways' (Ps. 81:13; 119:3; 128:1), 'in your truth' (Ps. 86:11), 'uprightly' (Ps. 84:11) or 'according to my [Yahweh's] rules' (Ps. 89:30). Conversely, a person can also walk 'in his guilty ways' (Ps. 68:21) or 'in darkness' (Ps. 82:5). The difference between 'walking' and 'walking before' is the latter's emphasis on intimacy (cf. Ps. 89:15).

[52] Sailhamer 1992: 156; similarly, Gunkel 1997: 263.

> I was blameless [*tāmîm*] before him,
>   and I kept myself from guilt.
> And the LORD has rewarded me according
>   to my righteousness [*şĕdāqâ*],
> according to my cleanness in his sight.
>   (2 Sam. 22:24–25; also Ps. 18:23–24)

Such claims by David and a number of his sons to have been blameless and to have walked before God with a whole heart seem incredible given what we know of their lives, not least of David's own life and the sin he committed with Bathsheba. Nevertheless, these claims need to be understood in the context of the sacrificial system that held together both God's call to faithfulness and his provision for mercy. Within the context of both commitment to Yahweh and trust in Yahweh's merciful provision, David could claim to have been blameless. Still, the desire for blamelessness cries out for a more substantial fulfilment. So too does God's promise in 1 Samuel 2:35 that he will raise up a faithful king for whom he will build a faithful house.

Perhaps, the greatest hint towards the fulfilment of that comes in Ezekiel 37:24, where the themes of walking and kingship also occur. Yahweh says, 'My servant David shall be king over them, and they shall all have one shepherd. They shall walk [*hlk*] in my rules and be careful to obey my statutes.' Yahweh promises a Davidic figure who will lead his people to 'walk' carefully in all God's ways and statutes.

The connection between God's fulfilment of the Abrahamic covenant and the Davidic covenant is not only restricted to the language of 'walking before me'. The connection can also be observed in the way that the OT takes up the language of the Abrahamic covenant in explicit connection with God's promise to David.[53] For instance, God tells Jeremiah, 'As the host of heaven cannot be numbered and the sands of the sea cannot be measured, so I will multiply the offspring [*zeraʿ*] of David my servant' (Jer. 33:22). The seed of Abraham and David are then explicitly brought together a few verses later:

> Thus says the LORD: If I have not established my covenant with day and night and the statutes of heaven and earth, then I will reject the seed [*zeraʿ*] of Jacob and David my servant, not taking

---

[53] See Alexander 1995.

37

from his seed [*zera'*] rulers for the seed [*zera'*] of Abraham, Isaac and Jacob. For I will restore their fortunes and have mercy on them. (Jer. 33:25–26, my tr.)

So too in Psalm 89 Yahweh promises numerous times to establish David's 'seed' and his throne for ever:

> I will establish your seed [*zera'*] for ever
> and I will build your throne for all generations.
> (Ps. 89:4, my tr.)[54]

While in Psalm 72, in a prayer concerning the king, we find the request

> May his name endure for ever,
> his fame continue as long as the sun!
> May people be blessed in him,
> all nations call him blessed!
> (Ps. 72:17)

This appears to be a reference to Genesis 12:3–4 and 22:18. Anderson comments:

> This verse seems to be an allusion to Yahweh's promise to Abraham (Gen 12:2f., 22:18), and the intention may have been to stress the fact that the divine promise to the patriarch has been fulfilled in the house of David.[55]

Alexander goes further:

> The similarity between Genesis 22:18a and Psalm 72:17b is striking and supports the idea that the 'seed' mentioned in Genesis 22:17b–18a does not refer to all Abraham's descendants, but rather to a single individual. While Genesis 22 does not directly indicate that this 'seed' will be of royal standing, it is noteworthy that Genesis 17 anticipates that kings will come from Abraham and Sarah through Isaac (Gn. 17:6, 16). This divine promise is later repeated to Jacob (Gn. 35:11).[56]

[54] See also Ps. 89:29, 36.
[55] Anderson 1972: 1:526; followed by Williamson 2000: 169.
[56] Alexander 1997: 365–366.

As Alexander notes, the promise that kings would come from Abraham is stated clearly in Genesis 17:6 and 16. That is not to say that Genesis 17 makes explicit the way in which God's promise to Abraham would find its fulfilment. Yet the vague mention of kings in Genesis 17 hints at the direction from which that fulfilment would come. So too the way that the OT uses the language of Genesis 17 and especially the language of 'walking before me' suggests that the OT as a whole expects that the way in which God's fulfilment of his promise to Abraham will come is through a Davidic king who will walk before Yahweh with all his heart.

'Walking before me' then speaks of privilege. But matched with the command to be 'blameless' it speaks of a relationship in which a person relates to God perfectly, according to his holiness and righteousness. Yet the direction that those ideas are taken in the remainder of the OT points to the idea that the fulfilment of that blameless relationship and the fulfilment of God's promise to Abraham is made a reality through a blameless sacrifice, but strangely also now, through a Davidic king who will walk before Yahweh with all his heart.

Circumcision and seed

The eventual fulfilment through the Davidic covenant is also hinted at in Genesis 17 through the text's emphasis on the single 'seed' of Abraham. An often overlooked question regarding Genesis 17 is, 'With whom is the covenant being established?' That, in turn, brings us back to the meaning of *hēqîm*.

As noted earlier, while God promises only once in Genesis 17 to 'give' (*ntn*) his covenant to Abraham, on three other occasions he promises to 'establish' (*hēqîm*) his covenant with Abraham and with his 'seed' after him (vv. 7, 19, 21). While the former simply means 'give', the latter, Hamilton notes, can mean anything from 'establish' to 'maintain' to 'fulfil'.[57]

The word *qwm* is used in connection with *běrît* (covenant) seventeen times in the OT,[58] where either a *běrît* is being established, or an aspect of a *běrît* is being established. On all but one occasion (Isa. 28:18) the verb is in the hiphil form (*hēqîm*). In Genesis 6 – 9 God tells Noah

---

[57] V. P. Hamilton 1990: 465.
[58] Gen. 6:18; 9:9, 11, 17; 17:7, 19, 21; Exod. 6:4; Lev. 26:9; Deut. 8:18; 2 Kgs 23:3; Neh. 9:8; Isa. 28:18; 49:8; Jer. 34:18; Ezek. 16:60, 62.

four times that he will 'establish' his covenant with him (6:18; 9:9, 11, 17). In Genesis 17 God tells Abraham that he will 'establish' his covenant with him and with Isaac. In Exodus 6:3–4 God tells Moses that he 'established' his covenant specifically with Abraham, Isaac and Jacob. Here the covenant initiation is an achieved fact, though what was promised in the covenant – the land of Canaan – was never received by any of the three patriarchs; they were merely 'sojourners' in it.[59] So while in Genesis 6 – 9 *hēqîm* could mean something like 'inaugurate', in the latter two cases the multiple generations with whom the covenant is 'established' suggests *hēqîm* must mean something more akin to 'perpetuate'.

In Leviticus 26:9 God also promises to 'establish' his covenant. In this context, the implication is that God will do what he has promised: God will multiply the Israelites, make them fruitful, walk among them and be their God. In the same vein, in Deuteronomy 8:18 God urges the people to remember that it is he who gives them the 'power to get wealth' for the purpose of 'establishing' the 'covenant' that he 'swore to your fathers'. That is, God gave them wealth in fulfilment of, or for the purpose of bringing to pass, the covenant promises he made to Abraham, Isaac and Jacob.

In Nehemiah 9:8 a number of the Levites recount that Yahweh 'cut' (*krt*) a covenant with Abraham and that Yahweh has 'kept' (*hēqîm*) his 'words'. What follows in the rest of chapter 9 is an account of *how* Yahweh has 'kept' his words: Yahweh has maintained his promise despite the sin of the people. In Nehemiah 9:8 we are told that Yahweh has kept his words because 'he is righteous', and in 9:33 we find out in what way he has been righteous: 'you have been righteous in all that has come upon us, for you have dealt faithfully and we have acted wickedly'. In this instance, *hēqîm* refers to God's commitment to do what he has promised or said.

In Ezekiel 16:60 and 62 Yahweh promises to 'establish' (*hēqîm*) an 'eternal covenant' or 'my covenant' as a result of the Israelites 'breaking' (*prr*) the covenant. He says:

> I will do to you just as you did, who despised the oath by breaking the covenant. Yet I will remember *my* covenant with you in the days of your youth, and I will establish with you an everlasting

---

[59] Exodus 6:4 therefore demonstrates that 'establish' cannot mean 'make a reality' or 'fulfil' in a person's 'historical reality' (as per Gentry and Wellum 2012: 155), since Yahweh 'established' his covenant with Abraham, Isaac and Jacob, but they did not receive the things promised (i.e. the land).

covenant. And you will remember your ways and be ashamed when you take your sisters, both your older and your younger, and I will give them to you, but not on the basis of *your* covenant. I will establish *my* covenant with you and you will know that I am Yahweh . . . (Ezek. 16:59–62, my tr.)

There is a play here between '*I* will remember' and '*you* will remember', as well as between '*my* covenant' and '*your* covenant'.[60] The 'broken' and 'despised' covenant now becomes *theirs*, while Yahweh's covenant, unilaterally entered into with Abraham in the days of their youth, is *his*. Most likely, the background for Ezekiel's comments is Leviticus 26, which we will consider in more detail in the next chapter. In Leviticus 26 Yahweh promises that when the people reject the Mosaic covenant he will remember and uphold his covenant with Abraham.[61] In this instance, *hēqîm* means something like 'bring to fulfilment'.

In Isaiah 28:18 the opposite can be found. Yahweh says to the people:

Then your covenant with death will be annulled [atoned?],
and your agreement with Sheol will not stand.

Here the parallelism suggests that annulling the covenant is synonymous with the covenant 'not standing'. In Jeremiah 34:18 the people did not 'keep' (*hēqîm*) the words of the covenant that they made, in which they promised to release fellow Israelites who were their slaves.

On two occasions a covenant is 'cut' (*krt*) or 'given' (*ntn*) to guarantee the establishment of something else. So in 2 Kings 23:3 Josiah 'cuts' a covenant with God 'to perform [*hēqîm*] the words of this covenant'. And in Isaiah 49:8, Yahweh 'gives' his servant as a 'covenant to the people, to establish [*hēqîm*] the land'.

It would appear then that in relation to *běrît*, *hēqîm* has a variety of meanings from 'perpetuate' to 'keep' to 'bring to reality'. That range of meaning would seem to support the contention of Dumbrell and others that *hēqîm* always refers to an existing covenant,[62] since

---

[60] *Mibběrîtēk* (v. 61) is sometimes translated 'my covenant with you' (e.g. NIV, NET; cf. HCSB), yet in the light of the parallelism begun in vv. 61 and 62, introduced by *wēzākartî* and *wēzākart* respectively, it makes more sense to translate it as 'your covenant'.

[61] Block 1997: 516–518.

[62] Dumbrell 2009: 25–26; Gentry and Wellum 2012: 155–161; Milgrom 2001: 2343–2346; cf. Gunkel 1997: 266.

to perpetuate, keep or bring a covenant to reality it must already exist! That, together with the definition of *ntn* as 'give what was promised', suggests, contrary to Williamson and others, that the covenant described in Genesis 17 is the same as the one in Genesis 15. Perhaps the most compelling reason of all, however, is that no later biblical author seems to deal with two Abrahamic covenants but only with one. As Wellum and Gentry note, 'Never in all the historical summaries in the Old Testament . . . is there a reference to two Abrahamic covenants. There is only one covenant with Abraham, confirmed to Isaac and Jacob.'[63]

Yet it remains to be seen what particular nuance *hēqîm* carries in Genesis 17. As already noted, while God promises only to 'give' (*ntn*) his covenant to Abraham once in Genesis 17, the expression *hēqîm bĕrît* is used three times. On the first occasion Yahweh says to Abraham, 'And I will establish my covenant [*wahăqimōtî 'et-bĕrîtî*] between me and between you and between your seed after you for their generations for an eternal covenant to be your God and the God of your seed after you' (Gen. 17:7, my tr.).

The second and third occurrences in verses 19 and 21 explain what God means when he says that he will establish his covenant between Abraham and his 'seed'. In verse 18 Abraham asks that Ishmael might 'live before you', which seems to be an echo of 'walk before'. But Yahweh replies, 'No, Sarah your wife will bear for you a son and you will call him Isaac, and I will establish my covenant with him [*wahăqimōtî 'et-bĕrîtî 'ittô*], for an eternal covenant for his seed after him' (Gen. 17:19, my tr.).

God's promise to establish (*hēqîm*) his covenant with Isaac and his 'seed' after him mirrors God's promise to Abraham in verse 7. In the first place, the intent is to distinguish Isaac from Ishmael. Verses 20 and 21 serve to contrast further Isaac and Ishmael's relationship to the covenant:

> As for Ishmael, I have heard you; behold, I have blessed him and will make him fruitful and multiply him greatly. He shall father twelve princes, and I will make him into a great nation. But I will establish my covenant with Isaac [*wĕ'et-bĕrîtî 'āqîm 'et-yiṣḥāq*], whom Sarah shall bear to you at this time next year. (Gen. 17:20–21)

---

[63] Gentry and Wellum 2012: 280. For other compelling arguments for understanding the two episodes as representing one covenant see ibid. 263–280.

Ishmael will indeed be blessed but Yahweh will establish his covenant with Isaac.[64]

However, the *hēqîm* language not only serves to distinguish Isaac (and Abraham) from Ishmael; it also serves to distinguish Isaac and Abraham from everyone else. In Genesis 17 God *establishes* his covenant with Abraham and Isaac only. Although the blessings bound up with the covenant come to others such as Sarah (17:15–16), Abraham's household (17:14),[65] and to Ishmael (17:20), the covenant is never said to be *established* with them, only with Abraham and Isaac.[66] Indeed, remarkably, such blessing and covenant status is almost, though not entirely, independent of the act of circumcision itself: Sarah is uncircumcised but enjoys the blessings of the covenant though the covenant is not established specifically with her, while Ishmael and the other males in Abraham's household are circumcised and enjoy some of the blessings of the covenant even though the covenant is not established with them.[67] Alexander comments:

> Although the male members of Abraham's household are circumcised, including Ishmael, the LORD emphasizes that the covenant will be established with Isaac, and him alone (Gen. 17:19, 21). The uniqueness of Isaac's position regarding the covenant is underlined by the exclusion of Ishmael even though he is also circumcised. This introduces an important distinction between those who may enjoy the benefits of this covenant and the one through whom the covenant will be established. Whereas the former includes all who are circumcised,[68] the latter appears to be restricted to a single line of descendants.[69]

---

[64] Arnold 2009: 174; Westermann 1995: 270. The use of *hēqîm bĕrît* in connection with Isaac rules out Williamson's proposal that the phrase refers to the establishment of a new covenant. Presumably whatever *hēqîm bĕrît* means for Abraham it means for Isaac as well, and another new covenant is not in view for Isaac.

[65] That the blessings of the covenant come to Abraham's household is clear since the failure to identify with the covenant promise through circumcision results in a person being 'cut off'. Moreover, as is clear from earlier promises, such as Gen. 12:2–4, while God's promise is to Abraham alone, those who identify with Abraham are caught up in the blessings of that promise.

[66] Bernat (2009: 19–20) notes that a *brk* versus *bĕrît* contrast is made in the passage between Abraham and Sarah first, and then Isaac and Ishmael.

[67] In a similar way, Cohen (2005: 13) refers to the *Sarah paradox* and *Ishmael paradox*: she is included but not circumcised, he is excluded but circumcised.

[68] Alexander is mistaken on this point, since Sarah enjoys the benefits of the covenant though she is not circumcised.

[69] Alexander 2012: 102.

God's promise to Abraham to establish his covenant with Abraham and his 'seed' after him will be fulfilled with the specific 'seed', Isaac.[70] Yet in verse 19 God promises Sarah that he will establish his covenant with Isaac and his 'seed' after him. The similarity between the language of verses 7 and 19 suggests that God intends to continue with Isaac's seed the pattern established by Abraham and Isaac. Which is to say that just as God established his covenant with a single descendant of Abraham, so God intends to establish his covenant with a single descendant of Isaac.[71] That principle is confirmed in the lives of Esau and Jacob when the covenant is continued through Jacob and *not* Esau. It is also confirmed by subsequent references in the OT to Yahweh's covenant with 'Abraham, Isaac and Jacob'.[72] For instance, Yahweh says to Moses:

> I appeared to Abraham, to Isaac, and to Jacob, as God Almighty, but by my name the LORD I did not make myself known to them. I also established [*hēqîm*] my covenant with them to give them the land of Canaan, the land in which they lived as sojourners. (Exod. 6:3–4)

Clearly, the covenant was not established with everyone, but specifically with these three.

In short, in the context of Genesis 17, *hēqîm běrît* is used to indicate the line of descent through which the covenant will pass; and perhaps, more particularly, to indicate that the covenant will follow a singular line of descent.[73]

Seed in Genesis

But the covenant sign of Genesis 17 must also be read within the framework established by Genesis. And so it is significant that this interest in a particular 'seed' is also borne out by the remainder of the Genesis narrative and its interest in individual figures. That is

---

[70] In that sense, the Abrahamic covenant actually operates in a similar way to the Davidic covenant: although it is made with a specific line of descendants, it has repercussions for the whole nation and all who join themselves with the Davidic/Abrahamic promise.

[71] When Yahweh says he will make his covenant with Abraham and his seed throughout '*their* generations' (17:9), the 'they' he has in mind is the generation of one seed after another.

[72] Alexander 2012: 102, n. 44.

[73] Ibid. 178, n. 7; Williamson 2000: 161–162.

demonstrated chiefly by four things: the division of the book according to the *tôlĕdôt* (descendants) formulas, the use of genealogies, the prevalence of the term 'seed', and the recurring narrative focus on one descendant over against another.[74]

As has been well noted, Genesis is clearly structured around the term *tôlĕdôt* (2:4; 5:1; 6:9; 10:1; 11:10, 27; 25:12, 19; 36:1, 9; 37:2).[75] The term most naturally refers to 'generations of X' and in most cases is followed either immediately by a genealogy (5:1; 10:1; 11:10, 27; 25:12; 36:9) or a narrative detailing the rise of that person's descendants (2:4;[76] 25:19; 36:1; 37:2).[77] In many cases both occur (e.g. 5:1; 10:1; 25:12; 36:1). These formulas serve to focus the narrative and to focus the narrative on a particular line of descent, but also on a particular character. Especially noteworthy are the *tôlĕdôt* of Jacob, which focus not on all twelve brothers, but on Joseph. As Hamilton observes:

> The cosmos's *tôledôt* has for its center Adam and Eve, as opposed to other parts of creation. Noah's *tôledôt* has for its center Shem as opposed to the other sons. Shem's *tôledôt* has for its center Terah, as opposed to other descendants. Terah's *tôledôt* has for its center Abram, as opposed to two other sons. Isaac's *tôledôt* has Jacob for its center, as opposed to another son. Jacob's *tôledôt* has Joseph for its center, as opposed to other brothers. Each of the *tôledôt*, then, focuses on one personality and weeds out lesser individuals.[78]

Moreover, two different kinds of genealogy are discernible: linear and segmented. The former focuses on a single line from A to Z (e.g. 5:1–32), while the latter branches off and considers the descendants of each of the children (e.g. 10:1–32).[79] The former is used to record the line from Adam, through Noah, to Abraham (5:1–32; 11:10–26;

---

[74] Alexander 1993; Alexander 1995: 22–23.

[75] E.g. V. P. Hamilton 1990: 2–11; Woudstra 1970; Cross 1973: 301–305; Skinner 1930: 39–41. *Tôlĕdôt* is also used twice in Genesis in a different way in a construction involving *lĕ* (10:32; 25:13). Both occur within existing genealogies.

[76] Gen. 2:4 is the most difficult case, but it seems sensible to take it as referring to the fact that the heavens and earth 'generated' Adam and Eve by God's power (Gen. 2:7). Skinner (1930: 41) notes, 'by analogy the phrase must describe what is generated by the heavens and the earth'.

[77] Cross 1973: 302.

[78] V. P. Hamilton 1990: 9–10.

[79] Ibid. 248–249; Alexander 1993: 258–259.

cf. 25:19–20; 37:2),[80] while the latter is used in relation to the minor characters such as Ishmael and Esau (e.g. 25:13–17; 36:10–40). Again these genealogies highlight not only the central *line*, but also the central *characters* through whom God works – Noah, Abraham, Isaac, Jacob, and Joseph – while moving quickly over characters who matter less to the central thread of the narrative.

The interest in descendants is also highlighted by Genesis' repeated use of the term *zera'* (seed). The term is used 59 times within Genesis compared to 170 times in the rest of the OT.[81] While *zera'* can be used in Genesis to refer simply to the seeds of plants and trees (1:11–12, 29; 8:22; 47:19, 23–24), on the remaining 48 occasions it is used to refer to descendants. In addition to its frequency, *zera'*, together with the genealogies and their associated narratives, also plays an important part in the unfolding plot of Genesis. In Genesis 3:15, after the fall of Adam and Eve, Yahweh says to the serpent, 'I will put enmity between you and between the woman and between your seed and her seed. He will bruise your head and you will bruise his heel' (my tr.).

The language here bears a striking similarity to that in Genesis 17:7 (see Table 2.1).[82]

Table 2.1

Genesis 3:15	Genesis 17:7
I will put enmity between you and between the woman,	And I will establish my covenant between me and between you
and between your seed and between her seed	and between your seed after you throughout their generations

That similarity, together with the other literary features noted here, suggests that it is in Yahweh's covenant with Abraham and his 'seed' that Yahweh's promise to destroy the serpent is being fulfilled.

Moreover, the language of Genesis 3:15 hints that perhaps a *particular* 'seed' is in view. Confusingly, the singular *zera'* can be understood either singularly or collectively. For instance, in Genesis 13:16 it is demonstrably plural when Yahweh refers to Abraham's

---

[80] The *tôlēdôt* of Gen. 25:19–20 and 37:2 are not really genealogies, yet both follow the 'segmented' genealogies of Ishmael and Esau respectively and serve to introduce the account of the children in the line of promise: Jacob and Joseph respectively.

[81] Alexander 1993: 259–260.

[82] My translations.

'seed' being 'as the dust of the earth'; while in 21:13, 'seed' is clearly singular and refers to Ishmael. Nevertheless, Collins has convincingly argued that where the singular verb is intended, 'it appears with singular verb inflections, adjectives, and pronouns',[83] as it does in Genesis 3:15.[84] Indeed, Eve's comment in 4:25 suggests she hoped that Yahweh's promise that her seed would crush the serpent's head might be fulfilled in Seth: 'God has appointed to me another seed [*zera'*] in the place of Abel, for Cain killed him' (my tr.).

What follows is the book of the *tôlĕdôt* of Noah, which begins with the (linear) genealogy tracing the particular line of descendants from Adam and Eve to Noah (5:1–32). The narrative then focuses on God's plan to begin again with the one man, Noah, and those with him. Significantly, after the flood Yahweh promises Noah, 'Behold, I am establishing my covenant with you and your seed after you' (9:9, my tr.). The promise once again bears a striking resemblance to that given to Abraham (see Table 2.2).[85]

Table 2.2

Genesis 9:9	Genesis 17:7
Behold, I am establishing my covenant with you	And I will establish my covenant between me and between you
and with your seed after you	and between your seed after you throughout their generations

Yet the two are also distinct in important ways. The key difference is the use of the second person plural ('with you [pl.]' and 'your [pl.] seed') in Genesis 9 compared with the use of the second person singular in Genesis 17. And in Genesis 9 the covenant is established with Noah and all his children and with all creation, while in Genesis 17 the covenant is established specifically with Abraham and his 'seed'.

Following the flood is the book of the *tôlĕdôt* of the sons of Noah, Shem, Ham and Japheth (10:1–32), charting the rise of many nations, which is then followed by the account of Babel. The judgment of God evident in Babel is then followed by the *tôlĕdôt* of Shem (11:10–26) and Terah (11:27–32), which ends with Abraham. The narrative then focuses on God's plan to bless the world through Abraham's seed.

[83] Collins 1997: 144.
[84] Notably the LXX takes *zera'* as a singular, translating it with *spermatos*. See R. A. Martin 1965; Collins 1997: 140–141.
[85] My translations.

When God first appears to Abraham, he promises to give the land to Abraham's 'seed' (12:7) and later to both Abraham and his 'seed' for ever (13:15). To that promise is added the promise to make Abraham's 'seed' exceedingly numerous (13:16). Those promises are reiterated in various forms to Abraham, Isaac and Jacob throughout the remaining chapters (15:5, 13, 18; 17:7–10, 19; 22:17–18; 24:7; 26:3–4, 24; 28: 4, 13–14; 32:13; 35:12; 48:4). The emphasis on Abraham's 'seed' is also highlighted in the narrative by the ongoing threat to childbearing in the form of barrenness (11:30; 25:21; 29:31), wives being taken by other men (12:10–20; 20:1–18; 26:6–16), and inter-'wife' conflict (16:1–15; 29:31 – 30:24). Moreover, as noted above, the narrative after Abraham focuses on individual characters to the exclusion of others: Isaac not Ishmael, Jacob not Esau, Joseph not his brothers.

While it is true that the *zera'* language and the related promises seem to alternate to some degree between a focus on individuals and whole groups, nevertheless, for our purposes, it is not necessary to determine exactly when it is singular and when it is plural. In some sense, clearly both are in view:[86] God plans to multiply Abraham but also to bless the world through a *particular* descendant. The move from two brothers with one chosen, in the case of Isaac and Ishmael and Jacob and Esau, to twelve brothers still with one chosen highlights the interrelation of the singular and plural 'seed'.

The promise both to Eve and to Abraham is that somehow through their offspring the curse of Genesis 3 will be undone and the world will be blessed. The focus of the genealogies and the narrative of Genesis on a particular line supports that. But, in addition, the focus in the unfolding narrative on particular individuals through whom God works suggests that the ultimate fulfilment of the promise lies not in the community as a whole but in a solitary figure. Those hints Genesis lays down are confirmed by later biblical history; not only by its fascination with central figures (e.g. Moses, Joshua, the judges, Samuel, etc.), but more importantly, in the establishment of the Davidic covenant that narrows the focus down to a particular seed of David through whom God will fulfil the Abrahamic covenant.

Why circumcision?

That focus on the 'seed' must inform our reading of circumcision. Indeed, it enables us to answer the very important question 'Why

---

[86] Similarly, J. M. Hamilton 2007: 261–262.

circumcision?' We return briefly then to the issue of circumcision itself. Several observations can be made.

First, one cannot but notice the connection between the nature of the sign – circumcision – and the focus on a particular seed through whom the blessing promised to Abraham will eventuate. The fact that the covenant is extended through a 'seed' and the inescapable reality that circumcision is conducted on the very instrument of procreation suggests that circumcision is bound up with the recollection of God's promise to Abraham of a 'seed', and more particularly his promise to bless the world through Abraham's 'seed'. Rupert of Deutz, in the twelfth century, asked why circumcision should be the sign and not something else, not least given that circumcision is a hidden sign by virtue of its position on the body. He surmises:

> Thus rightly, in the same way for Abraham, because he believed God saying that in his seed all nations would be blessed, in the place of the seed, that is, in the genital part of the body, a sign of that same faith was placed.[87]

The sign was not only a reminder of the promise, but also a reminder that the promise would become a reality through the promised seed.[88]

Second, receipt of the blessing was independent of the sign itself. The two opposite examples of Sarah and Ishmael make this point well. In the case of Sarah, she is specifically included in God's blessings promised to Abraham: like Abraham, Sarah receives a name change (17:15); God promises to bless her and to give Abraham a son by her; and together with Abraham she will be the progenitor of nations and of kings (17:16). Yet notably Sarah does not receive the sign of circumcision.

In contrast to Sarah, Ishmael received the sign of circumcision but is explicitly excluded from the covenant. As we saw above, God established the covenant with Isaac, not Ishmael. Ishmael will himself be blessed, but with different blessings from those promised in the

---

[87] Rupert Tuitiensis, *De Trinitate* 5.31 (PL 167:395, my tr.); for a brief discussion of Rupert's view see Cohen 2005: 194–195.

[88] In contrast, the twelfth-century rabbi Joseph Bekhor Shor argued instead that circumcision assists in procreation and hence in the fulfilment of God's promise to multiply Abraham (ibid. 193). Philo argued similarly (*Spec.* 1.7). Yet for the reasons I have outlined in this chapter (specifically, the focus on a 'seed' in Genesis, the focus on Isaac versus Ishmael in Gen. 17, and the connection with the Davidic king) I think the connection with a single 'seed' is much more likely. This is confirmed by how the NT writers take up circumcision.

covenant with Abraham: he will father princes, not kings, and he too will become a great nation (17:19–20). When Abraham pleads that God would establish his covenant with Ishmael (17:17–18), God replies that he will establish it with Isaac (17:21). The implication being that Yahweh will establish his covenant with Isaac and *not* Ishmael, though Ishmael is swept up in its blessings.[89] In the case of both Sarah and Ishmael the covenant blessing is independent of the sign.

Moreover, the curse of the sign is restricted only to males as well. In giving Abraham and his descendants the sign of circumcision God said that any who did not receive that sign would be 'cut off' (17:14). But implicitly such a curse can be applied only to the males. No female could receive the sign, and so it would be a nonsense to talk about a female failing to receive the sign and so being cut off. Such tensions suggest from the very outset important ideas about the 'sign' function of circumcision in relation to the covenant itself. They set limits on the efficacy of the sign and on how it was to be understood as relating to the covenant itself. They demonstrate, as will be confirmed in later chapters, that the sign of circumcision was precisely that: a sign. Though God commanded it to be done, the presence or absence of circumcision did not in itself speak to who would share in the blessings that the covenant promised.[90] Even at the very institution of the sign of circumcision that was clear by virtue of the relationship to the covenant and its sign of Sarah, Ishmael, and the rest of the household. Yet because it was a crucial signification and reminder of the promise, God commanded it to be done, and for parents to reject the sign must inevitably have spoken of their own ambivalence towards the promise and the hope.

Together those realities shed light on why only half the population ever received the sign of the covenant. First, because it was a *sign* of the covenant. And second, because it was the sign that through a male seed of Abraham God would bring about what he had promised.

Summary

We have seen in this chapter evidence to suggest that the sign of circumcision seems to hold together two competing ideas – complete obedience and trust in Yahweh. From the very outset, circumcision

---

[89] Blaschke 1998: 91–92.
[90] Williamson 2000: 185.

is connected with the idea of 'blamelessness' and its synonym 'righteousness'. The command to 'walk before me and be blameless' was a call to a special relationship with Yahweh – one exercised in complete and perfect obedience to him. Moreover, the fulfilment of all that God had promised Abraham was dependent on such a relationship being a living reality. Yet even before Yahweh commanded Abraham to be blameless/righteous, Abraham had been reckoned to be blameless/righteous on account of his trust in Yahweh.

I have proposed that those two competing ideas of promise and obedience were reconciled in the sacrificial system. The discrepancy between the ideal of blamelessness and its absence in a person's life was held together through the hope set forth in the sacrificial system of a 'blameless' substitute to atone for the moral incompleteness of the offerer. I hope to confirm that idea as we progress.

In addition, Genesis 17 together with the overarching narrative of Genesis suggested that God's covenant with Abraham would be fulfilled through a specific individual descended from Abraham. The use of language later in the OT in connection with the monarchy similar to the language found in Genesis 17 suggests that the specific seed of Abraham will be a Davidic king who will walk before Yahweh and do all that is in Yahweh's heart and mind.

Chapter Three

Circumcision in the Old Testament: the meaning of the sign developed

In this chapter we turn to consider references to circumcision found throughout the rest of the OT. We will focus first on Leviticus 26, Deuteronomy 10 and 30, and Joshua 5, before examining a number of other references in Exodus, Isaiah, Jeremiah, Ezekiel and Habakkuk. Along the way it will become clear that the connections I have suggested between circumcision and the themes of faith, blamelessness/ righteousness, mercy through sacrifice, and the focus on the Davidic seed of Abraham are supported by these other references to circumcision in the OT, both physical and metaphorical. The same ideal of perfect obedience together with trust in God's provision is maintained.

Leviticus 26

On a number of occasions circumcision is connected metaphorically with the heart. These uses of circumcision are important because they reveal the underlying theology of circumcision. A metaphor, by definition, uses what is true about one thing to make a statement about another. In the metaphorical uses of circumcision then we glimpse something of the OT understanding of physical circumcision.

The first occurrence of metaphorical circumcision applied to the heart is in Leviticus 26:41. In that context Yahweh is putting before the people blessings for obedience and curses for disobedience. In verses 1–12 Yahweh spells out what will be the result of their obedience to him: 'If you walk [*hlk*] in my statutes and observe my commandments and do them, then I will give you . . .' (26:3–4). Significantly, the call to obedience is couched in the language of 'walking'. The list of things that Yahweh will give in response to this obedience includes the rains in their season, fruitful harvests, security and dwelling in the land. But he also promises:

I will turn to you and make you fruitful and multiply you and will confirm my covenant with you . . . I will make my dwelling among you and my soul shall not abhor you. And I will walk [*hlk*] among you and will be your God, and you shall be my people. (Lev. 26:9–12)

The elements here are reminiscent of the covenant of Genesis 17. The ideas of fruitfulness, multiplication, confirming the covenant, walking with Yahweh, Yahweh's being their God and their being his people, are all found in Genesis 17. But added here is also the reciprocal notion of God's walking among them and making his dwelling among them.

The extent of obedience Yahweh requires in order for these Abrahamic blessings to be received is made clear by the next verse:

But if you will not listen to me and will not do *all* these commandments, if you spurn my statutes, and if your soul abhors my rules, so that you will not do *all* my commandments, but break my covenant . . . (Lev. 26:14–15, emphasis mine)

The obedience required is obedience not just to some of the commands but to *all* the commands and to the covenant as a whole.[1] The result of disobedience is judgment. Verses 16–39 depict an escalating series of judgments in which the following phrase, or one like it, is constantly repeated: 'And if by this discipline you are not turned to me but walk [*hlk*] contrary to me, then I will also walk [*hlk*] contrary to you, and I myself will strike you sevenfold for your sins' (Lev. 26:23–24; also 26:18, 21, 27–28).

The last judgment in this escalating series of judgments is exile and perishing among the nations (26:33, 38–39). As Wenham concludes, this judgment is essentially 'a denial of all the hopes enshrined within the covenant with Abraham, that his descendants would be a great nation, inherit the land of Canaan, and so on'.[2]

Yet after this series of warnings, another option is presented:

But if they confess their iniquity and the iniquity of their fathers in their treachery that they committed against me, and also in walking contrary to me, so that I walked contrary to them and

---

[1] Although only five commands are specifically mentioned (relating to idolatry, Sabbath and the sanctuary; 26:1–2), Milgrom (2001: 2276) convincingly argues they are a 'pithy summary of God's commands given heretofore'.
[2] Wenham 1979: 332.

brought them into the land of their enemies – if then their uncircumcised heart is humbled and they make amends for their iniquity, then I will remember my covenant with Jacob, and I will remember my covenant with Isaac and my covenant with Abraham, and I will remember the land. (Lev. 26:40–42)

In contrast to those who receive discipline and do not turn to Yahweh, there are those who confess their sin, their uncircumcised hearts are humbled, and they make amends for their iniquity. The result of these three actions is that Yahweh will remember his covenant with Abraham, Isaac and Jacob, and he will remember the land. If these conditions of confession, uncircumcised hearts being humbled and making amends for iniquity are met, then the covenant will be remembered, but not otherwise. In short, there are conditions to be met in order for the covenant with Abraham to be remembered.

Humility

On the surface, it is surprising that the uncircumcised heart here is not to be 'circumcised' (*mwl*) but rather 'humbled' (*kn'*). But as David Bernat notes, 'Since כנע "humbling, self-abasement" replaces מול as the action that solves the problem of the uncircumcised heart, it provides the exegetical key to our metonym.'[3] Yet it is not immediately clear whether to humble an uncircumcised heart is the same as to circumcise it. Indeed, Leviticus 26 itself, while offering hints cannot be used to draw a firm conclusion. Yet, as we will see later, Deuteronomy demonstrates that something similar *and* more comprehensive is in view.

The idea of humbling (*kn'*) does not surface within Leviticus apart from this one occurrence in 26:41. A broader look at the use of *kn'* throughout the OT provides a helpful picture of what is intended here. The basic meaning of *kn'* is 'subduing' or 'humbling'. About half the occurrences in the OT refer to people being subdued in battle, such as the enemies of Israel being subdued, and on occasion it refers to Israel being subdued by her enemies (Deut. 9:3; Judg. 3:30; 4:23; 8:28; 11:33; 1 Sam. 7:13; 2 Sam. 8:1; 1 Chr. 17:10; 18:1; 20:4; 2 Chr. 13:18; Neh. 9:24; Pss 81:14; 106:42; Isa. 25:5). Twice God is said to humble people because of their sinfulness (2 Chr. 28:19; Ps. 107:12). Of particular note is Psalm 107:12, where some who rebelled have their hearts 'humbled' with trouble, which leads them to cry to Yahweh in their

---

[3] Bernat 2009: 104–105.

distress. Yahweh hears their cry and then delivers them. The same note is present in Leviticus 26, where the programme of curses leads up to the repentance and confession mentioned in verse 41. Yet on a significant number of occasions, *kn'* refers to people humbling *themselves* before God in repentance (1 Kgs 21:29; 2 Kgs 22:19; 2 Chr. 7:14; 12:6–7, 12; 30:11; 32:26; 33:12, 19; 34:27). Investigating those occasions helps to create a picture of what God had in mind when he spoke of the uncircumcised hearts of the people being humbled.

For instance, Ahab is recorded as being a man of extraordinary wickedness (1 Kgs 21:25), yet when confronted by Elijah, he repents (1 Kgs 21:27). In response, God displays mercy, saying, 'Have you seen how Ahab has humbled [*kn'*] himself before me? Because he has humbled [*kn'*] himself before me, I will not bring the disaster in his days . . .' (1 Kgs 21:29).

Similar repentance is often displayed by various others, such as Hezekiah and the people with him (2 Chr. 32:26), and Josiah (2 Kgs 22:15–20; also 2 Chr. 34:27). But three episodes in particular are helpful for highlighting the nature of true humility.

In the days of Rehoboam, God sent Shishak, king of Egypt, up against Judah because they had been unfaithful. But the response of the king brings God's mercy:

When the LORD saw that they humbled [*kn'*] themselves, the word of the LORD came to Shemaiah: 'They have humbled [*kn'*] themselves. I will not destroy them, but I will grant them some deliverance, and my wrath shall not be poured out on Jerusalem by the hand of Shishak.' (2 Chr. 12:7)

Verse 14 sheds more light on the nature of this repentance: 'And he did evil, for he did not set his heart to seek the LORD.' That is, while Rehoboam repented in particular circumstances, he never repented regarding the whole shape and direction of his life, and with respect to his allegiance to Yahweh.

Manasseh, like other kings before him, leads the people into evil (2 Chr. 33:9) with the result that Yahweh brings Assyria against them and Manasseh is captured and taken to Babylon. Yet when Manasseh repents God shows mercy:

And when he was in distress, he entreated the favour of the LORD his God and humbled [*kn'*] himself greatly before the God of his fathers. He prayed to him, and God was moved by his entreaty and heard his plea and brought him again to Jerusalem into his kingdom. Then Manasseh knew that the LORD was God. (2 Chr. 33:12–13)

Manasseh not only finds mercy, but discovers that Yahweh is God. Manasseh's repentance goes further than that displayed by Rehoboam, who repented in particular circumstances, but never turned to Yahweh. Yet significantly, while Manasseh launches on a programme of reform, his reform is imperfect. Manasseh removes the foreign idols and altars from Jerusalem and throws them outside the city, he reinstitutes the thanksgiving and peace offerings and commands the people to serve Yahweh (2 Chr. 33:15–16). Yet it appears that he failed to destroy the high places outside Jerusalem, since people still made sacrifices there (2 Chr. 33:17). The imperfection of Manasseh's reform programme is significant because it highlights the fact that humility is not identical with perfection. That, in turn, reflects back on Yahweh's desire in Leviticus that the people's uncircumcised hearts be humbled. Whatever a circumcised heart might be, a humbled uncircumcised one is not a perfect one, but a repentant one that seeks mercy from the Most High God.

The account of Zedekiah provides a sobering foil to this pattern of hardship and prophecies of judgment, followed by humble repentance, followed by Yahweh's mercy and deliverance. Zedekiah provides an example of what happens when people do not humble themselves before Yahweh.[4] The chronicler records:

He did what was evil in the sight of the LORD his God. He did not humble [kn'] himself before Jeremiah the prophet, who spoke from the mouth of the LORD. He also rebelled against King Nebuchadnezzar, who had made him swear by God. He stiffened his neck and hardened his heart against turning to the LORD, the God of Israel. (2 Chr. 36:12–13)

Likewise, the people refused to humble themselves. The end result of that is catastrophic – exile and the destruction of Jerusalem (2 Chr. 36:14–21).

This whole principle of humble repentance followed by deliverance is embodied in the words of 2 Chronicles 7:14: 'if my people who are called by my name humble [kn'] themselves, and pray and seek my

---

face and turn from their wicked ways, then I will hear from heaven and will forgive their sin and heal their land.'

It is evident then that the fundamental commitment of Yahweh in Leviticus 26 is carried on through the remainder of the OT: when the people humbled their uncircumcised hearts, Yahweh relented from his judgment and showed mercy.[5] It is also clear that a humbled uncircumcised heart is not one that is made perfectly submissive to Yahweh, but (to state the obvious) one that is humbled and that repents of the desire to run contrary to Yahweh's will; while, as in the case of Zedekiah, the opposite of a humble heart is a hardened heart and a stiffened neck.

Confession and making amends

Still, humility alone is not sufficient to bring about the fulfilment of the Abrahamic promises – humility must be joined with atonement. That becomes clear as we examine the meaning of 'confess' (*ydh*) and also 'make amends' (*rṣh*). The precise meaning of these two concepts is not spelled out in Leviticus 26, yet it makes sense to suppose that their meaning has been established through their use in Leviticus so far. A search back through Leviticus shows that *ydh* and *rṣh* have already appeared in a number of theologically significant contexts.[6]

Ydh occurs only two other times in Leviticus, both in the hithpael, with the meaning 'confess'. The first occurrence is in 5:5–6, where a person who has unknowingly sinned discovers his or her sin. In that case,

> when he realizes his guilt in any of these and confesses [*wĕhitwaddâ*] the sin he has committed, he shall bring to the LORD as his compensation for the sin that he has committed, a female from the flock, a lamb or a goat, for a sin offering. And the priest shall make atonement for him for his sin.

The second occurrence is in 16:21–22 among the regulations for the Day of Atonement. There Yahweh commands:

> And Aaron shall lay both his hands on the head of the live goat, and confess [*wĕhitwaddâ*] over it all the iniquities of the people of

---

[5] The use of the niphal passive of *kn'* in Lev. 26:41 may be intended to suggest that it is God who brings about the humbling of their hearts (perhaps at least in part through exile and punishment). See Lemke 2003: 307–308; Meade 2014: 68.

[6] On the significance of the former see Bernat 2009: 111–113.

Israel, and all their transgressions, all their sins. And he shall put them on the head of the goat and send it away into the wilderness by the hand of a man who is in readiness. The goat shall bear all their iniquities on itself to a remote area, and he shall let the goat go free in the wilderness.

What is significant about both these occurrences is that it is not confession alone that is important, but confession tied with atonement; and in the latter case, atonement for breaking the covenant itself. It was on the Day of Atonement only that blood would be sprinkled on the Ark of the Covenant in which were held the tablets of stone that spelled out the pact between Yahweh and his people.

The meaning of $rṣh$ is more difficult. Barstad notes of $rṣh$, in general, that it is

> not only a central theological term expressing fundamental relationships between God and human beings, but also a technical term of the sacrificial cult. On Yahweh's favourable acceptance of the sacrifice depends the fate of Israel and those who worship Yahweh.[7]

Yet it is not immediately clear whether the phrase $yirṣû$ 'et-'$ăwōnām$ in Leviticus 26 means 'accept their iniquity/punishment' or 'make amends for their iniquity'. The confusion stems partly from a debate over whether there are two possible roots of $rṣh$.[8] The particular phrase $yirṣû$ 'et-'$ăwōnām$ occurs only here in verses 41, 43 and Isaiah 40:2. Though in Isaiah 40:2 the verb is in the niphal form. Perhaps the greatest flaw with the translation 'make amends' is that, as Milgrom points out, it 'impute[s] to Israel a further activity in securing its redemption'. Yet Leviticus 26 makes clear it is not that Israel sets out to make amends; rather, they must endure what God has in store for them by way of restitution. Milgrom continues, 'the implication is that Israel, in a state of remorse, must wait *passively* until its punishment is paid in full'.[9]

But in one sense, a choice between the two possible roots hardly matters. What is clear from the whole chapter is that what Israel must accept or endure is a punishment that fits their crime, and it is enduring

[7] Barstad 2004: 621.
[8] E.g. Averbeck 1997; Barstad 2004: 624–625.
[9] Milgrom 2001: 2333.

that punishment that makes amends for their sin. Leviticus 26:43 presents a useful confirmation of this point because *rṣh* appears twice there: 'And the land will be abandoned by them and it will *accept* [*rṣh*] its Sabbaths while it is deserted by them and they will *accept* [*rṣh*] their iniquity since they rejected my laws and their soul despised my statutes' (my tr.).

The land would 'accept/enjoy' its Sabbaths while the people 'accepted/endured/made amends' for their sin. In concrete terms, the land would lie desolate to make up for all the Sabbaths that were missed while the people were in the land (26:35). The Sabbath functioned as the sign of the Mosaic covenant par excellence (Exod. 21:12–18). Israel must suffer a penalty commensurate with the crime of desecrating the covenant most particularly exemplified by desecrating the Sabbaths. But once the sanctuary has been destroyed, there is no means of atonement apart from suffering the penalty themselves.[10] What is significant is that again confession and humility alone are insufficient: there must be atonement and recompense. Humility and atonement open the door for Yahweh to remember his covenant with Abraham, Isaac and Jacob (26:42). Strikingly, it is on the basis of the covenant with Abraham that Yahweh shows mercy.

Leviticus 26 then supports what we have already seen with respect to circumcision: that receipt of God's promise to Abraham requires complete obedience (i.e. blamelessness). But that in the absence of that 'blamelessness' the promise to Abraham is received through humble confession and atonement.

Deuteronomy 10

The next occurrence of heart circumcision is in Deuteronomy 10:16: 'Circumcise therefore the foreskin of your heart, and be no longer stubborn.'

This call for the people to circumcise their hearts is set within a series of calls for absolute obedience, once again couched in the language of 'walking'.[11] For instance:

> And now, Israel, what does the LORD your God require of you, but
> to fear the LORD your God, to walk [*hlk*] in all his ways, to love

---

[10] Ibid. 2333; Kiuchi 2007: 485. As Milgrom suggests, that may be why *rṣh* is used instead of *kpr*.

[11] DeRouchie (2004: 198) notes, 'Moses' exhortation to Israel in Deut. 10:12–13 parallels closely the Abrahamic commission.'

him, to serve the LORD your God with all your heart and with all your soul, and to keep the commandments and statutes of the LORD, which I am commanding you today for your good? (Deut. 10:12–13)

The scale of the obedience Yahweh is seeking is total: '*all* his ways . . . *all* your heart . . . *all* your soul'. Merrill surmises, 'Israel was to serve the Lord with unreserved and unqualified devotion . . . [and in] strict conformity to precise stipulations.'[12]

This theme recurs several times in the context (11:1, 8, 13, 22) and is explicitly linked with possession of the land (11:8–9, 13–17, 22–23) in a similar way to the blessing section of Leviticus 26. Thus Moses says:

You shall therefore keep the whole commandment that I command you today, that you may be strong, and go in and take possession of the land that you are going over to possess, and that you may live long in the land that the LORD swore to your fathers to give to them and to their offspring, a land flowing with milk and honey. (Deut. 11:8–9)

The 'whole commandment' Moses is speaking about is fleshed out later:

For if you will be careful to do all this commandment that I command you to do, loving the LORD your God, walking [*hlk*] in all his ways, and holding fast to him, then the LORD will drive out all these nations before you, and you will dispossess nations greater and mightier than you. (Deut. 11:22–23)

Possession of the land promised to their fathers is dependent on doing all of the commandment: loving God, walking in all his ways, holding fast to him and serving him with all their heart and soul.

Yet the command to circumcise their hearts is also set in contrast to 'no longer be stiff-necked' (*wĕ'orpĕkem lō' taqšû 'ôd*, my tr.). A survey of the use of the term *qšh* proves helpful. Twenty-nine times it is used to refer to stubborn hearts or people.[13] God 'hardens'

---

[12] Merrill 1994: 202. Tigay (1996: 107) describes the requirement as 'total obedience'.
[13] Exod. 7:3; 13:15; 32:9; 33:3, 5; 34:9; Deut. 2:30; 9:6, 13, 27; 10:16; 31:27; Judg. 2:19; 2 Kgs 17:14; 2 Chr. 30:8; 36:13; Neh. 9:16–17, 29; Job 9:4; Ps. 95:8; Prov. 28:14; 29:1; Isa. 48:4; Jer. 7:26; 17:23; 19:15; Ezek. 2:4; 3:7.

Pharaoh's heart (Exod. 7:3).[14] Pharaoh 'stubbornly' refuses to let God's people go (Exod. 13:15). God accuses the people of being 'stiff-necked' after the golden calf incident (Exod. 32:9; 33:3, 5; 34:9). Most significantly, Israel is described by Moses as 'stubborn' three times in Deuteronomy 9 (9:6, 13, 27).

What is particularly useful is observing the things with which 'stubbornness' (*qšh*) is contrasted. For instance, 'stubbornness' is set in contrast to obedience to Yahweh. So Nehemiah describes Israel in the exodus period and following as 'stubborn' because they refused to obey Yahweh (Neh. 9:16, 17, 29). Oftentimes 'stubbornness' is set against hearing Yahweh. So the people 'did not listen to me or incline their ear, but stiffened their neck' (Jer. 7:26).[15] Even more telling for the argument here, 'stubbornness' is twice set against 'humility' (*kn'*). In 2 Chronicles 30:8 Hezekiah sends out the decree calling on the people not to be 'stiff-necked', and while most laugh and mock, some from Asher, Manasseh and Zebulun 'humbled themselves' (2 Chr. 30:11). Similarly, in 2 Chronicles 36:12–13 we are told that Zedekiah did not humble himself before Jeremiah but stiffened his neck against turning to Yahweh. In 2 Kings 17:14 'stubbornness' is juxtaposed with 'trust' (*'mn*). There we are told that the fall of Israel was because 'they would not listen, but were stubborn, as their fathers had been, who did not believe [*'mn*] in the LORD their God'. In that context, the specific failure is identified as the people's refusal to turn from their 'evil ways' in repentance when confronted by Yahweh's prophets.

On a number of occasions, the remedy to being 'stubborn' is to plead with Yahweh for forgiveness. So after the golden calf episode Moses pleads with God:

> If now I have found favour in your sight, O Lord, please let the Lord go in the midst of us, for it is a stiff-necked people, and pardon our iniquity and our sin and take us for your inheritance. (Exod. 34:9)

These same events are rehearsed just before the command in Deuteronomy 10 for the people to circumcise their hearts and no longer be stubborn. Moses recounts to the people how he prayed to Yahweh: 'Remember your servants, Abraham, Isaac and Jacob. Do not regard the stubbornness of this people, or their wickedness or their sin' (Deut.

---

[14] God also 'hardened' the heart of Sihon, king of Heshbon (Deut. 2:30).
[15] See also Jer. 17:23; 19:15; Ezek. 2:4–5; 3:7.

9:27). Notably here forgiveness is anchored in an appeal to God's promise to Abraham, Isaac and Jacob. Indeed McConville makes a similar point, going so far as to note that the argument present in 9:1 – 10:11 (and earlier) 'in important respects, comes close to the Pauline doctrine of justification by faith, or righteousness that comes from faith', though he does not connect it in any meaningful way with the reference to circumcision a few verses later.[16]

The setting of Deuteronomy 10, together with an understanding of the broader use of *qšh*, suggests that to 'no longer be stubborn' means to adopt a position of humility and repentance before Yahweh. The parallel command 'circumcise the foreskin of your heart' should then be understood to mean the same; though it goes further, since by using the language of 'circumcision' it anchors the appeal for forgiveness in Yahweh's promise to Abraham, Isaac and Jacob, as Moses has done in chapter 9. Thus DeRouchie is only partly correct when he notes of Yahweh's command for the people to circumcise their heart:

> The challenge for Israel is to remove their heart's shell – to stop being stiff-necked – and in so doing to realize the ultimate signifi-cance of the oath of allegiance to which physical circumcision points – that is, the call to walk before God blamelessly (Gen 17:1).[17]

Circumcision symbolizes not only allegiance and the commitment to walk before Yahweh, but also humility and trust in Yahweh's promise that he will bring that about. Barker neatly combines the two, writing:

> a circumcised heart is a heart which is submissive, responsive to God and humble . . . [A] circumcised heart will recognise its inability and trust the all-powerful (10:14) Yahweh. Thus a circum-cised heart will rely on grace and not itself.[18]

Deuteronomy 10 confirms the pattern that we have already observed in both Genesis and Leviticus 26: possession of what was promised to Abraham requires complete obedience, yet in the absence of that complete obedience as a present reality there is hope in humility and repentance centred around God's promise to Abraham.

---

[16] McConville 2002: 192.
[17] DeRouchie 2004: 197.
[18] Barker 2004: 105.

Deuteronomy 30

In Deuteronomy 30 circumcision of the heart is mentioned again. Yet a significant and puzzling shift occurs. Instead of the people being commanded to circumcise their hearts, Yahweh promises that he will do it. In 30:5–6 Moses tells the people:

> the LORD your God will bring you into the land that your fathers possessed, that you may possess it. And he will make you more prosperous and numerous than your fathers. And the LORD your God will circumcise your heart and the heart of your offspring, so that you will love the LORD your God with all your heart and with all your soul, that you may live.

On this occasion the result of circumcising the heart is made clear: people will love Yahweh with all their heart and soul, in order that they might live. This idea is further expanded in verse 8: 'And you will return and you will obey the voice of Yahweh, and you will do all his commands which I am commanding you today' (my tr.).

Craigie notes, 'When God "operated" on the heart, then indeed the people would be able to love the Lord and live.'[19] But according to Merrill, 'This impossible standard was always understood as the ideal of covenant behavior, one to be sought but never fully achieved.'[20] What is envisaged then is more than just enablement to repentance, but wholesale spiritual surgery on the heart. As Thompson argues, 'God himself will carry out the inward renewal of Israel . . . so that Israel will love Yahweh with all their heart . . . Repentance in itself will not suffice.'[21] Barker asks even more pointedly whether or not the circumcision of Israel's heart would guarantee obedience. He notes, 'the certainty of the statements about Israel's love and obedience in vv6b, 8 suggests a sense of guarantee as well. Verses 6–8 function almost as a promise that Israel *will* love and obey, not just that they *can*.'[22]

Yet it is not at all clear how to reconcile this view with the view of chapter 10, where the people are called on to circumcise their own hearts, and where that circumcision appears to be less comprehensive – it envisages humility and trust rather than complete obedience. So

[19] Craigie 1976: 364; similarly, Lemke 2003: 309.
[20] Merrill 1994: 389.
[21] Thompson 1974: 311.
[22] Barker 2004: 178 (emphases his).

too the setting here is almost identical to that in Leviticus 26, with blessings and curses followed by hope through some operation being performed on Israel's uncircumcised hearts. That similarity suggests that the circumcised heart here is equivalent to the 'humbled' uncircumcised heart of Leviticus 26.

The same emphasis on repentance and trust is also evident in Deuteronomy 30, both at the beginning of the chapter, with the repeated emphasis on 'returning' (*šwb*), the language often used for repentance, but also at the end of the chapter. Although the command to love Yahweh with all their heart is utterly beyond the people, paradoxically Yahweh says that it 'is not too hard for you, neither is it far off' (30:11).[23] It is not in heaven, nor is it beyond the sea, such that the people should be unable to attain it. Rather, 'the word is very near you. It is in your mouth and in your heart, so that you can do it' (30:14). Yahweh's grace does not imply that the demand for obedience is relinquished (30:16). Instead, the gap is bridged by the word in their heart.

The word that is to be in their heart is the one embodied in circumcision and appropriated by a circumcised heart: Yahweh's promise to Abraham. A promise that included the prospect of walking before Yahweh blamelessly, and a promise that we have seen was foundational in Deuteronomy 10. That such is still in view is confirmed by the recollection of the Abrahamic promise at numerous times through the chapter (30:5, 9, 16, 20). As we will see in chapter 5, this is very much the view Paul propounds of keeping the law and having a circumcised heart.

In 'choosing life' the people are not promising to make themselves utterly obedient, but are embracing the promise of life and obedience held out in Yahweh's promise to Abraham. Yet even that trust and repentance is a gift from God (29:4). In contrast, the wrong response – choosing death – is exemplified in chapter 29:

> Beware lest there be among you a man or woman or clan or tribe whose heart is turning away today from the LORD our God to go and serve the gods of those nations. Beware lest there be among

---

[23] As Meade (2014: 78) notes, 30:11–14 is often understood either in relation to (1) the present – the law is not too hard to keep now; or (2) the future – the law will not be too hard to keep once Yahweh circumcises the people's hearts upon their return from exile (for the respective views see e.g. McConville 2002: 429; Coxhead 2006; Barker 2004: 182–187). However, my argument here is that both are in some sense true and the gap is bridged by humble trust in Yahweh's promise to Abraham.

you a root bearing poisonous and bitter fruit, one who, when he hears the words of this sworn covenant, blesses himself in his heart, saying, 'I shall be safe, though I walk [*hlk*] in the stubbornness of my heart.' This will lead to the sweeping away of moist and dry alike. The LORD will not be willing to forgive him, but rather the anger of the LORD and his jealousy will smoke against that man, and the curses written in this book will settle upon him, and the LORD will blot out his name from under heaven. (Deut. 29:18–20)

The opposite of 'choosing life' and approaching Yahweh in repentance and trust is to 'choose death' and to 'walk' in the stubbornness of one's own heart.

The notion of blamelessness evidenced in the sacrificial system and the promise signified by circumcision enables us to draw Deuteronomy 10 and 30 together. The need had always been for blamelessness. However, in the absence of blamelessness God had made provision for reconciliation and forgiveness through sacrifice accompanied by humble trust and submission, together with the hope that one day he would make the people truly blameless. What God calls Israel to do in Deuteronomy 10 is to seek the fulfilment of that through humble repentance and trust in God's promise to Abraham. What Deuteronomy 30 makes clear is that even that repentance and faith is a work of God. God promises in Deuteronomy 30 to drive his people back to take hold, by faith, of the Abrahamic promise through which he will make *actual* blamelessness a reality in the lives of his people. Flowing from this God-wrought faith-appropriation of God's promise to Abraham is their transformation into people who love him with all their heart.

Deuteronomy 30 supports what we have seen so far. The law maintained that possession of the land necessitated obedience. But, as both Deuteronomy and Leviticus make clear, that is unattainable. Deuteronomy 30 demonstrates that the people need to be *made* obedient by an act of God. That reality continually pushes people back to appealing humbly to God to fulfil his promises to Abraham.

Joshua 5

The passages we have considered in this chapter so far all pertain to metaphorical circumcision. Joshua 5 is one of the key OT passages that relates to physical circumcision. The reason for its significance lies not only in the massive extent of the circumcision undertaken, but also in the significance of its historical situation. The account occurs at a major turning point in redemptive history as the Israelites set foot in the Promised Land. The people had just crossed the Jordan to take possession of the Promised Land when Yahweh instructed Joshua to 'Make for yourself flint knives and circumcise again the sons of Israel a second time' (Josh. 5:2, my tr.).

Joshua is commanded to circumcise the sons of Israel 'a second time' because, as the rest of the passage makes clear, the practice had been in abeyance for the forty years in the wilderness. In coming to terms with Joshua 5 it is crucial to understand precisely why the practice of circumcision stopped for those forty years.[24]

---

[24] The situation is complicated by textual differences between the LXX and the MT. But there are good reasons for preferring the MT. First, it seems strange in the LXX for God to command circumcision to be done while sitting down, given there is no interest elsewhere in Scripture regarding the posture for circumcision. Second, the LXX displays a number of signs of carelessness and amateurish translation: it lists the time spent in the desert as forty-two years rather than the usual forty (see Auld 2004: 126); it names the desert as the Madbaritite desert (*tē erēmō tē Madbaritidi*), which seems to be an example of dittography combined with a total misunderstanding of the Hebrew language (Boling 1982: 193; cf. Auld 2004: 126); and the use of *dio* in v. 6 makes no sense: 'For forty-two years Israel wandered in the Madbaritite desert, *on account of which [dio]* many of those warriors who had come out from the land of Egypt were uncircumcised' (my tr.). How is it that forty-two years in the wilderness could have led to the *prior* uncircumcision of the adult males? Third, the LXX is inconsistent. Verse 7 recapitulates the message thus far, but instead of saying that Joshua circumcised *both* those who were born on the way *and* those who came out of Egypt (as it does in vv. 4–5), it simply says that Joshua circumcised those born on the way. The latter being exactly what the MT says. Fourth, the LXX displays evidence of theologizing. 'Purified' (*perikathairō*; v. 4) is used in the place of 'circumcised' (see similarly, the LXX of Lev. 19:23 and Deut. 30:6; cf. ibid. 126). But although circumcision is mentioned in the same context as uncleanness is in Lev. 12, circumcision and uncleanness are not strongly linked until the prophets (e.g. Isa. 52:1). It seems more likely that a later editor would have introduced rather than removed such a theologically freighted word. Fifth, the MT displays greater overall coherence. The MT plays on the terms *tmm* and *šb'* (on which see below). Moreover, a comparison of the differing messages of the two versions proves enlightening. The key difference in the LXX is that those who came out from Egypt were also uncircumcised. This implies that the 'reproach of Egypt', and the chief obstacle to entering the land, was the uncircumcision of the men while they were in Egypt. This is possibly confirmed by v. 6 of the LXX, where 'those who disobeyed the commands of God' is set in apposition to 'they were uncircumcised, many of the warriors who came up out of Egypt, *those who disobeyed the commands of God*' (my tr.). The implication is that their disobedience chiefly consisted of their failure to circumcise themselves and their children. In contrast, the only disobedience that the MT mentions is that those who came out of Egypt did not listen to the voice of Yahweh. Moreover, in the LXX it is the uncircumcised who die in the wilderness, while in the MT it is the circumcised who die in the wilderness and do not enter the land! It could plausibly be argued then that the MT represents the harder reading since it is those who possess the sign of the promise who fail to enter the land.

Hamlin suggests that the people omitted circumcision due to 'their preoccupation with the problems of freedom and survival'.[25] Hawk suggests the omission is symptomatic of Israel's disobedience:[26] it is one more breach of the covenant. But the circumcision event here in Joshua 5 is a response to Yahweh's command. Why did Yahweh wait forty years before issuing his command? Others suggest that there was no pause in the practice, but rather what is intended is a more comprehensive kind of circumcision. There is some evidence that Egyptian circumcision was less comprehensive than the one practised by the Israelites. Perhaps then what is being commanded is *Hebrew* not *Egyptian* circumcision.[27] Yet the text explicitly affirms that all those who came out of Egypt had been circumcised (5:5). It makes no distinction between an Egyptian and a Hebrew circumcision. Moreover, it was those *not* born in Egypt but in the desert who needed to be circumcised (5:7). In other words, the text makes no room for a different *kind* of circumcision.[28]

The problem with all these interpretations is that they ignore the explanation for the cessation and reintroduction of circumcision given by the text itself. Verse 4 begins, 'and this is the reason Joshua circumcised them' (my tr.). What follows in verses 4–6 is the reason for the reintroduction of circumcision but also the reason for why it was stopped in the wilderness. The reason can be broken down into three stages:

1. Although those who came out of Egypt were circumcised, they had died in the desert (v. 4b).
2. And although those who came out of Egypt were circumcised, those born on the way were not (v. 5).
3. *Because* those who came out of Egypt wandered in the desert until they were 'finished off' since they did not listen to the voice of Yahweh (v. 6a).

That is, verse 6 is explaining not only why those who came out of Egypt died on the way, but also why those who were born on the way

---

[25] Hamlin 1983: 32.

[26] Hawk 2000: 79–80.

[27] According to Sasson (1966: 474), 'Whereas the Hebrews amputated the prepuce and thus exposed the corona of the penis, the Egyptian practice consisted of a dorsal incision upon the foreskin which liberated the glans penis.' But there is evidence that the complete removal of the foreskin was also practised (Blaschke 1998: 36).

[28] Harstad 2004: 224.

were left uncircumcised: it was because the Egypt generation 'did not listen to the voice of Yahweh' (my tr.). Putting together the end of verse 5 with the beginning of verse 6 demonstrates that clearly:

> And all the people born in the desert on the way after coming out from Egypt were not circumcised *because* for forty years the sons of Israel wandered in the desert until the nation was finished off, those who did not listen to the voice of Yahweh. (my tr. and emphasis)

Why 'not listening to the voice of Yahweh' should lead to the lapse of *circumcision* seems a mystery until the second half of verse 6. There the juxtaposition of *šbʿ* (swear) points to the reversal of God's Abrahamic covenant with that particular generation. What Yahweh 'swore' to Abraham, he 'swore' to the wilderness generation they would not receive.[29] That then hints at the reason for the interruption of circumcision during the years of the wilderness wandering: to apply the sign of God's covenant with Abraham was inappropriate while the wilderness generation lived, those who had been specifically excluded from the blessings of that covenant.

That understanding is further supported by Yahweh's own interpretation of the mass circumcision event given in verse 9: 'Today I have rolled away the reproach of Egypt from you' (my tr.). The meaning of this phrase has been variously interpreted.[30] Reproach has already been connected with circumcision in the account of Genesis 34, where the sons of Jacob tell the Hivites that it would be a 'reproach' for their sister to marry someone uncircumcised. Based on that account, some suggest that the reproach of Egypt was the shame of being uncircumcised in Egypt.[31] But as Butler points out, that cannot be, since the text specifically says that those in Egypt were circumcised. Butler instead prefers to understand the reproach as the 'insulting social position as slaves to which Israel was degraded in Egypt'.[32] Yet both those views overlook the preoccupation of Joshua 5 with the disobedience of the wilderness generation as the central obstacle to both circumcision and entrance into the land.

In coming to terms with the phrase 'the reproach of Egypt', two questions present themselves. First, if the reproach of Egypt is *merely* the slavery in Egypt, why is Israel's reproach only now said to be

---

[29] Butler 2014: 1:335.
[30] For a survey see Noort 2005: 14–18.
[31] E.g. Nelson 1997: 76.
[32] Butler 2014: 1:336.

removed? Why not forty years earlier? Second, if the reproach is *merely* the disobedience of the people in the wilderness, why is Egypt mentioned?

The answer lies in looking back to Yahweh's covenant with Abraham in Genesis 15. There Yahweh swore that Abraham's descendants would be slaves in a land not their own for four hundred years, after which they would come out. However, having come out from slavery, they would possess the land God promised to Abraham (Gen. 15:13–16). The deliverance from Egypt then is the fulfilment of only half the promise; the other half is entrance into the land. Woudstra writes:

> Israel's bondage, which at the Exodus had been broken in principle, was finally and definitively removed now that the people were safely on Canaan's side, no longer subject to the words of shame of which Num. 14:13–16; Deut. 9:28 speak hypothetically.[33]

'Rolling away the reproach of Egypt' describes the whole episode from deliverance *out* of Egypt and *into* the land. That is confirmed by the reference four times to the people who had 'come out from Egypt' (5:4, 5 [twice], 6) and to events that had happened 'on the way' (5:4–5, 7), which presupposes not simply an exit from Egypt but a journey *to* somewhere in particular. However, that whole process was interrupted by the people 'not listening to the voice of Yahweh', and the journey to the Promised Land was completed only in Joshua 5.

Thus rolling away the reproach of Egypt incorporates both the defeat of those who held the people in slavery and the removal of the consequences of the people's disobedience, not least by the judgment of a whole generation. Creach writes:

> The phrase . . . refers either to the humiliation of Egyptian bondage, humiliation that did not end until Israel settled in its own land . . . or to the wilderness generation's lack of faith. These two interpretations are complementary. In Joshua's theological schema the wilderness generation never completely shook off the stigma of Egyptian bondage, because it was not willing to accept the freedom of land possession. The wilderness wanderers carried a disgrace they could not remove, since they had a 'life sentence' that disallowed their realization of the promise of Canaan.[34]

---

[33] Woudstra 1981: 102.
[34] Creach 2003: 57.

An examination of the development and later use of *ḥerpâ* (reproach) supports this. *Ḥerpâ* is used to refer to the general condition of reproach and shame (e.g. Gen. 30:23; Job 16:10; 19:5). But more often it is used in connection with the reproach and shame of being subjugated and defeated by enemies (e.g. 1 Sam. 17:26; Neh. 1:3; 2:17; 4:4). In the prophets, God's judgment against Israel is described in the language of reproach (e.g. Isa. 47:3; Jer. 24:9; 29:18; 42:18; 44:8, 12; 49:13; 51:51; Ezek. 5:14–15; 22:4; Dan. 9:16). Perhaps the most distressing of all the uses is in the prophecy in Daniel that 'many of those who sleep in the dust of the earth shall awake, some to everlasting life, and some to shame [*ḥerpâ*] and everlasting contempt' (Dan. 12:2). But *ḥerpâ* is also tied in other places to deliverance. Thus:

> He will swallow up death for ever;
> and the Lord GOD will wipe away tears from all faces,
> and the reproach [*ḥerpâ*] of his people he will take
> away from all the earth . . .
>
> (Isa. 25:8; see also Isa. 54:4;
> Ezek. 36:15, 30; Joel 2:19; Zeph. 3:18)

In other words, *ḥerpâ* often conveys more than embarrassment or social disgrace. It is often bound up with God's own judgment, the shock of the subjugation of God's own people, and the apparent conflict presented by the lack of fulfilment of God's own promises.

That God's judgment on the wilderness generation was the cause for the cessation of circumcision during the wilderness years is also suggested by the play on words between the generation who were 'finished off' (*tmm*) in the desert (v. 6), and Joshua's 'finishing off' (*tmm*) the circumcision of the subsequent generation (v. 8).[35] It was only once the wilderness generation itself was 'finished off' that the subsequent generation could reinstitute circumcision.[36] Thus it was not that circumcision removed the reproach;[37] rather, the removal of the wilderness generation removes the reproach of God's judgment and the interruption of the promise, thus making the practice of circumcision plausible again. In that light, Yahweh's command to Joshua to 'circumcise again the sons of Israel a second time'

---

[35] Cf. Nelson 1997: 77; Butler 2014: 1:335.
[36] Woudstra (1981: 101) notes, 'Perhaps the writer means that this period of wilderness wandering, caused by the people's disobedience, was a time of wrath during which the sign of the covenant between God and Israel could not be applied.'
[37] Contra Butler (2014: 1:336–337).

(my tr.) is a call to reintroduce the lapsed rite since it is now appropriate again.

Not listening to the voice of Yahweh

Joshua 5 functions then as a reflection on the link between circumcision and the reason that the wilderness generation failed to receive the Abrahamic promise. Before moving on, it will be useful to re-examine those reasons.

Here in Joshua 5:6 the reason given is simply that 'they did not listen to the voice of Yahweh' (*lō'-šom'û běqôl yhwh*, my tr.). The phrase here is not explained. However, the phrase 'listen to the voice of' typically means 'obey'. For example, in Deuteronomy 13:18, Moses says, 'if you obey the voice of the LORD your God [*tišma' běqôl yhwh*], *keeping all his commandments* that I am commanding you today, and *doing what is right in the sight of the LORD your God . . .*' (emphases mine). Thus 'listening to the voice of Yahweh' involves keeping the commandments. Or even more comprehensively:

> *I have not transgressed any of your commandments, nor have I forgotten them.* I have not eaten of the tithe while I was mourning, or removed any of it while I was unclean, or offered any of it to the dead. I have obeyed the voice of the LORD my God [*šāma'tî běqôl yhwh 'ĕlōhāy*]. I have done according to all that you have commanded me. Look down from your holy habitation, from heaven, and bless your people Israel and the ground that you have given us, as you swore to our fathers, a land flowing with milk and honey. (Deut. 26:13–15, emphasis mine)

Notably, on a number of occasions, as in the last example, receiving the promises given to Abraham is tied to that comprehensive obedience. This becomes most explicit in Deuteronomy 28, where the blessings and curses spelled out are linked to either 'listening' or not 'listening' to the voice of Yahweh (Deut. 28:1–2, 15, 45, 62). Perhaps even more telling is Deuteronomy 30, where Yahweh's promise to bring the people into the land is bound up with their 'listening to the voice of Yahweh' (*wěšāma'tā běqôl yhwh*; Deut. 30:8, my tr.), which itself flows out of his promise to circumcise the hearts of the people (Deut. 30:6).

Permanent possession of the land required obeying Yahweh. In Joshua 5 then circumcision is stopped for the period of the wilderness wanderings because the people were not obedient – they did not listen to the voice of Yahweh and were excluded from the land. So again, circumcision is tied closely to complete obedience in every aspect of life. Without obedience the wilderness generation could not enter the Promised Land. Indeed, their disobedience led to their being judged in the wilderness.

Yet it is important to consider not just the reason given in this text for that generation being excluded but also the reasons given elsewhere in the Bible. The account of the episode which led to that generation being excluded from the Promised Land is found in Numbers 13 and 14. After men are sent up to spy out the land, they return with stories of inhabitants the size of giants. Terrified, the people refuse to go up. Yahweh says to Moses, 'How long will this people despise me? And how long *will they not believe in me*, in spite of all the signs that I have done among them?' (Num. 14:11, emphasis mine).

When Moses recapitulates the reasons in Deuteronomy 1:32, he gives the same explanation: the people 'did not believe the LORD your God'. The reason for the wilderness generation being excluded from the Promised Land appears then to be disobedience and unbelief. Or perhaps better, disobedience that was grounded in their unbelief. The same twofold reason can be observed in the writer of Hebrews' reflection on the same events. He writes, 'And to whom did he swear that they would not enter his rest, but to those who were disobedient? So we see that they were unable to enter because of unbelief' (Heb. 3:18–19).

The text of Joshua then continues the pattern we have observed so far of holding together both the demand for full obedience and the necessity of faith in Yahweh. The writer of Joshua, however, does not explain how these two hold together, though the phrase 'Today I have rolled away the reproach of Egypt from you' (5:9) hints at a possible answer.

A survey of the use of *gll* (roll) proves helpful. The verb occurs only eighteen times. Most of the time it refers simply to rolling, whether it be rolling stones (Gen. 29:3, 8, 10; Josh. 10:18; 1 Sam. 14:33; Prov. 26:27), or rolling in blood (2 Sam. 20:12; Isa. 9:5), or rolling in more poetic language, such as the rolling up of the heavens (Isa. 34:4), the rolling down (i.e. destruction) of mountains (Jer. 51:25), or the rolling on of rivers (Amos 5:24). Once, somewhat curiously, it refers to Joseph's 'rolling' on his brothers in retribution (Gen. 43:18). Similarly, Job refers to those who 'roll on' him vindictively (Job 30:14).

More interestingly, it is used in Psalm 119:22 to refer, as in Joshua, to the 'rolling away' of reproach:

Roll [*gll*] away from upon me reproach [*ḥerpâ*] and shame,
for I have kept your testimonies.

(my tr.)

In the context, the reproach appears to be the rebuke of those 'who
wander from your commandments' (Ps. 119:21). Again, as in Joshua
5, the reproach is the judgment of God against those who disobey
him.

What is at first even stranger is the way that in a number of places
gll becomes a metaphor for trust.[38] In Psalm 22:8 David's enemies cry
out:

Roll [*gll*] onto Yahweh.
Let him rescue him.
Let him deliver him since he delights in him.

(my tr.)

So too in Psalm 37:5 David recommends:[39]

Roll [*gll*] your ways onto Yahweh,
and trust in him and he will act.

(my tr.)

It seems probable that there is a connection between these two
metaphorical uses of *gll*. For instance, Kidner, in his comment on
Psalm 37:5 notes that the image is 'getting rid of a burden' but that
the word eventually became a synonym for trust.[40] It seems possible,
though difficult to prove, that the metaphorical use developed out of
such a significant occasion as Joshua 5. On that occasion, Yahweh
rolled away the massive burden of slavery in Egypt and the disobedience of the wilderness generation and brought the people into the
land. Perhaps it was on that basis that appealing for Yahweh to 'roll
away' became a plea for Yahweh to roll away similar burdens, while
'rolling to Yahweh' became, from the opposite viewpoint, an expression
for looking to Yahweh to do the same.

Nevertheless, what is crucial in Joshua 5 is that it is Yahweh, not
the people, who rolled away the reproach of both slavery in Egypt

---

[38] Konkel (1997: 1:868) notes, 'Three times *gll* is used as a metaphor for trust . . .
This is a beautiful mental image of what it means to commit oneself to God.'
[39] See also Prov. 16:3.
[40] Kidner 1973: 150.

and his judgment against the disobedience in the desert and then also fulfilled his promise to Abraham. In that sense, circumcision becomes (again) not only a beacon of that promise to Abraham but a reminder of God's commitment to deal with disobedience (and slavery) in order that the promise *can* be fulfilled. The circumcision event in Joshua then serves to re-emphasize what was already encapsulated in the understanding of circumcision: both Yahweh's unyielding commitment to complete obedience and his unyielding commitment to fulfil what he had promised to Abraham.

Significantly too, the people's circumcision is not the precondition for entry into the land; rather, circumcision is the symbolic result of God's already accomplished deliverance of them into the land. Moreover, it must be noted that it is not those who are excluded from the land who are excluded from circumcision; it is their children who receive the land who are excluded for forty years from the sign of circumcision. That ordering suggests that it is not an individual's physical circumcision per se that is important. As Woudstra notes:

> Though circumcision was essential to the celebration of the Passover (Exod. 12:48), the signal manifestation of God's goodness as shown in the Jordan crossing was not as such dependent on the nation's circumcised or uncircumcised state. Insistence upon observance of the law under the Old Covenant, though in a very real sense a condition of the covenant, was not to be construed along the lines of righteousness by works.[41]

Circumcision is important, not for the sake of the individual, but for the message it sends to the community. That is, circumcision seems to function not individually but corporately. The lack of circumcision of the children was a sign to the circumcised parents of their failure to inherit the promise. The lack of circumcision of the children was also a sign to the children of the need for trust and obedience in order to possess the Promised Land. Indeed, it is remarkable to think that it was during the time in which circumcision was on hold in the wilderness that Moses delivered his Deuteronomic sermon calling the people to circumcise their hearts and promising that one day Yahweh would do it for them.[42] From this point on in Israelite history, if it were not already abundantly clear from Genesis, Leviticus and Deuteronomy,

---

[41] Woudstra 1981: 98.
[42] Harstad 2004: 225.

circumcision is linked in the most profound way with God's requirement for complete obedience; yet not only with the requirement for complete obedience, but also with the provision of grace for those who trust Yahweh.

Further witness from the Old Testament

We now turn to a number of other passages in the OT that deal with circumcision. What follows is not a comprehensive analysis of each passage but rather an attempt to sketch out the way that each passage confirms the elements we have already seen bound up with circumcision. Moreover, not all the remaining references to circumcision will be considered here, but only those that highlight the themes we have seen.

Exodus

Canonically speaking, the first reference to circumcision outside Genesis is in Exodus 4:

> At a lodging place on the way the LORD met him and sought to put him to death. Then Zipporah took a flint and cut off her son's foreskin and touched Moses' feet with it and said, 'Surely you are a bridegroom of blood to me!' So he let him alone. It was then that she said, 'A bridegroom of blood', because of the circumcision. (Exod. 4:24–26)

Circumcision also occurs on two other occasions in Exodus: in Exodus 6:10–30 to describe Moses' speech/lips, and in Exodus 12:43–51 in connection with the Passover. Although only brief, the passage in Exodus 4 has proven to be one of the most difficult circumcision passages in the Bible. Yet its brevity and complexity do not speak against its significance. There are a number of important links with the other circumcision passages in Exodus, which suggests that this is no passing episode, but that a deeper theological point is being made.

Numerous suggestions have been made as to what the account in Exodus 4:24–26 means.[43] Some suggest that Yahweh was seeking to kill Moses because Moses had not been circumcised or had been circumcised incompletely;[44] others that Yahweh was seeking to kill

---

[43] For useful surveys see Durham 1987: 56–57; Robinson 1986: 447–449.
[44] Durham 1987: 58–59.

Moses because Gershom had not been circumcised,[45] or to kill Gershom because Gershom had not been circumcised.[46] Or perhaps the son meant is not Gershom but Eliezer.[47] Some propose that Yahweh's anger stems from Moses' recalcitrance at the beginning of Exodus 4.[48] Propp believes the episode is related to Moses' bloodguilt for killing the Egyptian.[49] The list of views is almost endless.

The diversity of interpretations stems from a number of significant questions that the passage raises. First, it is not clear who Yahweh is threatening to kill. The third person pronominal suffixes (*wayyipgĕšēhû* and *hămîtô*) could refer either to Moses or to Gershom.[50] And if it is Moses, 'Why should Yahweh suddenly attack the man he has just commissioned to liberate Israel?'[51] Second, it is not clear whose feet Zipporah touches with the severed foreskin. Again the third person pronominal suffix (*lĕraglāyw*) could refer to Moses', Gershom's or even Yahweh's feet.[52] Third, it is not clear whether 'feet' really means 'feet'[53] or whether it is a euphemism for genitals.[54] Does Zipporah, for instance, circumcise Gershom and then touch Moses' genitals with the severed foreskin? Fourth, what does the curious phrase *hătan dāmîm* (bridegroom of blood) mean?

We cannot hope to address all the issues raised by this passage. Instead the aim is simply to show that the themes present in this passage are the same we have uncovered so far in connection with circumcision, and perhaps also to show that the understanding of circumcision presented here helps to make a great deal more sense of this passage, even if all the knots cannot be untied. With that in mind, several points can be made.

First, the passage follows the lengthy narrative running from chapter 2 that details the rise of Moses and then his commissioning

---

[45] V. P. Hamilton 2011: 82.

[46] Stuart 2007: 152–156; Sarna 1991: 25. Walters (2002) thinks that the passage is deliberately ambiguous and that both Moses and Gershom are intended interpretations of the passage.

[47] R. B. Allen 1996: 266–269.

[48] Walters 2002: 418–419; Robinson 1986: 456; Propp 1999: 196. R. B. Allen (1996: 260) points out that is unlikely given that situation was resolved.

[49] Propp 1999: 234–235; cf. Embry 2010: 182–185.

[50] It is unlikely that Eliezer could be intended since in the narrative of Exodus so far only Gershom has been introduced (Exod. 2:22). Moreover, the theme of the firstborn is important in the immediate context and Gershom is the firstborn (Robinson 1986: 450–451).

[51] Propp 1993: 499.

[52] For the latter see Hays 2007: 43–44.

[53] Kosmala 1962: 23–24; Walters 2002: 411–412.

[54] Sarna 1991: 26; Propp 1993: 506.

in chapters 3 and 4. That commissioning narrative is preceded by a reference to Yahweh's remembering his covenant with Abraham, Isaac and Jacob (Exod. 2:24). The theme of God's relationship with the three patriarchs is also scattered throughout chapters 3 and 4 (3:6, 15–16; 4:5) and continues after the circumcision episode (6:3, 8). These references to Abraham, Isaac and Jacob and the mention of the covenant suggest that circumcision is not at all out of place here in Exodus 4. The only other place where Abraham is mentioned in Exodus is in the golden calf episode (32:13; 33:1), where Yahweh relents from destroying the people on account of their 'stiff-neck' (*qĕšē-'ōrep*; 32:9; 33:3, 5; 34:9). Significantly, on both occasions the only hope for deliverance, either from 'harsh slavery' (*'ăbōdâ qāšâ*; 1:14; 6:9) or from a 'stiff neck', is Yahweh's faithfulness to his promise to Abraham.

Second, this episode comes immediately after Yahweh's comment that he will harden (*ḥzq*) Pharaoh's heart (4:21). Pharaoh's hardness of heart puts him at risk in the same way that Israel's hardness of heart later puts them at risk. Furthermore, we have seen how later in Deuteronomy 10, the remedy to a hard heart or stiff neck is to circumcise one's heart by grasping hold of Yahweh's promise to Abraham. So too in this episode Moses' or Gershom's life is endangered by a failure to take hold of that promise emblematized as it was in circumcision.

Third, the regulations for the celebration of the Passover later in Exodus 12:43–51 involve the themes of endangerment of the firstborn and circumcision, which are also prominent in the episode in Exodus 4:24–26.[55] Yahweh has just told Moses to say to Pharaoh, 'Israel is my firstborn son, and I say to you, "Let my son go that he may serve me." If you refuse to let him go, behold, I will kill your firstborn son' (Exod. 4:22–23).

In contrast, circumcision later in Exodus 12:43–51 becomes a prerequisite for participation in the Passover that celebrated the protection of Israel's firstborn while Egypt's firstborn perished. The regulations for the Passover in Exodus 12 are also preceded by the comment that the Israelites had been in Egypt 430 years. That time

---

[55] Sarna (1991: 24–25) argues that Exod. 4:22–26 and 12:23 – 13:15 form a 'thematically arranged chiasm'. E.g.:

    a. Firstborn (4:22–23)
      b. Circumcision (4:24–26)
      b. Circumcision (12:43–49)
    a. Firstborn (13:1, 11–15)

period immediately brings to mind Yahweh's covenant with Abraham in Genesis 15 where he promised that Abraham's descendants would be slaves for 400 years before being delivered (Gen. 15:13).[56] So too the regulations for the Passover in Exodus 12 are followed by detailed regulations on the consecration of Israel's firstborn to Yahweh (13:1, 11–16). The consecration of every firstborn, man and animal, will be a 'sign' (*'wt*) for them. Just as circumcision is a sign (*'wt*; Gen. 17:11), so is the consecration of the firstborn males. Suggestively too, just as Zipporah 'touched' (*ng'*) the 'feet' of Moses or Gershom, so the Israelites were to 'touch' (*ng'*) the blood of the Passover sacrifice on the doorposts and lintels of their houses (12:22).[57]

Curiously, Zipporah is said to 'cut [*krt*] the foreskin of her son' rather than circumcise. *Krt* is also used in Genesis 17, where those who are uncircumcised will be 'cut off' (Gen. 17:14).[58] The implication is perhaps that Gershom's circumcision rescues Gershom from that penalty; or, alternatively, Gershom's circumcision vicariously rescues Moses. The latter seems to make the most sense of Zipporah's touching Moses' feet/genitals with the severed foreskin, since one circumcision vicariously takes the place of another.[59] It also makes the most sense of the narrative and its context. As Durham notes, 'Moses is the center of Yahweh's concern everywhere else in the section . . . The sudden emergence to the forefront of Moses' son would make no sense whatever in such a sequence.'[60] Additionally, Hays points out, 'If it were the son, then Moses is not part of the story at all and so the son's identity would not need to be specified again when Zipporah cuts off his foreskin.'[61]

The most likely scenario seems to be that it is Moses himself who is threatened by Yahweh on account of his uncircumcision, but Zipporah intervenes and seeks God to uphold his promise to Abraham. She does this by circumcising Gershom and touching Moses' feet/genitals with the severed foreskin. Robinson writes:

> If it is Moses whose life is at risk, it is presumably Moses' feet or genitals that Zipporah touches with her son's foreskin. Moses is

---

[56] Exod. 13:5 also refers to the land that Yahweh swore to their fathers to give them.

[57] Fretheim 1991: 79; Sarna 1991: 26; V. P. Hamilton 2011: 82; Propp 1993: 511.

[58] Sarna 1991: 26.

[59] Durham 1987: 59; Fox 1974: 593; or symbolically, Propp 1993: 513; cf. R. B. Allen 1996: 263; Walters 2002: 412.

[60] Durham 1987: 58; cf. Kosmala 1962: 22–23.

[61] Hays 2007: 41–42.

saved by the smearing of blood. If I have been right to find in Ex. iv a foreshadowing of Ex. xii, the gist of this becomes a little clearer. Moses stands for Israel. Moses deserves to die, as the Pharaoh's son deserves to die; Israel deserves to die as the Egyptians deserve to die. The Israelites will, however, be spared because of the spilling and smearing of the blood of the Passover lamb, and this is symbolized by the smearing of the blood of Gershom.[62]

Fourth, Moses' next encounter with God in chapter 6 sees an unexpected shift from the phrase 'heavy mouth and heavy tongue' (*kĕbad-pe ûkĕbad lāšôn*; 4:10) to the phrase 'uncircumcised lips' (*'ăral šĕpātāyim*; 6:12, 30). Often the two phrases are seen to be equivalent, with uncircumcision being little more than a graphic picture of obstructed lips.[63] But there are good reasons to think otherwise. The proximity of the Zipporah incident is suggestive. In a book that mentions circumcision only three times it seems more than a coincidence.[64] Additionally, as with the events of chapter 4, the reference to circumcision is preceded by a recapitulation of Yahweh's promise to Abraham: Yahweh appeared to Abraham, Isaac and Jacob (6:3); he established his covenant with them to give them the land of Canaan (6:4); he has heard the groaning of his people and remembered his covenant (6:5); and he will bring them into the land he swore to give to Abraham, Isaac and Jacob (6:8). So it is strongly within the context of the Abrahamic covenant that Moses complains, 'Behold, the people of Israel have not listened to me. How then shall Pharaoh listen to me, for I am of uncircumcised lips?' (Exod. 6:12).

The same complaint is repeated by the narrator in 6:30. Sandwiched between these two references to uncircumcised lips is a genealogy. The structure of the passage suggests that the genealogy is quite important and serves to explain or answer Moses' complaint:

Yahweh's commitment to the covenant with Abraham,
    Isaac and Jacob (vv. 1–9)
  Moses' commissioning (vv. 10–11)
    Moses complains of uncircumcised lips (v. 12)
      Yahweh charges Moses and Aaron to bring the people
      out (v. 13)

---

[62] Robinson 1986: 457.

[63] E.g. Sarna 1991: 33; Fretheim 1991: 90; Keil and Delitzsch 1996: 1:304; cf. Propp 1999: 273.

[64] Stuart 2007: 174; DeRouchie 2004: 194–195.

Genealogy (vv. 14–25)
Summary statement (vv. 26–27)
Restatement of Yahweh's commission to Moses and
Aaron (v. 28)
Restatement of Moses' complaint about uncircumcised
lips (v. 30)[65]

The purpose of the genealogy is suggested by the summary statement in verses 26–27:

These are the Aaron and Moses to whom the LORD said: 'Bring out the people of Israel from the land of Egypt by their hosts.' It was they who spoke to Pharaoh king of Egypt about bringing out the people of Israel from Egypt, this Moses and this Aaron. (Exod. 6:26–27)

The statement implies that the purpose of the genealogy is to establish the credentials of Moses and Aaron.[66] Yet surprisingly, these credentials do not address Moses' ability to speak (as in 4:1–17) but his heritage. That indicates that Moses' complaint here is different from his complaint in chapter 4.

Such a shift makes complete sense. After all, Moses' previous objection has already been addressed – Yahweh is both the one who makes mouths and the one who provided Aaron to speak alongside Moses. In chapter 6 a different objection is raised, and it is answered in a different way by the genealogy that traces Moses back to Israel/ Jacob. Such genealogies, of course, are quite familiar from Genesis, where their purpose was to trace the line through which God would fulfil his promise to Abraham. This genealogy, as those, shows that Moses is within the promised line – he is Abraham's seed.

If it is true that the genealogy answers the complaint, and given that Yahweh has just outlined his intention to fulfil his promise to Abraham through Moses (6:1–8), then Moses' new fear may be not that he cannot speak because he is physically unable but that he cannot speak (and he will not be heard) because he is not in the line of promise through which God will fulfil his covenant with Abraham, Isaac and Jacob. His unique history – being brought up by the daughter of Pharaoh – may well have raised significant concerns about his identity. Zipporah's family obviously took him to be an Egyptian (2:19). This

---

[65] For a similar structure see V. P. Hamilton 2011: 107.
[66] Durham 1987: 83–84; cf. Bernat 2009: 88–89.

identity crisis would also have been exacerbated if the reason for the events in Exodus 4:24–26 was that Moses himself was uncircumcised. Nevertheless, the genealogy shows that Moses was indeed Abraham's seed.

Although we have not been able to answer every question related to Exodus 4, we have seen that many of the themes we have encountered before arise here too: Yahweh's faithfulness to his promise to Abraham as the ground for deliverance; taking hold of that promise rather than being hard-hearted as the remedy to endangerment; the connection between circumcision and sacrifice; and the connection between circumcision and the individual seed of Abraham through whom God would fulfil the promise. Yet the episode also highlights that although circumcision symbolized the need for trust in Yahweh's promise to Abraham, physical circumcision could not simply be discarded. It remained, for the moment, an important part of Yahweh's plan, reminding people of Yahweh's promise to Abraham and inviting them to participate in that promise.

Isaiah 52:1

In Isaiah 52:1 Yahweh foreshadows a day when Jerusalem will be free from the uncircumcised and the unclean:

> Awake, awake,
>   put on your strength, O Zion;
> put on your beautiful garments,
>   O Jerusalem, the holy city;
> for there shall no more come into you
>   the uncircumcised and the unclean.

Isaiah 52:1 is the third of three calls to 'awake', beginning in 51:9 (also 51:17). The first call to awake is addressed to Yahweh, while the latter two are addressed to the people. Nevertheless, together the three sections speak of restoration, as in the exodus (51:10), and the end of God's anger against Israel (51:22).[67] These three calls to 'awake' are preceded by three calls to 'listen' or 'give attention' at the beginning of Isaiah 51 (51:1, 4, 7).[68] The two sections are connected in that the

---

[67] The three units are linked by the use of double imperative and other literary and thematic connections, such as the emphasis in each section on deliverance (Oswalt 1998: 340; see also Melugin 1976: 163–167).

[68] Scholars disagree over the unity of these three sections, but the three are linked by the use of introductory imperatives, common vocabulary, similar phrases, common

people of God are called to listen and return to Yahweh in advance of his promised restoration.[69]

Especially notable is the mention of Abraham in the first call to listen in 51:1–2:

> Listen to me, you who pursue righteousness,
>   you who seek the LORD:
> look to the rock from which you were hewn,
>   and to the quarry from which you were dug.
> Look to Abraham your father
>   and to Sarah who bore you;
> for he was but one when I called him,
>   that I might bless him and multiply him.

Those who pursue and desire righteousness are to look to what God did for Abraham: just as from one man came a whole nation, Yahweh promises to do the same again. The speaker is the Isaianic servant, and the events of Isaiah 53 suggest that the servant himself is that one person from whom 'offspring' (*zera'*) will come (53:10). In that vein, the NT writers twice take Abraham as a type of Christ – as good as dead yet producing many descendants (Rom. 4:19; Heb. 11:12). So too it is through the sacrificial suffering of the righteous servant that many will be accounted righteous (53:9–11). These ideas bear deep resonances with those we have already seen in connection with circumcision.

The theme of righteousness also runs through the first half of Isaiah 51 (51:1, 5–8). But notably, in 51:7, those who know righteousness are described as those 'in whose heart is my law'. This represents the same kind of internalization that is present in other circumcision-related OT texts (e.g. Lev. 26; Deut. 10; 30). In that context, the statement in 52:1 that no more uncircumcised people will enter Jerusalem begins to look more and more like a statement not so much about physical circumcision but, similar to what we will see in the other prophets, a statement about those who pursue righteousness through trust in God's promises to Abraham. Thus Oswalt observes regarding 52:1:

---

form of address, the same speaker (Yahweh), as well as other connections (Melugin 1976: 157–159; also Oswalt 1998: 333; Motyer 1993: 402–407).

[69] Numerous features connect the two sections: the language of comfort (51:3, 12, 19; 52:9); Zion's joy and gladness (51:3, 11; cf. 52:8–9); and deliverance from exile and punishment (e.g. 51:3, 7, 11, 14, 17, 22; 52:2–4). See Motyer 1993: 402.

Their salvation is not a matter of God's willingness . . . nor of the severity of their punishment . . . It is a matter of their faith. Will they rise from their apathetic lethargy and lay hold of what is theirs?[70]

That may be confirmed by the coupling of uncircumcised with unclean. Uncleanness is a major biblical topic, but much like circumcision it is one that in the later prophetic writings takes on symbolic significance – uncleanness is ultimately a matter of the heart. Most notable is the language found in Ezekiel 36 in which Yahweh promises to sprinkle, wash and cleanse his people, giving them a new spirit and causing them to walk in his ways (Ezek. 36:25–29). But Oswalt also notes the link with the cleansing of Zion found earlier in Isaiah 4:[71]

And he who is left in Zion and remains in Jerusalem will be called holy, everyone who has been recorded for life in Jerusalem, when the Lord shall have washed away the filth of the daughters of Zion and cleansed the bloodstains of Jerusalem from its midst by a spirit of judgement and by a spirit of burning. (Isa. 4:3–4)

Here cleansing is bound up with holiness, as it is in 1:16–17 and 35:8, and refers not merely to Jerusalem's enemies,[72] but to her own people as well. Thus Oswalt writes of Isaiah 52:

The promise that the uncircumcised and the unclean will no longer come in to the city continues the theme of 4:2–6. The greatest hope for Zion is not that she will be rich, famous, and mighty, but that she will be the city of God, sharing his character . . .[73]

Isaiah 52:1 suggests that it is not primarily those who are circumcised who will enter Jerusalem, but those who pursue righteousness through trusting Yahweh's promise to Abraham and who receive righteousness through the righteous suffering servant.

---

[70] Oswalt 1998: 359.
[71] Ibid. 360.
[72] E.g. McKenzie 2008: 127; Westermann 1969: 247; Blenkinsopp 2002: 340.
[73] Oswalt 1998: 360.

Jeremiah 4:4

In Jeremiah 4:4 Yahweh says to the people of Judah and Jerusalem:

> Circumcise yourselves to the LORD;
>> remove the foreskin of your hearts,
> O men of Judah and inhabitants of Jerusalem;
> lest my wrath go forth like fire,
>> and burn with none to quench it,
>> because of the evil of your deeds.

It is immediately clear that the issue which circumcising their hearts is intended to address is the evil deeds of the people. Moreover, this plea to circumcise themselves to the Lord comes amid a series of calls to repent. In 3:12 Jeremiah is commanded to proclaim to the northern tribes:

> Return, faithless Israel,
> declares the LORD.
> I will not look on you in anger,
>> for I am merciful,
> declares the LORD;
> I will not be angry for ever.

The same calls to repent are repeated in 3:14 and 23. The nature of that 'returning' is explained more fully by verse 13:

> Only acknowledge your guilt,
>> that you rebelled against the LORD your God
> and scattered your favours among foreigners under
>> every green tree,
>> and that you have not obeyed my voice,
> declares the LORD.

Repentance involves the acknowledgment of their guilt, rebellion and disobedience. Significantly, these calls to repentance follow the denials of sin in chapter 2. For example:

> How can you say, 'I am not unclean,
> I have not gone after the Baals'?
>> (Jer. 2:23)

you say, 'I am innocent;
  surely his anger has turned from me.'
Behold, I will bring you to judgement
  for saying, 'I have not sinned.'

(Jer. 2:35)

As Lemke notes, what is required is 'genuine deeds of penitence that move beyond externals to matters of the heart'.[74] More positively, the required repentance involves removing their idolatry and returning to trust in Yahweh. As Yahweh says right before the call to circumcise their hearts:

If you return, O Israel,
declares the LORD,
  to me you should return.
If you remove your detestable things from my presence,
  and do not waver,
and if you swear, 'As the LORD lives,'
  in truth, in justice, and in righteousness,
then nations shall bless themselves in him,
  and in him shall they glory.

(Jer. 4:1–2)

The language of swearing an oath ('as the LORD lives') is reminiscent of covenant inauguration. So too the last phrase of verse 2, 'then nations shall bless themselves in him, and in him shall they glory', is remarkably similar to Genesis 12:3, 18:18, 22:18 and 26:4.[75] Holladay notes that the contexts of the latter two references also share the language of 'swearing' (*šb'*; Gen. 22:16; 26:3).[76] That, together with the reference to circumcision in verse 4, suggests that Yahweh's covenant with Abraham is in view here in Jeremiah. Moreover, Sailhamer has argued that the 'in him' of 4:2 refers not to Israel or God but to the promised king from the house of David. In the Genesis texts, the 'him' in whom the nations will be blessed is the Abrahamic 'seed', whom I have argued is ultimately a descendant of David.[77] That is, the repentance for which Jeremiah is calling involves not only a return to and embrace of Yahweh's covenant with Abraham, but also

---

[74] Lemke 2003: 303.
[75] Lundbom 1999: 331; Thompson 1980: 213, n. 28; DeRouchie 2004: 199.
[76] Holladay 1986: 128.
[77] Sailhamer 2009: 482–499.

hope in Yahweh's commitment to see the promises of that covenant enacted, in which not only Israel but the nations will be blessed through the promised Davidic king.[78] So also, following their repentance, Yahweh promises to put away his anger (3:12), give them shepherds after his own heart who will lead them (3:15), and heal their faithlessness (3:22) such that no longer shall anyone follow their own evil heart (3:17).

Again we have circumcision of the heart linked with humble repentance involving an acknowledgment of sin and a return to trust in Yahweh and his covenant with Abraham, together with Yahweh's commitment that if they return to him he will lead them into faithfulness.

Jeremiah 6:10

In Jeremiah 6:10 Yahweh launches another similar criticism through his prophet Jeremiah:

> To whom will I speak
> and will I warn and they will listen?
> Behold their ears have a foreskin
> and they are not able to listen.
> Behold the word of Yahweh is an object of scorn.
> They do not delight in it.
>
> (my tr.)

Conveniently here Jeremiah explains what it means that the people's ears have a foreskin: they are not able to listen in the sense that the words do not penetrate their minds and hearts.[79] Allen proposes that the problem is 'a blatant refusal to take correction seriously. Uncircumcised ears are those wilfully closed to prophetic indictments.'[80] But it goes deeper than that. The issue is not simply the inability to hear prophetic rebuke, but also that Yahweh's word more generally is an object of scorn to them and they do not delight in it. The mention of delight in Yahweh's word pushes the idea beyond the present rebuke (after all, who delights in rebuke?) and moves to God's word in its broadest sense (cf. Ps. 119:35).[81] This statement follows on from the

---

[78] Lundbom (1999: 327) writes, 'It is the Abrahamic covenant being fulfilled, not the Mosaic covenant being obeyed, and the beneficiary once repentance has taken place will be both Israel and the nations.'

[79] Craigie et al. 1991: 103.

[80] L. C. Allen 2008: 86.

[81] Cf. Lundbom 1999: 425–427.

one in Jeremiah 4. Both arise from the same essential criticism that the people refuse to turn from their sin and listen to Yahweh.

The first half of chapter 6 represents a series of warnings on account of the sin among the people of Jerusalem:

> As a well keeps its water fresh,
>   so she keeps fresh her evil;
> violence and destruction are heard within her;
>   sickness and wounds are ever before me.
> Be warned, O Jerusalem,
>   lest I turn from you in disgust,
> lest I make you a desolation,
>   an uninhabited land.
>
> (Jer. 6:7–8)

Such indictments are also found after Yahweh's condemnation of the people for having uncircumcised ears:

> For from the least to the greatest of them,
>   everyone is greedy for unjust gain;
> and from prophet to priest,
>   everyone deals falsely.
>
> (Jer. 6:13)

It is in that context that Yahweh asks, 'To whom will I speak and will I warn and they will listen?' Yahweh speaks to warn in order that the people might repent (as in Jer. 4), yet no one hears. They refuse to turn from their sin.

It is common to view the meaning of 'uncircumcised ears' as primarily referring to a kind of metaphorical foreskin that encases the ears and makes them impenetrable.[82] While that imagery is convenient and may be in play, in the light of what we have seen, it makes sense to understand the reference to circumcision not primarily as related to metaphorical flaps of skin that cover the ear, but as an implicit reference to the Abrahamic covenant. The people must turn from sin and trust God as Abraham trusted God, and they must look for the deliverance God promised Abraham would come about through his seed and was foreshadowed in the regular sacrifice of blameless animals. That is, it is not the physical notion of

---

[82] E.g. Thompson 1980: 257; L. C. Allen 2008: 86; Lundbom 1999: 330.

circumcision being applied to the ear to construct the metaphor, but the metaphorical/theological meaning of circumcision being applied to the ear.[83] Yet, irrespective of how the metaphor is constructed, the key point is that once again circumcision/uncircumcision is linked with sin and repentance.

Jeremiah 9:25–26

In Jeremiah 9:25–26 Yahweh looks to a day when there will be judgment for those who are circumcised only in the flesh and not also in the heart. He declares:

> Behold, the days are coming, declares the LORD, when I will punish all those who are circumcised merely in the flesh – Egypt, Judah, Edom, the sons of Ammon, Moab, and all who dwell in the desert who cut the corners of their hair, for all these nations are uncircumcised, and all the house of Israel are uncircumcised in heart. (Jer. 9:25–26)[84]

The cause for the impending judgment is made clear earlier in the chapter in response to the question 'Why is the land ruined and laid waste like a wilderness, so that no one passes through?' (9:12).[85] To which Yahweh responds:

> Because they have forsaken my law that I set before them, and have not obeyed my voice or walked in accord with it, but have stubbornly followed their own hearts and have gone after the Baals, as their fathers taught them. (Jer. 9:13–14)

---

[83] See Bernat, who argues concerning Lev. 26 that circumcision has become as 'dead metaphor' (Bernat 2009: 109–111).

[84] A complexity arises in this passage given that all or some of the nations mentioned seem to have practised circumcision and yet they are called 'uncircumcised' (Lundbom 1999: 573–574; Holladay 1986: 319). L. C. Allen (2008: 121) suggests that this is a reference to the partial circumcision practised by these nations where the foreskin was cut but not amputated. Yet that explanation presupposes that all that matters is circumcision itself. Irrespective of the physical details of how these nations practised circumcision, they were not practising circumcision *as a sign of the Abrahamic covenant*. In that sense, they were circumcised but uncircumcised. In the same way, the nation of Israel had been circumcised as a sign of the Abrahamic covenant but they had not appropriated that covenant within their heart; hence they were circumcised but not circumcised in the heart (similarly, Holladay 1986: 320).

[85] Lundbom (1999: 569) and L. C. Allen (2008: 119–121) note several connections between 9:23–26 and 9:12–16 (cf. Craigie et al. 1991: 152–153; McKane 1986: 213; Thompson 1980: 317–318, 321).

Here again we encounter stubborn hearts, as in Deuteronomy 10. The remedy Yahweh prescribes for this is first of all to consider and mourn (Jer. 9:17–20). The other part of the remedy is to boast, not in personal achievements, but in the knowledge of Yahweh:

> Thus says the LORD: 'Let not the wise man boast in his wisdom, let not the mighty man boast in his might, let not the rich man boast in his riches, but let him who boasts boast in this, that he understands and knows me, that I am the LORD who practises steadfast love, justice, and righteousness in the earth. For in these things I delight, declares the LORD.' (Jer. 9:23–24)

It is those who do evil, who refuse to obey Yahweh, who stubbornly follow their own hearts and who boast in their own achievements who are uncircumcised of heart; while it is those who consider, mourn and boast in knowing Yahweh and his love, justice and righteousness whose hearts are circumcised.

Ezekiel 28:10

In Ezekiel 28:10 Ezekiel receives the word of Yahweh concerning the king of Tyre[86] that

> You shall die the death of the uncircumcised
> by the hand of foreigners;
> for I have spoken, declares the Lord GOD.

Yet circumcision is simply a metonym for something else. As Joyce notes, 'Like most other peoples of the ancient Near East, the Phoenicians did in fact practise circumcision; so Ezekiel is using the term "uncircumcised" metaphorically, to signal uncleanness and cultural inferiority.'[87]

However, the reason given for God's judgment is not 'cultural inferiority' but the king's pride. For example:

> your heart is proud,
> and you have said, 'I am a god,

---

[86] Ezek. 28:2 refers to the 'prince of Tyre', while 28:12 refers to the 'king of Tyre'. There is some disagreement as to whether the same figure is meant. The decision largely rests on whether one sees 28:1–10 and 28:11–19 as being of a piece. Block (1998: 88–90) provides compelling evidence that the two are connected, sharing many themes and words.

[87] Joyce 2007: 178.

I sit in the seat of the gods,
in the heart of the seas,'
yet you are but a man, and no god,
though you make your heart like
the heart of a god . . .
(Ezek. 28:2)

Curiously, in the next section Ezekiel is called to lament the demise of the king of Tyre in language reminiscent of Adam in the Garden of Eden.[88]

You were the signet of perfection,
full of wisdom and perfect in beauty.
You were in Eden, the garden of God;
every precious stone was your covering . . .
(Ezek. 28:12–13)

More significant, however, for our purposes are the words in 28:15:

You were blameless [*tāmîm*] in your ways
from the day you were created,
till unrighteousness was found in you.

As Block notes, Ezekiel's use of *tāmîm*, following the use of *hlk* (28:14),

invites comparison with Noah, who was also 'blameless' and 'walked with God' (Gen. 6:9), and Abraham, who was charged by God: 'Walk (*hithallēk*) before me and be blameless (*tāmîm*)' (Gen. 17:1).[89]

But the context also suggests an equation of sorts between blamelessness and the sinless pre-fall Edenic state of Adam and Eve. Although the identity of the character in 28:11–19 is disputed,[90]

---

[88] Block 1998: 105–106.

[89] Ibid. 116. Zimmerli (1983: 86, 93) even suggests that *hithallākĕttā* should be read as belonging to the beginning of v. 15, as with the Syriac: 'You walked blameless on your way . . .'

[90] Some think the person referred to is the king of Tyre, others a cherub, still others Satan (for a summary of issues see Cooper 2001: 264–265).

together with the background of the imagery,[91] the language of 'Eden' (28:13) links the imagery in Ezekiel 28 strongly with Genesis 1 – 3 (Gen. 2:8, 10, 15; 3:23–24; 4:16). As does, (1) the language of creation (*br'*; 28:13, 15), which is often used in the OT to refer to the initial creation (e.g. Gen. 1:1, 21, 27; 2:3–4; 5:1–2; Isa. 40:28; 42:5); (2) the reference to a cherub (28:14, 16; see Gen. 3:24), albeit in a different role; as well as (3) the pattern of a perfect creature who falls into unrighteousness.[92] Nevertheless, for our purposes it is sufficient to note that *some* connection between blamelessness and Genesis 1 – 3 is intended, whoever is meant and whatever the background.

Without solving all those difficulties, we can still observe that here again circumcision is set in opposition to pride and is linked with (walking in) blamelessness/righteousness understood in terms of pre-Edenic sinlessness.

Ezekiel 44:6–9

In Ezekiel 44 during Ezekiel's vision of the new temple, he is commanded:

> And say to the rebellious house, to the house of Israel, Thus says the Lord GOD: O house of Israel, enough of all your abominations, in admitting foreigners, uncircumcised in heart and flesh, to be in my sanctuary, profaning my temple, when you offer to me my food, the fat and the blood. You have broken my covenant, in addition to all your abominations. And you have not kept charge of my holy things, but you have set others to keep my charge for you in my sanctuary.
>
> Thus says the Lord GOD: No foreigner, uncircumcised in heart and flesh, of all the foreigners who are among the people of Israel, shall enter my sanctuary. (Ezek. 44:6–9)

In a similar way to Isaiah 52, where no uncircumcised people would enter the restored Zion, here no uncircumcised person will enter the restored temple. What is interesting is the combination of uncircumcision of the flesh and heart. The necessity of circumcision

---

[91] Some understand the background to be Genesis (Block 1998: 117–120; Greenberg 1997: 590–593); others a kind of parallel fall for Satan or other angels (Barr 1992: 220), while others think the imagery stems from pagan myths (Eichrodt 1970: 392; Cooke 1951: 315). Yet, as Greenberg points out, that Ezekiel was using 'Israelite mythical motifs familiar to his audience is the most plausible assumption'.

[92] See Block 1998: 117–118; Joyce 2007: 178–179; L. C. Allen 1990: 94.

of the flesh points back to Genesis 17 and the need to be seen to have embraced Yahweh's covenant with Abraham; while the necessity of circumcision of the heart points to the need for a more than skin deep appropriation of the covenant.[93]

Habakkuk 2:16

Habakkuk also mentions circumcision:

> Woe to him who makes his neighbours drink –
> you pour out your wrath and make them drunk,
> in order to gaze at their nakedness!
> You will have your fill of shame instead of glory.
> Drink, yourself, and show your uncircumcision!
> The cup in the Lord's right hand
> will come round to you,
> and utter shame will come upon your glory!
>
> (Hab. 2:15–16)

Assuming the reading of 'uncircumcision' here is correct,[94] these two verses show that in response to the sin of the Babylonians who plot to expose the nakedness of their neighbours (v. 15), God himself will reveal their own shame, not simply by exposing their nakedness in return, but by exposing their uncircumcised state (v. 16).[95] The idea is one of reversal.[96] The shame intended here may be nothing more than the shame of being physically uncircumcised, but it seems quite likely that more is intended. The exposure of their (hidden) uncircumcision simultaneously exposes their utter disobedience to God. As Robertson puts it, 'Shame attaches to uncircumcision only because it represents a lack of submission to the God of all the earth.'[97]

Yahweh's words through Habakkuk in 2:15–16 are part of a speech that begins in 2:2 and stretches to verse 20.[98] It details the sins for

---

[93] Cf. Lemke 2003: 312.

[94] The DSS have *r'l* (stagger) instead of *'rl* (foreskin), and the LXX, Vulgate, Syriac and Aquila assume a similar reading. Curiously, the Qumran commentary on 2:16 seems to support the MT (Robertson 1990: 202). Yet emending the text to 'stagger' breaks the reciprocity between the sin and the judgment (Miller 1982: 63–64; cf. Smith 1998: 109).

[95] Ward 1911: 17.

[96] Andersen 2001: 246; Roberts 1991: 124–125.

[97] Robertson 1990: 202.

[98] Andersen 2001: 15–18.

which the judgment of Yahweh is coming upon the people. However, the foundational problem is highlighted in 2:4–5:

> Behold, his soul is puffed up; it is not upright within him,
>> but the righteous shall live by his faith.
> Moreover, wine is a traitor,
>> an arrogant man who is never at rest.
> His greed is as wide as Sheol;
>> like death he has never enough.
> He gathers for himself all nations
>> and collects as his own all peoples.
>
> (Hab. 2:4–5)

The core issue is arrogance and pride. The opposite of pride is 'faith/faithfulness' (*'ĕmûnâ*).[99] Such a person is righteous and will live. Although there is some debate as to the meaning of *'ĕmûnâ* and to what it refers (Yahweh's faithfulness, the faithfulness of the vision, or the faith/faithfulness of the person),[100] the fact that it is set in opposition to *'pl* (puffed up) implies that what is in view is humility[101] – the kind of humility that expresses itself in faith/trust.[102]

But as Robertson points out, this comparison is pivotal for the five 'woes' that follow. He notes, '[Yahweh] gives him a vision which contrasts the righteous by faith with the resolutely proud (2:2–5). Then he offers five proverbial bywords which ridicule the haughty (2:6–20).'[103] In other words, the five 'woes' of 2:6–20 reflect on the failure of the proud to trust. In that light the threat to expose the circumcision of the Babylonians is a threat to expose their lack of humble (and obedient) trust in Yahweh. But it also then exposes their lack of the righteousness and life that comes through humble faith in Yahweh.

Once again we have circumcision being brought up in a context where the emphasis is on humility, faith and righteousness. Moreover, it is noteworthy that on two occasions in the NT Paul makes reference to Habakkuk 2:4 in close proximity to discussions about circumcision. The first is in Galatians 3:11 as Paul discusses justification by faith in

---

[99] The noun *'ĕmûnâ* here is a cognate of the verb *'mn*, used to describe Abraham's faith in Gen. 15:6.

[100] For a discussion of the issues see Andersen 2001: 211–215.

[101] Robertson 1990: 174–175, 178; Bruce 2009: 860.

[102] This contrast between pride and faith stands whether one understands Habakkuk to be referring to faith explicitly (i.e. *'ĕmûnâ* = faith) or implicitly (i.e. trust in Yahweh's/the vision's faithfulness).

[103] Robertson 1990: 167–168.

attempting to counter his opponents' demand for circumcision. The second is in Romans 1:17 in a quotation that sets up his discussion of the pride of humanity, which in turn leads to his explanation of the significance of circumcision. We will look at the context of both of these in more detail in subsequent chapters. Nevertheless, it may be that Paul too saw something of the connection between Habakkuk 2:4 and the matter of circumcision raised in 2:16.

Summary

We saw in the previous chapter evidence that circumcision was bound up from the very beginning with the ideas of faith and blamelessness/ righteousness within the context of the Abrahamic covenant. I suggested that the demand and promise of blamelessness/righteousness was held together through the hope of a 'blameless' sacrifice. We have now seen how these ideas are carried throughout the remainder of the OT. In Leviticus 26 the same demand for obedience is presented, while it is simultaneously acknowledged that demand will not be met. The only hope for the people is to humble their uncircumcised hearts and put their trust in Yahweh's promise to Abraham and in his provision of atonement foreshadowed in the sacrificial system. Similarly, in Deuteronomy Yahweh calls the people to obedience, yet that obedience is found through humility and repentance centred around Yahweh's promise to Abraham, emblematized by the idea of circumcision of the heart. In Deuteronomy 10 Moses' call to obedience and love follows his recounting of the golden calf episode and of how he interceded on the people's behalf by calling on Yahweh to remember his promises to Abraham, Isaac and Jacob. In Deuteronomy 30 Yahweh promises that one day the people will love and obey him completely. Yet such obedience and love is not beyond the people: it is found in Yahweh's word of promise to Abraham. Unlike the stubborn heart that hears the words and thinks, 'I'll be safe though I go my own way,' the circumcised heart repents and trusts in Yahweh's words.

Joshua 5 reveals that circumcision was stopped throughout the period of the wilderness wanderings on account of the people's dis-obedience and failure to trust Yahweh. As a result, the circumcised generation died in the wilderness, while it was the uncircumcised generation that Yahweh brought to the Promised Land. On the cusp of the Promised Land the people were circumcised as a reminder of how Yahweh had 'rolled away' the reproach of their unbelief. In that way, physical circumcision represents the same basic idea embodied in circumcision of the heart. Physical circumcision is a sign of God's requirement and promise of blamelessness and a reminder of the need for that promise to be embraced in the heart by repentance and faith.

So too in the rest of the OT circumcision is often connected with the ideas of faith, repentance, sacrifice and blamelessness/ righteousness. Less prominent in those passages is the notion of the promised seed. Yet it is not entirely absent. In Exodus 4 – 6 there is a glimpse of the importance of a particular seed of Abraham. And Isaiah 52's vision of a renewed and holy Jerusalem is set within the context of the hope that, just as Abraham was only one man and God made him many, so God's righteous servant in Isaiah 53 will be cut off as a sacrifice but will see many descendants and will make many to be accounted righteous. Finally, we noted the possibility that Jeremiah 4:4 envisages that the blessing of the nations promised to Abraham will come through a Davidic seed.

Chapter Four

Circumcision in the New Testament: the themes of the Old Testament continued

Given the apparent shift in the latter half of the OT towards the metaphorical use of circumcision, it is surprising that the NT has a very large number of references to physical circumcision. For instance, Luke refers to the circumcision of both John the Baptist and of Jesus (Luke 1:59; 2:21), and to Paul's circumcision of Timothy in order to deliver the message of the Jerusalem council (Acts 16:3). Often 'circumcision' (*peritomē, peritemnō*) and 'uncircumcision' (*aperitmētos, akrobystia*) are used simply to differentiate between those who were circumcised – the Jews – and those who were not – the Gentiles.[1] In fact, out of the 74 references to circumcision/uncircumcision in the NT only 10 refer to metaphorical circumcision.[2]

In this and the following chapters we will consider circumcision in the NT by focusing on the major passages that discuss circumcision, whether physical or metaphorical. However, in an attempt to understand how the NT view of circumcision is anchored in the OT, we begin not with circumcision, but by examining how the NT writers take up those themes that are connected with circumcision in the OT – 'walking' and 'being blameless'. Only then will we turn to consider a number of NT circumcision passages. The first is Philippians 3, where Paul draws together circumcision, righteousness and blamelessness. The other two passages are from Colossians and Ephesians, that contain many of the same themes as Philippians 3.

Blamelessness in the New Testament

We begin with the language of blamelessness. The primary interest is to establish how the NT writers use this language; however, along the

[1] Acts 10:45; 11:2–3; Rom. 3:30; 4:9, 12; 15:8; Gal. 2:7–9, 12; 6:13; Eph. 2:11; Col. 3:11; 4:11; Titus 1:10.
[2] Acts 7:51; Rom. 2:25–26, 28–29; Phil. 3:3; Col. 2:11 (three times), 13.

way, we will also consider a few references to contemporary Jewish writings that confirm the understanding of this language for which I have argued on the basis of the OT.

Amōmos

To understand how the writers of the Greek NT use language that reflects the Hebrew term *tāmîm* it is useful to see how *tāmîm* was translated in the LXX. For the most part, in the LXX *tāmîm* is translated by the Greek term *amōmos*. Of the 91 occurrences of *tāmîm* in the OT, 67 times it is translated by *amōmos*. Conversely, on the 3 occasions where *amōmos* is used in the LXX and it does not translate *tāmîm*,[3] it translates a cognate of *tāmîm*.[4] In other words, *amōmos* essentially translates no other Hebrew word.

Amōmos is even further slanted towards sacrificial usage than is *tāmîm*. On 57 occasions it refers to sacrificial animals being 'without blemish',[5] once it refers to the 'whole tail' (Lev. 3:9) and in the remaining 19 instances it is used as a moral category. I suggested earlier that the use of *tāmîm* in the sacrificial context underpinned its use in overtly moral contexts. This idea is confirmed by the way the NT writers use *amōmos*.

Amōmos is used only 8 times in the NT, but on several occasions it is used to refer to Jesus as a sacrifice 'without blemish'. Peter writes, 'you were ransomed from the futile ways inherited from your forefathers, not with perishable things such as silver or gold, but with the precious blood of Christ, like that of a lamb without blemish [*amōmos*] or spot' (1 Pet. 1:18–19).

Jesus as the lamb 'without blemish' is contrasted with the 'futile ways' of Peter's readers, suggesting that Jesus' blamelessness refers to his moral perfection. Similarly, the writer of Hebrews argues, 'how much more will the blood of Christ, who through the eternal Spirit offered himself without blemish [*amōmos*] to God, purify our conscience from dead works to serve the living God' (Heb. 9:14).

In the context the writer is making a point about the internal efficacy of the sacrificial work of Christ versus the external efficacy of the OT

---

[3] This is not including the occasions where there is no equivalent Hebrew term, on which see n. 5.

[4] Ps. 19:14 (*tmm*); Ps. 64:4 (*tām*); Prov. 20:7 (*tōm*).

[5] Of the 8 occasions where *amōmos* is used and there is no equivalent in the Hebrew Bible, in all but one of those instances it has been inserted in sacrificial contexts with the sense of 'without blemish' (Exod. 29:38; Lev. 4:14; 12:6; 23:18; Num. 7:88; 15:24; 28:27; cf. Prov. 22:11).

sacrificial system. In that vein, it makes sense to understand that the 'perfection' of Christ is an internal, moral blamelessness in contrast to the external, physical 'perfection' of the bulls and goats. The writer is revealing his understanding of the symbolism of the old covenant sacrifices: just as the 'spotless' sacrifices were offered to bring external cleansing, the moral, internal 'spotlessness' of Jesus cleanses the consciences of those who trust in him.

Notably too, a few uses of *amōmos* in the NT carry the sense of 'before God'. That is, just as Abraham was called to walk 'before God', and just as in the old covenant the sacrifices were presented to God 'without blemish', the NT writers convey the sense that Jesus presents his people 'before God' as blameless. So in Ephesians 1:4, believers have been chosen in Christ 'that we should be holy and blameless [*amōmos*] before him'. In Ephesians 5:27 Jesus' purpose was to 'present the church to himself in splendour, without spot or wrinkle or any such thing, that she might be holy and without blemish [*amōmos*]'. In Colossians 1:22 we have been reconciled to God by the death of Christ in order that he might 'present you holy and blameless [*amōmos*] and above reproach before him'. And in Jude 24, God is the one who is able 'to present you blameless [*amōmos*] before the presence of his glory'. In each case the presentation in view is eschatological.[6] Perfect blamelessness is not a present reality but a future one. Moreover, it is clear in each case that what is in view is the moral perfection necessary to live in the presence of God.

Numerous times blamelessness is also paired with holiness in a way which suggests that the two are virtual synonyms (Eph. 1:4; 5:27; Col. 1:22). Conversely, in Colossians 1:22, 'blamelessness' is set in contrast to a 'hostile mind' and 'evil deeds', while in Philippians 2:15 it is set against a 'crooked and twisted generation'. In Jude 18 'blamelessness' is contrasted with 'scoffers, following their own ungodly passions', 'worldly people', and 'the garment stained by the flesh' (v. 23). In Revelation 14:4–5 the saints are 'blameless' in that 'in their mouth no lie was found' and they 'have not defiled themselves with women'.[7] In other words, the category is not relational or covenantal but moral. Blamelessness relates to the moral perfection required to live in the presence of God – there must be no hint of that which God hates. But more than that, according to the NT writers, it is the sacrifice of Jesus, the blameless one, that opens the way for Jesus the high priest to offer his people to God as blameless.

---

[6] Hauck 1967: 831; Gathercole 2002b: 186.
[7] For the identification of these as the saints see Beale 1999: 737–741.

Aside from the NT, *amōmos* is also used in contemporary Jewish literature. One example worthy of particular attention is in the *Testament of Benjamin*, where *amōmos* is used in a prophecy regarding Joseph:

> In thee shall be fulfilled the prophecy of heaven [concerning the Lamb of God, and Saviour of the world], and that a blameless one [*amōmos*] shall be delivered up for lawless men, and a sinless one [*anamartētos*] shall die for ungodly men [in the blood of the covenant, for the salvation of the Gentiles and of Israel, and shall destroy Beliar and his servants]. (*T. Benj.* 3.8 *APOT*)

Jacob's prophecy is a direct response to Joseph's request that his brothers not be held accountable for their sin against him: 'For Joseph also besought our father [that he would pray for his brethren], that [the Lord] would not impute to them as sin [whatever evil they had done unto him]' (*T. Benj.* 3.6 *APOT*).

Several items are worthy of note regarding this verse. First, a blameless person dies on behalf of sinners. Here we have again the idea of a blameless substitute that is so prominent in the OT sacrificial system. Second, the blameless substitute is a descendant of Abraham. We have already seen that hinted at in the focus on the particular seed of Abraham, though here it is ascribed to Joseph rather than to Judah/David. Third, blamelessness is equated with sinlessness (*anamartētos*).

What is unclear is whether this text is pre-Christian or not.[8] Yet, it hardly matters whether it is Christian or Jewish, pre-Christ or post-Christ; either way it highlights that others picked up on the same themes we have noted in the OT: a blameless/sinless (*amōmos*/*anamartētos*) descendant of Abraham dying on behalf of sinners. An idea also clearly present among the NT writers.

Amemptos

While *amōmos* is the Greek term that usually translates *tāmîm*, the term used in the crucial text of Genesis 17:1 is *amemptos*. That term is used only twice to translate *tāmîm* (Gen. 17:1; Job 12:4). Nevertheless, it occurs in the NT in a number of very significant contexts. The most significant is Luke 1:6, where almost all the language of Genesis 17:1 is applied to Zechariah and Elizabeth:

---

[8] For a brief discussion see Hengel 2004: 137–138.

> And they were both righteous before God, walking blamelessly in all the commandments and righteous requirements of the Lord. (my tr.)

> *ēsan de dikaioi amphoteroi enantion tou theou, poreuomenoi en pasais tais entolais kai dikaiōmasin tou kyriou amemptoi.*

Several points should be noted. First, they are described as 'righteous before God'. Second, that expression is paralleled by 'walking blamelessly'. Although the term used is not the more cultic term *amōmos*, it is the term used in Genesis 17:1 (*amemptos*). This second phrase explains the first: Zechariah and Elizabeth are righteous *in that* they walk blamelessly. Third, Elizabeth and Zechariah walk blamelessly 'in *all* the commandments and righteous requirements of the Lord'.

This description of Zechariah and Elizabeth confirms a number of our observations made when looking at the OT: first, the equivalence of righteousness and blamelessness; and second, the moral content of blamelessness – it is connected with the 'commandments and righteous requirements of the Lord'. If anything is missing, it is the emphasis on sacrifice and atonement and the hope in the seed of Abraham. And yet while that emphasis is not explicit, it can hardly be overlooked that Zechariah is faithfully serving as a priest. In other words, Zechariah and Elizabeth's righteousness and blamelessness cannot be abstracted from their faithful observance of the sacrificial system provided by God, in part, to make atonement for sins. As Dunn notes:

> For the terms of the covenant included demand for repentance and provision of sacrifice and atonement for sin. So to live in accordance with the law must have included availing oneself of the ritual and cultic provisions of the law when impurity and sin blighted the covenant life. Such I imagine to be the character and quality of life attributed to Zechariah and Elizabeth in Luke 1:6.[9]

So too in Zechariah's song we find his hope of a 'horn of salvation' from the Davidic house. A hope he links with the covenant God swore to Abraham (Luke 1:67–79).

Besides Luke 1:6, there are only four other NT occurrences of *amemptos*. In 1 Thessalonians 3:13 Paul links blamelessness with

---

[9] Dunn 2008: 479.

the second coming: 'that he may establish your hearts blameless [*amemptos*] in holiness before our God and Father, at the coming of our Lord Jesus with all his saints'. Again we can observe the link with holiness and the presentation of believers before God at the eschaton. In Hebrews 8:7 the writer notes that 'if that first covenant had been faultless [*amemptos*], there would have been no occasion to look for a second'. The emphases of Hebrews will be considered in the next section. The only other two NT occurrences are in Philippians 2 and 3, which are considered in more detail below.

Teleios

Another word used in the LXX to render *tāmîm* is *teleios*. The two words clearly operate within the same sphere of meaning: *teleios* generally means 'perfect' or 'complete'. It is used only four times in the LXX to render *tāmîm*: in Genesis 6:9 to describe Noah as 'perfect' in his generation; in Exodus 12:5 to describe a lamb 'without blemish'; in Deuteronomy 18:13 in the command to be 'perfect before the Lord your God' (my tr.); and in David's psalm in 2 Samuel 22:26: 'with a perfect man you will be perfect' (my tr.).[10] The use of *teleios* in apocryphal writings mirrors the moral use found elsewhere. Sirach 44.17 takes up the language of Genesis 6:9, noting that 'Noah the righteous was found blameless' (*APOT*).[11] Likewise, Wisdom 9.6 observes, 'For even if a man be perfect among the sons of men, yet if the wisdom that cometh from thee be not with him, he shall be held in no account' (*APOT*).

Even on occasions where *teleios* does not directly translate *tāmîm*, the thought is still a high moral standard. As Sabourin notes, 'The Septuagint employs *teleios* to characterize the conduct of men above all in phrases applied to the kings of Israel, whose hearts were or were not "wholly true" to the Lord all their days, with *teleios* translating *shālēm*.'[12] For example, the Lord says to Solomon, 'Let your heart therefore be wholly true [*teleios*/*šālēm*] to the LORD our God, walking in his statutes and keeping his commandments, as at this day' (1 Kgs 8:61).[13] Beyond these references, *teleios* is used in the OT to refer only to David's 'complete' hatred (Ps. 139:22), to my 'perfect one' (Song

---

[10] On two occasions the cognate *teleiotēs* is used to render *tāmîm* (Judg. 9:16, 19). Both refer to the people of Israel acting in 'integrity'.

[11] The Greek phrase is *Nōe heurethē teleios dikaios*, which translates the Hebrew phrase *nwḥ ṣdyq nmṣ' tmym*, for which see Beentjes 1997: 176.

[12] Sabourin 1980: 267.

[13] See also 1 Kgs 11:4; 15:3, 14; 1 Chr. 28:9.

5:2; 6:9), to Judah's being taken 'wholly' into exile (Jer. 13:19) and to a 'teacher' (1 Chr. 25:8).

While the meaning of *teleios* in the LXX is much broader than that of *tāmîm*, nevertheless there are numerous occasions in the NT where the meaning reflects that of *tāmîm*, referring to the perfections of God or the perfection of the new age. So, for instance, 'when the perfect [*teleios*] comes, the partial will pass away' (1 Cor. 13:10). Or in Ephesians 4:13, 'until we all attain to the unity of the faith and of the knowledge of the Son of God, to mature manhood [*andra teleion*], to the measure of the stature of the fullness of Christ'. Here the measure of 'mature manhood' is the 'measure of the stature of the fullness of Christ'. In Colossians 1:28 Paul's hope is to present everyone 'perfect in Christ' (*teleion en Christō*, my tr.). And James 1:25 refers to the 'perfect law' (*nomon teleion*).

Perhaps foremost in this category is Matthew 5:48, where Jesus says, 'You therefore must be perfect, as your heavenly Father is perfect.' As Luz observes:

> The key to understanding the verse is the word 'perfect' . . . Some have correctly emphasized that the concept must be interpreted not on the basis of the Greek doctrine of virtues but on the basis of its Jewish background.[14]

The command echoes Leviticus 19:2, 'You shall be holy, for I the LORD your God am holy,' perhaps also being influenced by Deuteronomy 18:13. It is a call to the perfections of God[15] and Jesus is evidently picking up on the strand of OT thought we have uncovered thus far: that to enter the kingdom of heaven in the fullest sense one must not simply be forgiven or even merely be committed, but be perfect.[16] Notable too is that within the context Jesus is talking about 'righteousness' (*dikaiosynē*). Verse 48 is the conclusion of a section begun with the statement that one's 'righteousness' must exceed that

---

[14] Luz 2007: 289.

[15] Carson (2010: 194–195) writes: 'Many judge its force to be nonmoral here in v.48, which becomes an exhortation to total commitment to God (e.g., Bonnard). But this makes a fairly flat conclusion of the antithesis. A better understanding of the verse does justice to the word *teleios* but also notes that the form of the verse is exactly like Leviticus 19:2, with 'holy' displaced by 'perfect', possibly due to the influence of Deuteronomy 18:13 . . . the perfection of the Father, the true eschatological goal of the law, is what all disciples of Jesus should pursue.'

[16] Numerous commentators on Matt. 5:48 note the cultic background of *teleios*. E.g. ibid. 194; Nolland 2005: 271.

of the Pharisees (Matt. 5:18–20). Then in 6:1 Jesus goes on to talk about not doing 'righteousness' before others. Once again the notion of blamelessness/perfection circles around together with righteousness.

Another place where the language of perfection is used in the NT is Hebrews, where the related *teleioō* (make perfect) helps carry the theology of the book.[17] For example, in the first half of Hebrews *teleioō* is used with respect to Christ: he was made perfect through suffering (2:10); he learned obedience through what he suffered and was made perfect (5:9); and he is the perfect Son who does not share the weaknesses (i.e. sin; cf. 4:15; 5:2) of the other high priests (7:28). *Teleioō* is also used in the middle chapters of Hebrews to describe the failure of the old covenant: it could not make anything perfect (7:18); its sacrifices could not perfect the conscience of the worshipper (9:9); and again its endless sacrifices could not make perfect those who draw near (10:1). Last of all, *teleioō* is used to describe believers under the new covenant: by a single offering Jesus has perfected them (10:14); the OT saints never received what was promised but are only now made perfect together with 'us' (11:40); and the spirits of righteous men made perfect now gather in the heavenly Jerusalem (12:23). Once again, in 12:23 righteousness and perfection are located together.

The pivot point between the perfection of Christ and the perfection of believers is the new covenant section in chapters 8–10. In the new covenant the law is written perfectly on the heart because God has finally made decisive atonement for sin through the spotless sacrifice of the perfect high priest in the perfect temple. Therefore, although the precise word is different (*teleioō* rather than *teleios* or *amōmos*) the theological categories are strikingly similar: a perfect sacrifice, a perfect high priest, an old covenant that could not deliver perfection, a new covenant that operates decisively on the heart, and a new people who are made perfect like the perfect Christ.

The last place of note where the language of perfection occurs in the NT is in Philippians 3:12, where Paul says that he has not yet been made 'perfect'. That passage also contains references to circumcision, righteousness, and blamelessness. We will turn to consider Philippians 3 in a moment. First, however, we will consider the language of

---

[17] A number of cognates of *teleioō* also occur in Hebrews: solid teaching is for the 'mature' (*teleios*; 5:14); the readers are to go on to 'maturity/perfection' (*teleiotēs*; 6:11); 'perfection' (*teleiōsis*) was not attainable through the Levitical priesthood (7:11); Jesus entered the more 'perfect' (*teleios*) tent (9:11); Jesus is the 'founder and perfecter [*teleiotēs*] of our faith' (12:2). Nevertheless, the basic structure seems to be carried by the verb. For a detailed study of perfection in Hebrews see Peterson 2005.

'walking' in the NT, before considering both circumcision and the language of 'walking blamelessly' within the Qumran material.

Walking in the New Testament

In the LXX, *hlk* is translated by an enormous array of Greek verbs, many occurring only a few times. In the vast majority of instances *hlk* is translated by *poreuō* (to go) or the passive/middle *poreuomai* (approx. 1,000 out of 1,500). *Poreuō* does not occur at all in the NT, while *poreuomai* occurs 153 times. For the most part, it carries the non-metaphorical meaning and means 'go' more than 'walk'.[18] The metaphorical meaning referring to a way of life occurs in a handful of places (Acts 9:31; 14:16; 1 Pet. 4:3; 2 Pet. 2:10; 3:3; Jude 11, 16, 18), but the most notable is in Luke 1:6, highlighted above, where it is said of Zechariah and Elizabeth, 'And they were both righteous before God, walking [*poreuomenoi*] blamelessly in all the commandments and righteous requirements of the Lord' (my tr.).

Of course, our interest is primarily in the phrase 'walk before me' that occurs in Genesis 17:1. There *hlk* is translated by *euaresteō*. That term is used in a similar way on a number of other occasions (Ps. 55:14; 116:9), not least to refer to Enoch's and Noah's walking with God (Gen. 5:22, 24; 6:9) and to Abraham and Isaac walking before God (Gen. 24:40; 48:15). Yet *euaresteō* is used only 3 times in the NT – in Hebrews, where it means 'to please' (Heb. 11:5–6; 13:16).

As Ebel notes, the term used more frequently in the NT to capture the metaphorical sense of 'walking' is *peripateō*, even though in the LXX it translates *hlk* only a meagre 20 times and only occasionally in the metaphorical sense (2 Kgs 20:3; Prov. 8:20; Eccl. 11:9).[19] Yet in the NT, *peripateō* is used 95 times. In the Gospels and Acts it mostly refers to someone 'walking', with no metaphorical connotations. The exceptions are two occasions that refer to walking 'according to' trad-itions or customs (Mark 7:5; Acts 21:21), and in John when Jesus refers to those who 'walk' either in light or in darkness (John 8:12; 11:9–10; 12:35).

However, in the epistles the reverse is true, so that on only one occasion does it refer to 'walking' in a non-figurative sense

---

[18] Ebel 1986: 946–947.
[19] Ibid. 935, 943, 947. Ebel (ibid. 933–935) also notes that *anastrephō/anastrophē* (2 Cor. 1:12; Gal. 1:13; Eph. 2:3; 4:22; 1 Tim. 3:15; 4:12; Heb. 13:7, 18; Jas 3:13; 1 Pet. 1:15, 17–18; 2:12; 3:1–2, 16; 2 Pet. 2:7, 18; 3:11) and *agōgē* (2 Tim. 3:10) are also used to convey the figurative notion of 'walking'.

(1 Pet. 5:8). Otherwise, one can walk 'according to/in the flesh' (Rom. 8:4; 2 Cor. 10:2–3); 'in a human way' (1 Cor. 3:3); 'following the course of this world' (Eph. 2:2); 'as the Gentiles do, in the futility of their minds' (Eph. 4:17); 'as enemies of the cross' (Phil. 3:18); 'in idleness' (1 Thess. 3:6, 11); deceptively (2 Cor. 4:2); 'in darkness' (1 John 1:6; 2:11); and in all kinds of sins (Col. 3:5–7). One can also walk, 'according to the Spirit' (Rom. 8:4; 2 Cor. 12:18; Gal. 5:16); 'in newness of life' (Rom. 6:4); 'by faith, not by sight' (2 Cor. 5:7); 'as children of the light' (Eph. 5:8); 'in him' (Col. 2:6); 'in love' (Rom. 14:15; Eph. 5:2); in 'good works, which God prepared beforehand' (Eph. 2:10); 'in a manner worthy of the calling to which you have been called' (Eph. 4:1; also 1 Cor. 7:17); 'in a manner worthy of the Lord/God' (Col. 1:10; 1 Thess. 2:12); 'to please God' (1 Thess. 4:1); 'according to the example you have in us' (Phil. 3:17); wisely (Eph. 5:15; Col. 4:5); 'properly as in the daytime' (Rom. 13:13); 'in the light' (1 John 1:7); 'in the truth' (2 John 4; 3 John 3, 4); 'according to his commandments' (2 John 6); and 'in the same way that [Jesus] walked' (1 John 2:6).

Notably absent, however, is the notion of 'walking before' or 'walking with'. The Thessalonians are told to 'walk properly before outsiders' (1 Thess. 4:12). But the only references to walking with/ before *God* are in Luke 1:6, where Zechariah and Elizabeth being 'righteous *before* God' is explained as their 'walking blamelessly', and in Revelation.

In Revelation *peripateō* is used once in the non-figurative sense (Rev. 9:20) and once in the figurative sense to describe a manner of life (Rev. 16:15). But more often 'walking' is used to refer to privileged access to God: the one who 'walks among the seven golden lampstands' (Rev. 2:1); or those who 'will walk *with* me in white, for they are worthy' (Rev. 3:4); and the nations 'walking' by the light of the glory of God in the renewed creation (Rev. 21:24).

Overwhelmingly then 'walking' in the NT is a moral activity. Although Revelation picks up on the OT theme of privilege, for the most part the meaning is bound up with walking in a particular manner. Just as in Genesis 17:1 Abraham is called to 'walk before me *and* be blameless', in the NT Christians are called to walk *in* ways that honour God.

Circumcision and walking blamelessly at Qumran

Before turning to a number of major circumcision passages in the NT, it is also fruitful to consider briefly some of the material from

Qumran.[20] Blamelessness and 'walking blamelessly' were significant categories there also; categories they picked up from the OT and developed. The use of that language at Qumran confirms some of the concepts we have uncovered in the OT, though it also presents some differences from the perspectives found in the OT and NT. Those differences will become more apparent when we study 'blamelessness' language in Philippians 3, in particular. However, before considering the language of 'blamelessness' and 'walking blamelessly' at Qumran it is useful to examine how circumcision itself is treated within the Qumran material.

Somewhat surprisingly, circumcision is mentioned relatively few times within the Qumran material. It seems to play a far less significant role than the language of blamelessness and walking blamelessly. Reference is made occasionally to physical circumcision or uncircumcision,[21] but more often the reference is metaphorical. It can refer to circumcision/uncircumcision of the heart,[22] lips[23] or ears,[24] or it can be associated with uncleanness, as we saw in Isaiah 52.[25] A number of instances will demonstrate the way that circumcision was understood.

In CD 16.6 Abraham's circumcision of himself is understood in connection with a commitment to do the law of Moses: 'Therefore, one will impose upon himself to return to the law of Moses, for in it all is defined . . . This is why Abraham circumcised himself on the day of his knowledge' (CD 16.1–6).[26]

This aligns with the interpretation of circumcision of the heart in 1QS, where part of the requirement laid out for the person joining the community is that he should not

walk in the stubbornness of his heart in order to go astray following his heart and his eyes and the musings of his inclination.

---

[20] Noting Gathercole's caution (2002b: 188): 'it is extremely difficult to define with any precision what these terms – "blamelessness," "sinlessness," and "perfection" – actually meant . . . because the terms are never discussed at any length (let alone in any *systematic* way) in the texts themselves.' The aim here is merely to highlight a number of similarities and differences between the Qumran understanding of 'walking blamelessly' and the one I have argued for on the basis of the OT.

[21] CD 16.6; 4Q458 fr. 2 2.4.

[22] 1QS 5.5, 26; 1QpHab 11.13; 4Q434 fr. 1 1.4.

[23] 1QH^a 10.7, 18.

[24] 1QH^a 21[top].5.

[25] 1QH^a 14.20.

[26] Unless otherwise indicated all translations of the DSS are taken from García Martínez and Tigchelaar 1997–8.

Instead he should circumcise in the Community the foreskin of his tendency and of his stiff neck in order to lay a foundation of truth for Israel, for the Community of the eternal covenant. (1QS 5.4–5)

As in the OT, metaphorical circumcision is juxtaposed with a stubborn heart and stiff neck. Within the context it is clear that to 'circumcise the foreskin of one's tendency' means, 'to convert from all evil and to keep themselves steadfast in all he commanded in compliance with his will' (1QS 5.1).

Or put another way, 'He shall swear with a binding oath to revert to the Law of Moses, according to all that he commanded, with whole heart and whole soul . . .' (1QS 5.8–9).

Again to circumcise one's heart refers to the commitment to do the Mosaic law. Conversely, in an interpretation of Habakkuk 2:16, the judgment falls on 'the Priest' for his failure to circumcise his heart and instead he 'walked on paths of excessiveness' (1QpHab 11.13–14). Elsewhere, to listen to someone with uncircumcised lips is to follow a person who will lead them away from God (1QH^a 10.18).

The emphasis on doing the Mosaic law does not mean that the grace of God is absent. There is in places some sense of the grace of God. God gives the reply of the writer's uncircumcised lips (1QH^a 10.7). So too God is the one who has 'circumcised the foreskin of their hearts and has saved them because of his grace' (4Q434 fr. 1 1.4).

Having considered circumcision within the Qumran material, we now turn to the language of 'blamelessness' and 'walking blamelessly'. The term *tāmîm* and its cognates are common in the Qumran literature. The verb *tmm* is of little interest and is almost always used with the meaning 'to bring to an end'.[27] Yet *tāmîm* and *tōm* continue, and even extend, the moral meaning that seems to have arisen out of the sacrificial system. Within the Qumran material as a whole *tāmîm* occasionally is used to refer to a period of time (e.g. a 'full year')[28] and to 'whole sacrifices',[29] but for the most part the meaning is distinctly moral and refers to 'perfect holiness' (*tmym qwdš*)[30] or a

---

[27] The exceptions are (at least) 1QS 8.25; 10.21; 11.17; 1QH^a 12.32.
[28] E.g. CD 15.15; 1QS 6.17; 11Q19 18.11; 19.12; 21.13.
[29] E.g. 11Q19 13.11; 17.14.
[30] E.g. CD 7.5; 20.2, 5, 7; 1QS 8.20.

'perfect path' (*tmymy hdrk*),[31] and often 'walking perfectly' (*hwlkym tmym*),[32] while *tōm* is used exclusively in the moral sense.[33]

The frequency with which *tāmîm* is used in 1QS indicates that the notion was quite fundamental to the community. Their use of the expression 'walking blamelessly'[34] suggests that they understood *tāmîm* in terms of Genesis 17:1 and as being intimately connected with God's covenant with Abraham. It also suggests that they saw themselves as being the proper inheritors of those promises.

The strictness with which *tāmîm* was understood is conveyed by the following:

> These are the regulations by which the men of perfect holiness shall conduct themselves, one with another. All who enter the council of holiness of those walking in perfect behaviour as he commanded, anyone of them who breaks a word of the law of Moses impertinently or through carelessness will be banished from the Community council and shall not return again; none of the men of holiness should associate with his goods or his advice on any matter. (1QS 8.20–24)

'Walking blamelessly' has to do with the law of Moses. Even breaking 'one commandment' is an offence. Where that is done deliberately, there is no possibility of restoration. In the case of carelessness or oversight he must undergo a two-year probation period after which he may be restored (1QS 8.24 – 9.2). The absolute nature of the perfection required by the community is also suggested by its pessimism regarding humanity's ability to walk perfectly. So:

> What is flesh compared to this? What creature of clay can do wonders? He is in iniquity from his maternal womb, and in guilt of unfaithfulness right to old age. But I know that justice does not belong to man nor to a son of Adam a perfect path. To God Most High belong all the acts of justice, and the path of man is not secure except by the spirit which God creates for him to perfect the path of the sons of Adam so that all his creatures come to know the

---

[31] E.g. 1QS 4.22; 8.10, 18, 21; 9.2, 5, 9; 1Q28a 1.28; 1QH^a 9.36; 11Q5 27.3. Similarly, 1QS 2.2, 3.9–10.

[32] E.g. CD 2.15; 1QS 1.8; 2.2; 3.9; 8.18, 21; 9.6, 8, 9, 19; 1Q28b 1.2; 5.22.

[33] The expression is always 'perfect paths' (1Q28a 1.17; 1QH^a 12.29; 1QS 1.13; 5.24; 11.2, 11).

[34] Even the expression 'blameless paths' connotes 'walking blamelessly'.

strength of his power and the abundance of his compassion with all the sons of his approval. (1QH[a] 12.29–33)

Only by God's power can there be 'perfection of way'. And where there is not, God's mercy atones for iniquity (1QH[a] 12.33–37).

The sacrificial background to the language of 'perfection' is evident in 1QS 9.3–5:

When these exist in Israel in accordance with these rules in order to establish the spirit of holiness in truth eternal, in order to atone for the guilt of iniquity and for the unfaithfulness of sin, and for approval for the earth, without the flesh of burnt offerings and without the fats of sacrifice – the offering of the lips in compliance with the decree will be like the pleasant aroma of justice and the perfectness of behaviour will be acceptable like a freewill offering . . .

Blameless behaviour is understood to be the import of the unblemished sacrificial animal. Additionally, the blameless behaviour of one small group atones for the rebellion and sin of another. Seifrid notes:

This transposition of the atoning function of the Temple sacrifices into the obedient life of the community results in an unmistakable attribution of salvific value to human behavior. The proper observance of *Torah* maintained by the community was thought to atone for sins . . .[35]

The key distinction is their understanding of the 'seed of Abraham'. It is not the holy seed (singular) who will be blameless and suffer but these outstanding men.[36] The same is demonstrated in 1QS 8.1–10, where a smaller group of twelve men and three priests provide atonement for the land by the blameless sacrifice of their obedience.

The point is that the understanding of OT blamelessness language I have proposed is not entirely without precedent. The Qumran community too saw 'blamelessness' language as highly significant.

---

[35] Seifrid 1992: 94.

[36] According to Wright (1996: 581), 'though it is very unlikely that anyone at Qumran thought in terms of a suffering Messiah, it is clear that there was a wider belief that the sufferings of the sect in general, and of one of its founders in particular, were pointers towards the coming liberation, and perhaps part of the means of its arrival.'

They saw it as being grounded in the command to 'walk blamelessly' in Genesis 17:1, and they understood it through the lens of the sacrificial system. The major difference is the means by which 'blamelessness' would finally come. They viewed it as being through the community itself and their diligence in keeping the commandments.

Finally, as in the OT, the language of blamelessness is often linked with that of righteousness (e.g. 1QS 3.3; 8.1–2; 9.5). Seifrid observes:

> It is crucial for modern commentators to bear in mind that the righteousness in which the member of the Qumran community participated was conceived of in behavioral, not merely forensic terms. 'Righteousness' is regularly coupled with 'perfection of way' and 'holiness' in 1QS as a description of the ideals of conduct for the members of the community.[37]

So although there are some significant differences in the way that the Qumran material treats circumcision and walking blamelessly and the way the OT and NT treat them (e.g. the emphasis on the Mosaic law in the place of faith and humility, and the anchoring of atonement in the behaviour of the community), there are also significant commonalities. Circumcision is tied with the goal of an obedient people, blamelessness is a stringent moral category but it is also linked with the sacrificial system, and righteousness is linked with blamelessness.

Philippians 3

In the remainder of this chapter we will consider three of the major circumcision passages in the NT. We begin with Philippians 3. Philippians 3 is a remarkable passage because it draws together nearly every strand of thought that we have uncovered so far. In it Paul contrasts those who continue the practice of circumcision with those who are the 'real circumcision' (*hē peritomē*) – those 'who worship by the Spirit of God and glory in Christ Jesus and put no confidence in the flesh'. He goes on to contrast his 'righteousness under the law' (*dikaiosynēn tēn en nomō*) with the 'righteousness from God that depends on faith' (*tēn ek theou dikaiosynēn epi tē pistei*). In regard to the first, Paul says that he was 'blameless' (*amemptos*). This is not the more common word *amōmos*, though as we have seen the two are intimately related. And indeed, Paul himself uses the two almost

---

[37] Seifrid 1992: 97.

interchangeably one chapter earlier when he says, 'that you might be blameless [*amemptos*] and pure, children of God without blemish [*amōmos*]' (2:15, my tr.). So once again, righteousness and blamelessness are linked. But of particular interest is that they are linked in the context of circumcision.

Confidence in the flesh

Paul, for his part, begins by arguing that 'the circumcision' – those who will share in the promises made to Abraham – are those who worship by the Spirit and boast in Christ Jesus. In contrast, those who trust in the flesh (*en sarki pepoithotes*) are not 'the circumcision' – they will not share in the promises made to Abraham. The things that characterize confidence in the flesh in Paul's case are being 'circumcised on the eighth day', 'from the people of Israel', 'of the tribe of Benjamin', 'a Hebrew of Hebrews', 'according to the law, a Pharisee', 'according to zeal, persecuting the church', 'according to righteousness in the law, being blameless' (*kata dikaiosynēn tēn en nomō genomenos amemptos*).[38]

The first characteristic of Paul's confidence in the flesh, 'circumcised on the eighth day', is the sign of the promise of God to Abraham. The next three are bound up with purity of genealogical descent from Abraham to Paul. The fifth, 'according to the law, a Pharisee', identifies Paul's genuine diligence to the prescriptions of the law. To take 'Pharisee' pejoratively – as 'legalistic' and inherently moribund – misses the point. Paul is using it to establish his former credentials among people who clearly would view being a Pharisee as highly commendable. His argument is moving along the lines that what they value he now considers rubbish.[39] Wright summarizes the basic world view of the Pharisee:

> The Pharisee was passionately concerned about the ancestral traditions, particularly the law of Moses and the development of that into oral law, and about the importance of keeping this double Torah not simply because it was required, or in order to earn the divine favour, but because a renewed keeping of the law with all one's heart and soul was one of the biblically stated conditions (as

[38] My translations.
[39] In that sense, reconstructions of first-century Judaism matter surprisingly little. Whether Paul was a 'legalist' or a 'covenantal nomist', either way he now considers all that rubbish.

in Deuteronomy 30) for the great renewal, the eschaton and all that it would mean.[40]

According to Wright, the hallmark of the Pharisaic world view was that diligent obedience to the law by Israel (not merely the individual)[41] could usher in the promises of Deuteronomy 30.

The sixth characteristic of Paul's confidence in the flesh, 'according to zeal, persecuting the church', follows on from Paul's Pharisaism. Paul's zeal for the law led him to persecuting the church for its flagrant disregard for the law. The reference to zeal has echoes of Phinehas, whose zeal for the law assuaged God's wrath against his people (Num. 25:6–13). Phinehas's zeal became the template for later zealots and was a hallmark of devotion to the law or God.[42] More significantly, Phinehas's display of zeal was credited to him as righteousness (Ps. 106:28–31), much as Abraham's faith was credited to him as righteousness. Likewise, *Jubilees* 30.17 draws on the language of Genesis 15:6 to present the zeal of Levi as his righteousness.[43] It would seem that Paul is also presenting his persecuting zeal as grounds for his righteousness.[44]

But Paul here sets up a conundrum. A core part of his previous 'confidence' led him to persecute the church. As Deidun cleverly observes:

> his former righteousness, seemingly at the very point of its perfection, made him a zealous persecutor of the Church. His mention of it here makes it difficult to understand Sanders' inferences from this passage, namely, that Paul considered his righteousness to be '*in and of itself a good thing*' . . . But it is surely not too much to suppose that Paul could never have considered to be intrinsically good the righteousness which drove him to do what he was most to regret . . .[45]

In other words, his former existence is mutually exclusive with his present one. How could it not be? If Paul was zealous for the law as

---

[40] Wright 2013: 195–196.

[41] Ibid. 193–194.

[42] E.g. Sir. 45.23; 1 Macc. 2.26, 54; 4 Macc. 18.12, also 1 Macc. 2.58; *T. Ash.* 4.5. See Hawthorne and Martin 2004: 186; Bockmuehl 1997: 198–201.

[43] Dunn 1988: 2:586–587.

[44] Nevertheless it is not simply zeal for *personal* holiness that Paul has in mind, but like Phinehas, zeal for the whole nation's allegiance to the Torah (Ortlund 2012: 154).

[45] Deidun 1986: 51 (emphasis his). See 1 Tim. 1:12–15.

Phinehas was, how could he not end up persecuting the church that for all intents and purposes appeared to disregard the law? Paul creates an enormous wedge between the law and Christ, since even the righteous actions of Phinehas replayed this side of the coming of the Christ would lead to the persecution of the church. The implication is that ongoing vigilance with respect to the law is incompatible with faith in Christ.

The last and perhaps most vexing example of 'confidence in the flesh' is, 'according to righteousness in the law, being blameless'. Shockingly, Paul says that the very thing to which God called Abraham – blamelessness – did not make Paul a member of the circumcision and he now considers his former blamelessness rubbish.

At first glance there seems little reason to doubt Paul's claim to blamelessness. Noah was described as such (Gen. 6:9). Abraham was called to it (Gen. 17:1). David was described and described himself as such (2 Sam. 22:24; 1 Kgs 9:4 [tōm]; Pss 7:8 [tōm]; 26:1 [tōm]). And in the NT the term is used to describe Zechariah and Elizabeth (Luke 1:6).[46] Despite that strong background, it has been common to view Paul's description of himself as bound up with a 'Pharisaic' interpretation of the law.[47] So Fee states:

> the key to 'faultless' lies with the cultic overtones of this word (cf. 2:15). Paul has no 'blemishes' on his record, as far as Torah observance is concerned, which means that he scrupulously adhered to the pharisaic [sic] interpretation of the Law, with its finely honed regulations for sabbath observance, food laws, and ritual cleanliness. His former blamelessness in these matters makes his Christian pronouncements on these items all the more telling.[48]

Fee rightly notes the cultic background but ties it with a 'pharisaic interpretation of the Law'. But the OT background of blamelessness raises the possibility that Paul's claim is entirely reasonable: that Paul was genuinely 'blameless' under the terms of the law itself, not merely through a 'Pharisaic' interpretation of it. Not because he was sinless, but rather because the law provided forgiveness for those who sinned through the sacrifices that were offered in faith. We cannot accept

---

[46] E.g. Wright 2013: 1034; Dunn 2008: 479.
[47] O'Brien 1991: 380; Schreiner 1985: 260–262.
[48] Fee 1995: 309.

the OT reality of blamelessness and yet reject Paul's claim out of hand.

Indeed, more recently it has been suggested that Paul's claim was legitimate; not least by Sanders. Sanders argued that Paul's righteousness under the law *was* valid but *became* invalid with the coming of Christ.[49] Similarly, Wright contends that Paul was not 'claiming here a lifetime of sinless perfection, but rather a status kept "without blame" by the usual method of repentance and sacrifice'.[50]

But if Paul's pre-Christian blamelessness was legitimate, we are left wondering what it is that he now considers rubbish. More interestingly perhaps, what is the difference between the blamelessness Paul urges his Philippian readers to pursue (2:15) and his own former blamelessness, which he now considers rubbish? And why is it that Paul has chosen to describe his moribund religion in terms steeped in the Abrahamic covenant?

Two basic options for understanding Paul's former blamelessness present themselves. First, Paul's pre-Christian blamelessness was of itself moribund because it was a distortion ('legalistic' or otherwise) of what God had revealed. Or second, because of the coming of Christ Paul's pre-Christian blamelessness, which had been adequate, is now inadequate since the reality is found in Jesus.

It will become clear that there are elements of truth in both. That is, the coming of the resurrected Christ has demonstrated definitively that blamelessness is through him. There is no blamelessness apart from him (nor was there ever). That leaves the 'works of the law' as unnecessary and redundant. But the coming of the resurrected Messiah/seed also shows Paul's pre-Christian blamelessness for what it was: a blamelessness from the flesh, apart from God and apart from the hope of the Christ.

Despite all his previous 'advantages', Paul says they are rubbish and do not make one part of the circumcision. But if these things do not make one part of 'the circumcision', what does? Paul's answer is simple: knowing Christ. Knowing Christ surpasses all his former attainments. In order to understand what was wrong with Paul's former blamelessness it is essential to understand why knowing Christ surpasses it and why knowing Christ alone makes one a member of 'the circumcision'.

---

[49] Sanders 1985: 43–45, 139–141.
[50] Wright 2013: 989; similarly, Thielman 1994: 155.

Knowing Christ

While Paul previously put his confidence in the flesh, now he considers that a loss 'for the sake of Christ' (*dia ton Christon*). Three times Paul reaffirms that all his previous possessions are a loss to him, and four times in the long statement that stretches from verse 7 to 11 he affirms his desire to know Christ:

But whatever gain I had, I counted [*hēgēmai*] as loss [*zēmian*]

for the sake of **Christ**.

Indeed, I count [*hēgoumai*] everything as loss [*zēmian*]

because of **the surpassing worth of knowing Christ Jesus my Lord**.

For his sake I have suffered the loss [*ezēmiōthēn*] of all things and count [*hēgoumai*] them as rubbish,

in order that [*hina*] I may **gain Christ** and be **found in him**,

not having a righteousness of my own that comes from the law, but that which comes through faith in Christ, the righteousness from God that depends on faith [*epi tē pistei*] –

that I may **know him** [*tou gnōnai auton*] and **the power of his resurrection**, and may **share his sufferings**,

becoming like him in his death, that by any means possible I may attain the resurrection from the dead.

The structure of these verses is contested. The most difficult issue is the relationship of the genitive articular infinitive *tou gnōnai auton* (that I may know him) that begins verse 10 with what precedes. There are four primary possibilities:[51] (1) it is connected with *epi tē pistei* ('depends on faith'; v. 9);[52] (2) it expresses the ultimate purpose of

[51] O'Brien (1991: 400–401) and Hansen (2009: 242, n. 129) list three, omitting the first. Reumann (2008: 498) lists five, adding the possibility that the clause refers back to *hēgoumai skybala* (consider rubbish) at the end of v. 8. But apart from the first option, all the options are further explicating why Paul considers all his former attainments rubbish.

[52] Some see *tou gnōnai auton* further explaining the nature of faith (e.g. Wright 2013: 988; Collange 1979: 131). But not only does that view suppose that Paul here uses the genitive articular infinitive in a way in which he uses it nowhere else (Hawthorne and

verses 8–9, while the *hina* clause expresses the penultimate purpose;[53] (3) it parallels the preceding *hina* clause such that verses 9 and 10 provide two distinct motivations for embracing Christ and considering his former advantages as rubbish; or (4) it is epexegetical and further explains the meaning of the *hina* clause.[54] Of these, the last is the most likely.

The uncertainty is created by the fact that there are three parallel statements predicated on the same two words, *hēgoumai* and *zēmia/ zēmioō*, while there are four purpose clauses:

1. 'for Christ' (*dia ton Christon*; v. 7, my tr.)
2. 'because of the surpassing worth . . .' (*einai dia to hyperechon*; v. 8)
3. 'in order that I may gain Christ . . .' (*hina Christon kerdēsō*; vv. 8–9)
4. 'that I may know him . . .' (*tou gnōnai auton*; v. 10)

Notably all four are introduced differently, which suggests that the distinction between them may be stylistic.[55] Even though there are only three parallel statements in which Paul says he considers all things loss, the obvious parallelism between the four purpose statements suggests that they should all be understood in the same way. In addition, the similar structures of the third and fourth purpose clauses, with both being further explained by participial phrases, suggests that the two should be taken as in parallel rather than the latter conveying a sense of ultimate purpose (as in view 2).

The most significant point, however, is that the themes of Paul's purpose statements are all intimately related. Paul uses seven ways of describing his pursuit of Christ for which he considers everything rubbish:

1. 'for Christ' (v. 7, my tr.)
2. 'because of the surpassing worth of knowing Christ Jesus my Lord' (v. 8)

Martin 2004: 196), it also puts the emphasis on faith rather than 'knowing Christ', whereas the latter seems to be more significant for Paul in this section.

[53] Fee 1995: 327.

[54] Melick 2001: 135.

[55] Analysis of v. 10 (*tou gnōnai auton* . . .) is often limited to a comparison with the *hina Christon* clause, leading to questions about why Paul has not used a double *hina*. Those questions evaporate once it is observed that there are four purpose clauses, not merely two.

3. 'in order that I may gain Christ' (v. 8)
4. 'in order that I may . . . be found in him' (vv. 8–9)
5. 'that I may know him' (v. 10)
6. 'that I may know . . . the power of his resurrection' (v. 10)
7. 'that I may know . . . the fellowship of his sufferings' (v. 10, my tr.)

The first, 'for Christ' (*dia ton Christon*, my tr.), is the most ambiguous: does Paul mean to please Christ or to gain him? What he means is explained in verse 8: Paul considers everything rubbish 'because of the surpassing worth of knowing Christ Jesus my Lord'. But again, exactly what that means is ambiguous. Paul goes on to show that the knowledge is not merely academic but existential.

In verse 10 Paul explains what he means by knowing Christ. 'Knowing Christ' (v. 10) clearly picks up on the theme of verse 8 ('knowledge of Christ'). Strictly speaking, the verb *gnōnai* (to know) governs three objects: 'him', 'the power of his resurrection' and 'the fellowship of his sufferings'.[56] The *kai* following *tou gnōnai auton* is most likely epexegetical.[57] That is confirmed by the fact that the two experiences that Paul lists next are each modified by the possessive *autou* and represent a sharing in an experience (resurrection, suffering) or quality (power), suggesting that this is what Paul has in mind by 'knowing him'. In addition, the double expression 'the power of his resurrection and the fellowship of his sufferings' (*tēn dynamin tēs anastaseōs autou kai [tēn] koinōnian [tōn] pathēmatōn autou*) is most likely governed by one article.[58] The implication is that these experiences are the two sides of the one coin, which is 'knowing Christ'.[59]

Sandwiched in the middle of all these expressions is Paul's desire to 'gain Christ' and 'be found in him'. While the language is different, both these expressions contain the same desire for an existential experience of Christ. In particular, they look ahead to the end time when Paul will be raised (v. 10) and conformed to the likeness of Jesus (v. 21).[60]

---

[56] Silva 2005: 163; cf. Fee 1995: 328.
[57] O'Brien 1991: 402; Hawthorne and Martin 2004: 197; Silva 2005: 163; Fee 1995: 328.
[58] The earliest manuscripts omit the article *tēn* (e.g. P46 ℵ* A B).
[59] O'Brien 1991: 402–403; Bockmuehl 1997: 214; Hawthorne and Martin 2004: 197.
[60] The perspective is not entirely future, since the resurrection power of Christ has broken into Paul's present existence. These themes are taken up in the next section.

While each of these components may not be exactly identical, and though some may be subsets of the larger whole, it still seems clear that Paul is attempting to explain one reality, not several, and not stages or conditions that build upon one another, as though to 'know him and the power of his resurrection' is the ultimate attainment somewhere beyond 'gaining Christ'.

Significantly, in none of what we have examined so far has Paul explained *why* knowing Christ is better than his past experiences. The reason why Paul prefers to know Christ rather than his previous experiences is explained by the two participial clauses. It is relatively clear that both the participial clauses 'not having . . .' (*mē echōn*) and 'becoming like him . . .' (*symmorphizomenos*) ought to be construed differently from the purpose clauses. Not least because as participial clauses they are grammatically distinct from all four of the purpose clauses. But additionally, their objects are also markedly different. There is a subtle shift away from knowing Christ to the *benefits* of knowing Christ. In verse 9 the ultimate object is 'the righteousness from God', and in verse 11 the ultimate object is resurrection from the dead. Moreover, both these expressions are essentially the only expressions in the long statement stretching from verse 8 to 11 that do not contain a direct reference to Christ.

The first participial clause is sometimes taken as causal, expressing the means by which Paul may know Christ. O'Brien opts for modal,[61] but result seems to be the best option. That is, the reason Paul desires to know Christ is so that he may not possess merely his own righteousness but the righteousness from God. The strong parallelism with the second participial clause supports this.

The second participial clause appears to express purpose.[62] The phrase 'if somehow I may gain' (*ei pōs katantēsō*) excludes the possibility that the clause is to be taken as causal or modal since the event

---

[61] O'Brien 1991: 393.

[62] The relationship of the participial clause to what precedes is disputed. Fee (1995: 329) sees a chiastic relationship:

    A the power of his resurrection
      B and fellowship in his sufferings
      B' being conformed to his death
    A' if somehow I might attain to the resurrection from the dead.

O'Brien highlights four objections to this structure. The most significant of which is that it drives a wedge between A and B which are closely joined syntactically, as noted above. Moreover, as Fee concedes, grammatically the participle is dependent on the infinitive (ibid. 333). These two facts suggest that the participle qualifies all of what precedes it in v. 10 (O'Brien 1991: 407; Koperski 1996: 269–272).

envisaged is in the future. That is, Paul desires to know Christ so that, being conformed to his death, he may somehow attain to the resurrection from the dead.

Without these participial phrases Paul's argument for why he has rejected his past attainments and thrown his lot in with Christ would amount to little more than 'Knowing Jesus is better because it just is.' Which, it must be granted, would be a wholly unconvincing argument for Paul's Philippian readers against circumcision and for Christ. It makes much more sense to understand that Paul is explaining or proving *why* knowing Christ is better. It is better because Paul receives a righteousness from God, and it is better because he is being continually conformed to Christ's death that by some means he may attain the resurrection from the dead. It will be helpful to consider in turn those two benefits of resurrection and righteousness.

Resurrection

Paul's desire in verse 10 is that he may know Christ intimately and experientially. The reason is so that 'being conformed to his death, I may somehow attain to the resurrection from the dead' (my tr.). The structure of verses 10–11 suggests that the ultimate goal is the resurrection. Sharing in Christ's sufferings and being conformed to his death are not endless experiences but present realities on the way to the final resurrection when Christ 'will transform our lowly body to be like his glorious body' (3:21).

Notably, that same goal can be described by the term 'perfection' (*teleioō*). In 3:12 Paul continues by saying, 'Not that I have already obtained this or am already perfect' (*ouch hoti ēdē elabon ē ēdē teteleiōmai*).[63] The object missing from the transitive verb *elabon* has prompted a number of suggestions as to Paul's meaning. He may be referring to:[64] (1) the 'prize' (v. 14);[65] (2) resurrection (v. 11);[66] (3) the

---

[63] A textual variant suggests that the goal can also be described as righteousness: *elabon ē ēdē dedikaiōmai ē ēdē teteleiōmai* ('obtained it or am already righteous or already perfect', my tr.). Nevertheless, the strong external evidence supports omitting *dedikaiōmai* (Silva 2005: 187; O'Brien 1991: 417–418; Metzger 1994: 547–548; cf. Reumann 2008: 534–535).

[64] This list is taken principally from O'Brien (1991: 421). Reumann (2008: 533–534) lists nine possibilities. He distinguishes between 'Christ' and 'knowing Christ'. He also includes (1) martyrdom; and (2) (moral or spiritual) perfection. It seems strange, however, to take perfection as the object of *elabon* and so have Paul saying, 'I have not received perfection nor have I been made perfect.'

[65] Collange 1979: 133.

[66] Melick 2001: 137–138.

righteousness that comes from God (v. 9);[67] (4) everything in verses 8–11;[68] (5) a general sense of incompleteness in contrast to those who thought they had already 'made it';[69] or (6) gaining Christ.[70]

The most obvious candidate is what Paul has only just mentioned: resurrection. But we have seen that resurrection (view 2) is the outcome of gaining Christ (view 6). Moreover, it makes sense to understand that the 'prize' (view 1) for which Paul presses forward is the eschatological goal of both resurrection (view 2) and gaining Christ (view 6). At the resurrection, when Paul's body is transformed to be like Jesus' glorious body, he will have gained Christ fully.[71] Furthermore, as we will see below, righteousness (view 3) is intimately connected with the resurrection. In a sense then, Paul's emphasis lands on resurrection but also incorporates the other elements of what has gone before.

This is supported by the fact that the expression 'not that I have already obtained this' is parallel with 'made perfect' (*teleioō*)[72] – a term we have already considered in the NT and OT more broadly. On the basis of our study of that term outside Philippians, one would expect Paul is saying something to the effect that while Christ has taken hold of him to make him blameless, he is not yet completely blameless and perfect. And indeed, that understanding is confirmed by the broader theology of Philippians.

Even if we ignore the background to the term *teleioō*, within the framework of biblical eschatology the chief goal of 'completion' is the eradication of sin from humanity and the world (e.g. Rev. 21:27). That eschatological goal is on display throughout Philippians. Throughout the letter Paul often looks ahead to the 'day of Christ' and to the perfection of believers at that time. So in 1:6, Paul again uses the language of completion/perfection: 'And I am sure of this, that he who began a good work in you will bring it to completion [*epiteleō*] at the day of Jesus Christ.'

The nature of that completed work is captured a few verses later in 1:10–11: 'so that you may approve what is excellent, and so be pure [*eilikrinēs*] and blameless [*aproskopos*] for the day of Christ, filled with the fruit of righteousness that comes through Jesus Christ'.

---

[67] Klijn 1965: 281.

[68] Bockmuehl 1997: 220.

[69] Schmithals 1972: 97; Collange 1979: 133.

[70] O'Brien 1991: 421–422.

[71] Fee 1995: 343.

[72] Fee (ibid. 344–345) observes, 'this verb seems intended to further clarify the first one'.

While *eilikrinēs* and *aproskopos* are words we have not met before, the meaning is similar to that of *teleios*. The first refers to something 'unmixed, without alloy'.[73] Büchsel suggests that the term literally means 'tested by the light of the sun' and hence 'completely pure' and 'spotless'.[74] Such a meaning would fit the context, where on 'the day of Christ' believers are presented to God absolutely spotless. *Aproskopos* is a metaphor derived from the idea of not stumbling or tripping. And is usually taken to mean without stumbling/offence, or without causing-to-stumble/giving-offence.[75]

What Paul has in mind is growing towards perfection – that the Philippians would abound more and more in knowledge, discernment and love so that they would be spotless on the last day. It is their perfection that will enable them to stand on the day of Christ. The same idea is present in 2:15–16:

> that you may be blameless and innocent, children of God without blemish in the midst of a crooked and twisted generation, among whom you shine as lights in the world, holding fast to the word of life, so that in the day of Christ I may be proud that I did not run in vain or labour in vain.

Paul's hope is that the good work begun now will be shown to be what it is by its perfection on the last day.

The pinnacle of these ideas is reached in 3:20–21:

> But our citizenship is in heaven, and from it we await a Saviour, the Lord Jesus Christ, who will transform our lowly body to be like his glorious body, by the power that enables him even to subject all things to himself.

The resurrection body in which Paul and the other believers will share is not simply a body that is not subject to physical decay, but one that is not subject to moral distortion. It is perfect and spotless. To see 'blameless' and 'pure' and 'without blemish' as merely 'sincere' is to miss the point profoundly. Likewise, it would be a mistake to think that Paul is simply speaking about a kind of abstract moral perfection. Paul's hope is for them to share in the complete transformation of

---

[73] *LSJ* 486.
[74] Büchsel 1965: 397.
[75] *LSJ* 230; Stählin 1968: 747–748.

believers into the likeness of Christ by sharing in his resurrection from the dead – which is to gain Christ and to know him.[76] To be perfect is to be like Christ.[77]

That which Paul has not received (*elabon*; 3:12) then is most likely 'resurrection' (3:11). Both on the grounds that it is the thing Paul has only just mentioned, and also because it is the pinnacle of Paul's idea. Yet Silva is right when he asserts that though the object of *elabon* in 3:12 is most likely resurrection, the theological implications mean that it includes much more: 'the ultimate spiritual redemption of our bodies'.[78]

With that in mind, we can begin to grasp more clearly what was inadequate about Paul's former life and his 'confidence in the flesh' that did not make him a member of the circumcision proper. Against the backdrop of ultimate perfection, spotlessness and blamelessness that can endure the penetrating gaze of God, a perfection that comes through sharing the death and resurrection of the Messiah, Paul's previous attainments begin to look distinctly shabby. While Paul may have had a *kind* of blamelessness according to the law, it is not one that would culminate in resurrection or perfection. The 'flesh' does not lead to resurrection. How can it?[79] In contrast to the powerful resurrection of the Christ, circumcision and ethnicity and the law are of the flesh, and at best physical mutilations. They cannot raise the dead. Klijn observes:

> It is clear that the Jews offered a way to perfection. This was extremely important, because this perfection could be gained on earth. Paul also preached a way to perfection, but that perfection should come sometime in the future, at Christ's coming . . . What Paul is trying to say is that the perfection offered by the Jews is senseless. It really gives perfection, but an earthly perfection . . . [E]arthly perfection comes to an end with the earth. It does not

[76] Silva's comments (2005: 174–175) are apropos: 'That the person of Christ himself stands in the background of Paul's comments [in 12a] is confirmed by verse 12b, where the inverse relationship involves Christ's seizing of Paul.'

[77] D. K. Williams (2002: 203) links the three references to 'perfection' in ch. 3 together to make the same point: 'The verb τελειόω, the adjective τέλειος (v. 15), and the noun τέλος (v. 19) refer back to vv. 10–11 in terms of the full realization of life in Christ's resurrection and the full eschatological realities of life in Christ, which is parallel to vv. 20–21.'

[78] Silva 2005: 175.

[79] Reumann (2008: 477) rightly observes, '*sarx* denotes the whole person, human life destined for demise and destruction before God, not something on which real life and future hopes can be built'.

offer the total renewal of man. For this reason one has to give up his efforts. The only way to receive a total restoration is given in the community with Christ's death and resurrection.[80]

Righteousness

We now turn to the other benefit of knowing Christ: righteousness. In verse 9 Paul states that the benefit of knowing Christ and being found in him is 'not having my own righteousness from the law, but the one through faith in Christ, the one from God which is on the basis of faith' (my tr.). Paul draws a contrast between his pre-Christian righteousness and his Christian righteousness. The chiastic structure highlights the comparisons:[81]

mē echōn	not having
emēn	my own
dikaiosynēn	righteousness
tēn ek nomou	from the law
alla tēn dia pisteōs Christou	but through faith in Christ
tēn ek theou	from God
dikaiosynēn	righteousness
epi tē pistei	on the basis of faith (my tr.)

His new righteousness is 'on the basis of faith' rather than 'my own'; and it is 'from God' rather than 'from the law'. The reason is because this new righteousness is *dia pisteōs Christou*. The meaning of that phrase is contested, but there are good reasons, here at least, for understanding it to mean 'faith in Christ', rather than 'the faithfulness of Christ'.

The evidence for either reading is sharply contested. While Bockmuehl confidently asserts, 'there is no case where *pistis Christou* (or equivalent phrases) unambiguously means faith "in" Jesus Christ',[82] others are less certain. Silva avers that 'Paul never speaks unambiguously of Jesus as faithful (e.g. *Iēsous pistos estin*) or believing (*episteusen Iēsous*), while he certainly speaks of individuals as believing in Christ.'[83] In favour of the subjective genitive ('faithfulness of Christ') is the fact

---

[80] Klijn 1965: 284.

[81] O'Brien 1991: 394; Schenk 1984: 310. Koperski (1996: 222–224, n. 140) rejects the chiasm and contends that 'the real contrast is indicated by the opposition of μή and ἀλλά'. But the pairings in the passage strongly support the identification of a chiastic structure with a definite centre.

[82] Bockmuehl 1997: 211.

[83] Silva 2005: 161. Though see 2 Tim. 2:13.

that on every occasion where *pistis* is used with a genitive of a person (who is not Christ) it refers to the faith or faithfulness *of* that person, rather than to faith *in* that person.[84] Yet as Westerholm cleverly points out, such is to be expected, since once 'Jesus', 'Christ', 'Jesus Christ' and 'Son of God' are removed, what other object of faith could there be except God?[85] The Hellenistic Jewish usage would also seem to support understanding *pistis* as 'faithfulness' rather than 'faith'.[86] Yet Matlock, reviewing studies of the evidence among patristic writers, argues convincingly that there is no evidence among these writers of a subjective reading of *pistis Christou*, nor any discussion of it, suggesting that despite the typical Hellenistic use of *pistis* the objective reading was merely taken for granted.[87]

In terms of the passage itself, Paul's emphasis on his own faith is introduced in the final phrase *epi tē pistei*, suggesting that *dia pisteōs Christou* may perhaps have another meaning.[88] While redundancy alone is not sufficient evidence of a distinction,[89] the chiastic structure also suggests a distinction in meaning of some kind between the central phrase and the last phrase.

The OT background of circumcision could support either the subjective or objective reading. That is, circumcision signified God's promise of a blameless (faithful?) 'seed' of Abraham/David through whom the promised righteousness would come, which supports the reading 'faithfulness of Christ'. Yet that promise had to be appropriated by faith, which supports the reading 'faith in Christ'.

In many ways the *theological* difference between the two is almost inconsequential.[90] However, several points can be made in favour of the objective reading. First, it would be a confusion of categories for Paul to use the language of 'faithfulness' to refer to the blameless/righteous seed. In terms of the background we have uncovered it would make 'faithfulness' here equivalent to righteousness. This in turn would introduce an even more tortuous redundancy, with righteousness effectively occurring three times in the one verse.

Second, Paul's emphasis here is not on the obedience of Christ but on participation with him, and not participation in his obedience

---

84 O'Brien 1991: 398; Bockmuehl 1997: 211.
85 Westerholm 2004: 305, n. 18.
86 E.g. Howard 1974: 213–214.
87 Matlock 2009: 86–88.
88 Bockmuehl 1997: 211–212.
89 See Hawthorne and Martin 2004: 195; Silva 2005: 161; Fee 1995: 325, n. 44.
90 See Westerholm 2004: 305, n. 18.

but in his sufferings and resurrection. Of course, Christ's obedience is related to his death and resurrection (not least in 2:8), but the point is that obedience is not in the foreground in 3:9. Moreover, Paul shows in 1:29 that he is able to distinguish between faith and suffering.[91] Instead, Paul's focus is on 'gaining Christ', 'knowing Christ' and 'being found in him', which seems more appropriately taken up under the rubric of 'faith *in* Christ'. After all, Paul must answer the question 'How can one gain, know and be found in Christ?' It is through this faith-appropriation of Christ himself that Paul shares in the benefits of Christ and so in the righteousness from God rather than from the law.[92] That crucial answer finds its proper place at the apex of Paul's chiasm.

But what should we make then of the apparent redundancy of *pistis*? Koperski is helpful here. Comparing the faith of Abraham to Christian faith she writes:

> The only difference is that Abraham, according to Paul, was justified by believing (= trusting) that God would fulfil the divine promise in the future, while the one who believes in Christ trusts that God has already acted in the resurrection of Jesus Christ. So Christian faith is belief in God, but precisely belief that God has been faithful in and through the resurrection of Jesus from the dead . . . the exaltation of Jesus as Lord and the righteousness available to humanity depend not only on the action of God but also on the action of Jesus Christ . . . This may well be the reason for the 'redundancy' of the *pistis Christou* expressions. When Paul speaks of justification on the basis of faith, perhaps he wants to make it quite clear that, though Abraham may be a model of faith and essentially the faith that justifies is a trust in the faithfulness of God such as Abraham had, it is faith that God has acted in the resurrection of Jesus Christ and with the cooperation of Jesus Christ so decisively that henceforth faith in God cannot be expressed except as a faith in Christ which amounts to the confession *Jesus is Lord*.[93]

That is, the centre of the chiasm demonstrates categorically that it is not generic faith in God that is crucial but faith in the long-awaited

---

[91] Koperski 1993: 205.

[92] Schreiner (1998: 183) also points to the similarly structured phrase *tēs gnōseōs Christou Iēsou* (3:8) as evidence for the objective reading.

[93] Koperski 1993: 211–213.

crucified and risen Christ. Thus there is not so much a distinction in meaning between *dia pisteōs Christou* and *epi tē pistei*, rather the former clarifies the latter – it is not merely faith in God in the abstract, but faith in the crucified and risen Christ that matters.

In verse 10 then Paul qualifies the righteousness he now has as to (1) its origin ('from God'); (2) the means by which it is received ('on the basis of faith'); and (3) the object of that faith by which it is received ('through faith in Christ').[94] But in the passage as a whole Paul also contrasts the *nature* of the righteousness available under the law versus that through Christ. Paul's former righteousness was not merely 'in/from the law' (*en nomō/ek nomou*) but also 'in the flesh' (*en sarki*), since that was the initial basis of the contrast begun in verse 3. As we will see, the law and the flesh were both saddled with the same problem: they did not lead to resurrection.

The parallelism between verse 9 and verses 10–11 advocated above also helps us to understand what the problem was with Paul's former righteousness. If it is correct that Paul's desire to 'gain Christ and be found in him' is synonymous with his desire to 'know' Christ and 'the power of his resurrection' (or if they are at the very least two sides of the same coin), then it also makes sense to view the participial phrases as synonymous (or as two ways of describing the same reality). Thus, diagrammatically, see Figure 1.

in order that I may gain Christ and be found in him	⇒	not having a righteousness of my own that comes from the law, but that which comes through faith in Christ, the righteousness from God that depends on faith
‖		‖
that I may know him and the power of his resurrection, and may share his sufferings	⇒	becoming like him in his death, that by any means possible I may attain the resurrection from the dead.

Figure 1

If this equation of the two participial clauses is correct, then the distinction between Paul's former righteousness and his righteousness from God by faith in Christ is that the latter shares in Christ's death and culminates in resurrection. Or conversely, that Paul's own

---

[94] This is a modification of O'Brien 1991: 396. The modification is necessary because O'Brien takes *pisteōs Christou* as a subjective genitive.

in-the-flesh-righteousness and in-the-law-righteousness did not culminate in resurrection. Fee observes:

> Obedience under that covenant could issue in blameless Torah observance, but it lacked the necessary power – the gift of the eschatological Spirit (v. 3) who alone brings life (2 Cor 3:6) – to enable God's people truly to know him and thus bear his likeness (being 'conformed to Christ's death,' that is, living a cruciform existence – which is true 'righteousness' in the 'right living' sense).[95]

This is supported by the fact that the righteousness Paul gains from God by faith flows out of 'gaining Christ' and 'being found in him'. This experiential language matches closely the language Paul uses to describe sharing in Christ's resurrection (3:10–11), being made perfect (3:12) and being transformed into his likeness (3:21). In short, for Paul in Philippians 3, righteousness is not primarily the imputation of Christ's obedience to Paul's account;[96] it is the consequence of participation in God's promise to Abraham through faith in the Messiah: participation in a partly inaugurated promise through sharing in the death and resurrection of the Messiah. A promise that confers both a present status but also ends in Paul's being transformed into Jesus' likeness.[97] This is not to say that righteousness is a declaration of being 'in the covenant';[98] it is the very heart of what the covenant promises and achieves.

We are the circumcision

Thus Paul highlights two problems with his former 'righteousness from the law'. First, it sprang from a confidence in the law as a source of righteousness rather than trust in the promised Messiah as the source of righteousness. And second, it did not lead to resurrection and perfection. Notably the second only is a problem endemic to the law and bound up with the new era of salvation history inaugurated

---

[95] Fee 1995: 326–327.

[96] E.g. Silva 2005: 160; Bockmuehl 1997: 210.

[97] Ziesler (2004: 150) astutely observes, 'although the forensic or acceptability aspect is present in the passage, and although the man who has righteousness from God is by this acceptable to God, the context shows a need for more than this. It suggests the new being in Christ, dying and rising with him, knowing the *power* of his resurrection. One wonders why all this is needed if the basic point is simply the imputation of righteousness' (emphasis his).

[98] E.g. Wright 2013: 989–990.

by Christ.[99] The fact that the law could not bring resurrection meant that it was at best only temporary and that something better was needed. This, indeed, was one of the distinct failings of the Pharisees' world view – they mistakenly believed that their obedience to the law (either individually or corporately) could bring the renewal of Deuteronomy 30 to pass.

These problems with Paul's righteousness arose due to a *misappropriation* of the law and circumcision. Paul says that 'the circumcision', properly conceived, are not those who are physically circumcised, descended from Abraham and having a fervent zeal for the law, but those who appropriate by faith in Christ the righteousness from God. Circumcision, properly received, pointed away from the individual Israelite and from Israelite heritage to the blameless Messiah/seed who was to come, while the law properly received pointed to the Messiah as the blameless substitute for sins.[100]

What Paul is countering is an emaciated view of the law that views the law apart from Christ and apart from faith. As we saw in our study of the OT, true righteousness was not possessed from the practice of the law *alone* but by a person looking beyond the law to the God who stood behind it and trusting in his promise to Abraham. The OT people who did that were reckoned to be blameless, though they were not yet fully blameless in reality. But then they were not blameless 'in the law' but 'from God' and 'through faith in Christ' – through faith in the seed who was to come. So, for instance, when Moses appealed for deliverance for the people after the golden calf episode it was not on the basis of the law covenant and the forgiveness that was available within it, but on the basis of God's covenant with Abraham and the promise of a blameless seed. So too Abraham himself possessed a righteousness and blamelessness that were not 'in the law' but 'from God' and through faith in the promised seed. After all, in Abraham's day the law had not been given yet. Or one can think of Simeon, who was righteous and devout and was patiently awaiting the consolation of Israel (Luke 2:25).

The coming of Christ, together with his death and resurrection, merely highlighted to Paul the purpose of the law and circumcision

---

[99] Cf. Sanders 1985: 140.

[100] In that sense, Wright (2013: 989) is wrong to say that in Philippians 3 Paul is redefining covenant membership 'in, through and around Messiah himself', since participation in the blessings of the covenant have always been in and through the Messiah/seed of Abraham. That, I am arguing, was the symbolic significance of circumcision all along.

that he had misunderstood and the moribund nature of his former righteousness: it was not from God, but was his own; not by faith, but according to his perishing flesh.

When Paul says 'we are the circumcision' he means that the true recipients of God's promises to Abraham are and always have been not those who put their confidence in the flesh – in ethnicity, or diligence to the law – but those who put their hope in the Messiah/seed of Abraham; whether the seed who was to come (the seed promised in the covenants and in the law), or the Messiah/seed Jesus who has now been revealed. Confidence in the flesh could not bring righteousness – the righteousness and perfection needed to appear at the day of judgment – or resurrection. Only the resurrected Messiah could bring those. And those who put their hope in him are the recipients of God's promises to Abraham. Both membership in the people of Israel and obedience are worthless – what counts is faith in the Messiah/seed of Abraham. Just as in the OT where true circumcision (circumcision of the heart) involved trust in God's promise to Abraham, now that the seed has come, the true circumcision are those who embrace that seed: Jesus.

Colossians 2

Although Colossians 2 does not use the language of blamelessness or righteousness it nevertheless contains many of the same themes that appear in connection with circumcision in Philippians 3 – death, resurrection and the failure of the flesh. Paul's reference to circumcision in Colossians 2 comes in the context of his desire to see the Colossians built up in their faith and not led astray by 'plausible arguments' (2:4). To that end Paul encourages them to continue 'rooted and built up' in Christ and not to be drawn away into empty traditions (2:6–8). Paul grounds this encouragement in four parallel statements about the nature of the gospel and the person and work of Christ in 2:9–15 among which is a statement about circumcision:[101]

For

in him [*en autō*] all the <u>fullness</u> [*plērōma*] of the deity dwells <u>bodily</u> [*sōmatikōs*]

and **in him** [*en autō*] you have been <u>filled</u> [*peplērōmenoi*]

---

[101] I have modified the ESV here.

who is the head of every ruler and authority.

In whom also [*en hō kai*] you were circumcised [*perietmēthēte*] with a circumcision made without hands.

in the putting off of the <u>body</u> [*sōmatos*] of flesh,

in the circumcision of Christ

having been buried with him in baptism,

in whom also [*en hō kai*] you were raised [*synēgerthēte*]

through faith in the working of God who raised him from the dead.

Each statement begins with *en* plus a pronoun (*autō* or *hō*).[102] The first two statements are clearly in parallel. In the first, the 'fullness' (*plērōma*) of God dwelled 'in him'; while in the second, the Christians have been 'filled' (*peplērōmenoi*) 'in him'.[103] The third and fourth are also clearly in parallel.[104] Both not only begin with *en hō kai*, but that phrase is followed closely in both by an aorist passive second person plural indicative (*perietmēthēte, synēgerthēte*). The parallelism between the two 'in him' statements and the two 'in whom' statements is demonstrated by the common interest in the body. The fullness of God dwelt in Christ 'bodily' (*sōmatikōs*), while the Colossian Christians were 'circumcised . . . by putting off the body [*sōmatos*] of the flesh'. Identifying these connections will help in coming to terms with Paul's statement that the Colossians have been 'circumcised'.

By using two prepositional phrases that also appear to be in parallel Paul explains how the Colossians have been circumcised:

- 'in putting off the body of the flesh' (*en tē apekdysei tou sōmatos tēs sarkos*); and
- 'in the circumcision of Christ' (*en tē peritomē tou Christou*)

---

[102] Dunn 1996: 146.

[103] O'Brien 1998: 103.

[104] The fourth phrase (*en hō kai synēgerthēte*) is taken by some not to be referring to Christ but back to baptism in the immediately preceding phrase (*syntaphentes autō en tō baptismō*) and hence not in parallel (e.g. Moo 2008: 203; Harris 2010: 93). But the 'in him' theme is so prevalent in this section of Colossians and the structure is so careful that a reference to baptism seems unlikely (Dunn 1996: 160–161; O'Brien 1998: 118–119; Barth and Blanke 1994: 320–321; Pao 2012: 167–168).

We will examine the meaning of the first phrase, before returning to consider the second and the nature of the 'circumcision made without hands' (*peritomē acheiropoiētō*).

Putting off the body of flesh

Although Paul uses the noun *apekdysis* (put off) only once, he uses the related verb *apekdyomai* several times to refer to the removal of the 'rulers and authorities' (2:15) and again to refer to putting off the 'old man together with his deeds' (3:9, my tr.).[105] In contrast, in 3:10 Paul says that the Colossians have 'put on' (*endyō*) the 'new man'. This 'new man', whom the Colossians have put on as a result of the 'old man' being removed, is 'being renewed in knowledge after the image of its creator'. In addition, Paul urges the Colossians a few verses later to themselves 'put on' (*endyō*) virtues that conform to the 'new man' (3:12).

The similarities with Philippians 3 are striking. As in Philippians 3, the great hope is of being renewed in the image of Christ (cf. Phil. 3:20), something that is somehow both a present reality ('you *have* put on') and also a future one ('which is *being* renewed'; 3:10). Furthermore, as in Philippians 3, Paul urges the Colossians to strive for what is already in some sense a reality: they *have* put on the new man who is being renewed in the image of Christ and they *ought* to put on virtues consistent with that (3:12). In addition, bracketed between these two, Paul once again refers to circumcision in 3:11: 'Here there is not Greek and Jew, circumcised and uncircumcised, barbarian, Scythian, slave, free; but Christ is all, and in all.' Again, as in Philippians 3, social circumstances or birthrights have no bearing. What matters is being part of the new creation – the new humanity in Christ.

The same ideas can be seen in an investigation of Paul's use of the phrase 'the body of the flesh' (*tou sōmatos tēs sarkos*), in 2:11. As in Philippians 3, Paul expresses scepticism with respect to the flesh in the context of a discussion about circumcision: true circumcision puts off 'the body of the flesh' (cf. Phil. 3:3). Although *sarx* in Colossians so far has referred merely to the physical body (1:22, 24; 2:1, 5), in 2:13 Paul clearly shows what he has in mind when he says that circumcision puts off the body of death: 'And you, who were dead in your trespasses and the uncircumcision of your flesh [*akrobystia tēs sarkos hymōn*] . . .'

---

[105] Dunn 1996: 167; Moo 2008: 212; cf. Pao 2012: 166.

The root problem that (spiritual) 'circumcision' seeks to address is that the flesh is dead in sin. Similarly, Paul says in 2:23, 'These have indeed an appearance of wisdom in promoting self-made religion and asceticism and severity to the body [sōma], but they are of no value in stopping the indulgence of the flesh [sarx].'

The strange worship practices of those trying to influence the Colossians (asceticism, the worship of angels, visions, strict regulations; 2:18–22) have no effect in addressing sinful flesh.[106] But it is not only the creative worship practices of the Colossian false teachers that are ineffective; it is even the regulations from the old covenant – food and drink, festivals, new moons and Sabbaths (2:16).

Paul's comments are part of a larger discussion about the 'body' that has begun in chapter 1. Christ is the head of the 'body' (1:18). He has reconciled us in the 'body of his flesh' (1:22, my tr.). Paul suffers for the sake of Christ's 'body' (1:24). The fullness of deity dwelt 'bodily' (2:9). The Colossians were circumcised by putting off the 'body of the flesh' (2:11). From Christ, the head, the whole 'body' is nourished and grows (2:19; cf. 3:15). In 2:17 Paul also makes the rather enigmatic statement that the OT practices of food and drink, festivals, new moon and Sabbath are 'a shadow of the things that are coming, but the body is Christ' (skia tōn mellontōn, to de sōma tou Christou, my tr.). While it is possible that here Paul intends only to contrast 'shadow' and 'reality',[107] given Paul has been consistently emphasizing the 'body', it seems more likely that he means to do the same here too.[108] A look at how Philo uses the shadow–body contrast (Conf. 190; Migr. 12) suggests the way in which Paul is using the pairing.[109] For Philo, the shadow is what is caused by the body (skian sōmatōn; Migr. 12). The shadow gives insight into the body, but it is the body itself, not the shadow, that is being investigated, since 'monstrous it is that shadow should be preferred to substance or a copy to originals' (Migr. 12). In the same way Paul is saying that the OT regulations were merely the shadows created by the body of Christ.

To summarize the argument of 2:16–23, the OT practices are only shadows; it is in Christ that the body grows, since severity to the

---

[106] Although the exact nature of some of the practices is contested (Pao 2012: 187–891; O'Brien 1998: 141–146), that has little impact on understanding the overall argument.

[107] E.g. O'Brien 1998: 141; Best 1955: 121.

[108] Also Lohse 1971: 117; Bruce 1984: 117. Best (1955: 121) objects that this requires having sōma appear twice ('the "body/reality" is the "body of Christ"') and with two meanings. But that misunderstands the nature of the body–shadow contrast/metaphor.

[109] Lohse 1971: 116–117.

(physical) body has no value in dealing with the flesh. The combined effect of Paul's references to the body in Colossians is to show that through the incarnation Christ has effected a bodily redemption of his people that the OT religious practices were unable to accomplish. Lohse summarizes:

> The old life, in which 'flesh' determined the conduct of the 'body,' has been put aside. Putting off the body of flesh, however, . . . does not mean contempt for earthly life. Rather it means being active in this life in obedience to the Lord.[110]

It is also important for our understanding of 2:11 to see that the exact phrase 'the body of the flesh' (*tou sōmatos tēs sarkos*) is also used in 1:22. Paul says that those who were once hostile and alienated from God, '[Jesus] has now reconciled in his body of flesh [*tō sōmati tēs sarkos autou*] by his death, in order to present you holy and blameless [*amōmous*] and above reproach before him . . .'

It is through the death of Christ's 'body of flesh' that the Colossians will be presented blameless before God. The mechanism by which that takes place is not spelled out in 1:22. That, however, is the precise point taken up again in 2:11 – 3:11.

Returning to 2:11, the question remains as to what 'putting off the body of flesh' means. As O'Brien points out, the interpretation of 2:11 is more or less divided along two lines:[111] (1) those who see putting off the 'body of flesh' as referring to the Colossians' putting off the old nature,[112] versus (2) those who see it as referring to the death of Christ.[113]

Paul's use of the phrase 'body of flesh' in 1:22 suggests that the 'body of flesh' being referred to in 2:11 is not that of the Colossians but that of Christ (view 2). That is also suggested by the parallelism between 'the body of the flesh' (2:11) and the fullness of God that dwelt 'bodily' *in Christ* (2:9). Yet Paul's use of 'body' and 'flesh' also seems to suggest that he has in mind the removal of sinful human flesh and renewal of the body (corporately) in the image of Christ (view 1).

It seems strange, however, that we should have to choose between the two.[114] The answer, of course, lies in observing that throughout

---

[110] Ibid. 103.
[111] O'Brien 1998: 116–117.
[112] E.g. Moo 2008: 200; Lohse 1971: 103.
[113] E.g. Dunn 1996: 157; Pao 2012: 165–166; O'Brien 1998: 116–117; Barth and Blanke 1994: 365.
[114] Similarly, Barth and Blanke 1994: 318.

this section Paul is emphasizing how the Colossians share in what is true of Christ. Paul constantly uses the language of 'in him' (2:9–12), 'with him' (2:13, 20; 3:3–4), as well as 'with' verbs (*synthaptō* [2:12]; *synegeirō* [2:12; 3:1]; *syzōopoieō* [2:13]). Moreover, the way the language of 'body', 'flesh' and 'putting off' is connected both to Christ and to the believer does not allow us to separate the work of Christ and the effects of that work in the believer.

Thus the answer to the question raised by 1:22 – how we are reconciled to God and presented blameless to him – is that in Christ the fullness of deity dwelt bodily, in his death (the putting off of his body of flesh) our body of flesh was also put off, we have been raised with him, we share in his body, and will be renewed in his image. As we will see, that is what circumcision symbolized.

The circumcision of Christ

We return now to the language of circumcision in 2:11 and to the meaning of the phrases 'circumcision without hands' and 'circumcision of Christ'. The precise relationship between Paul's statement that the Colossians have been circumcised and the two prepositional phrases is contested. Certainly, 'you were circumcised with a circumcision made without hands' refers to the experience of the Colossians. But the two prepositional phrases 'in putting off the body of the flesh' and 'in the circumcision of Christ' are more complex.

Pao lists three possibilities for the relationship between the two parallel prepositional phrases:[115] (1) both describe what is done to believers; (2) the first describes the experience of believers, the second, the experience of Christ; or (3) both describe the experience of Christ. In the light of what we have seen, none of these options is quite right. The third option is almost right, but the situation is also slightly more complex.

As discussed above, the first prepositional phrase, 'in putting off the body of the flesh', clearly describes the experience of Christ. The parallelism between the two prepositional phrases therefore suggests that 'the circumcision of Christ' refers to Christ's 'putting off the body of flesh' in his death.[116] But we have also observed that the Colossian

---

[115] Pao 2012: 165.

[116] Barth and Blanke (1994: 319) note that the genitive in the expression *tē peritomē tou Christou* could be (1) *objective*: the circumcision which Christ underwent, either his death (e.g. Dunn 1996: 158; O'Brien 1998: 117; Pao 2012: 166) or, less likely, his circumcision on the eighth day; (2) *subjective*: the circumcision performed by Christ (e.g. Bruce 1984: 104); or (3) *qualitative/possessive*: the Christian circumcision as

believers share in that experience. When Christ put off his body of flesh, they participated in that, which effected the putting off of their body of flesh. They shared in Christ's experience and his experience was effective for them. That is also confirmed by the way 'body', 'flesh' and the 'put on/off' language is used in connection with the Colossians in the immediate context.

'Putting off the body of flesh', therefore, refers to the experience *both* of the Colossians and of Christ. Additionally, both the circumcision of the Colossians and the circumcision of Christ represent the putting off of the body of flesh, but the circumcision of the Colossians takes place *in* the circumcision of Christ.[117] Or to put it another way, the Colossians put off the body of flesh in Christ's putting off of the body of flesh. The first prepositional phrase then becomes a kind of transitional phrase, linking the two circumcision phrases. That may also be the reason that the expression 'the body of the flesh' in 2:11, as is frequently noted, lacks the personal pronoun present in 1:22,[118] since it refers *both* to the Colossians and to Christ.[119] Whatever the case, what is significant for our purposes is the observation that again the fulfilment of circumcision comes through the sacrifice of the Messiah/Christ.

Circumcision and resurrection

One apparent difference, however, between Colossians 2 and Philippians 3 is that Paul here seems to link circumcision only with the death of Christ, not also the resurrection. Although resurrection is also part of the context here, the parallelism between Colossians 2:11 and 2:12 seems to suggest a distinction.

The nature of the parallelism is not immediately clear. For instance, does verse 12 express the same thought as verse 11, only in different words, or is there a development? Considering the four parallel statements in 2:9–12, it can be seen that verse 10 advances the idea of verse 9: in Christ the 'fullness' of God dwelt and in him the Colossians have been 'filled'. So too Paul seems to move from death in verse 11 to resurrection in verse 12.[120]

(note 116 *cont.*) opposed, say, to the Mosaic kind (e.g. Harris 2010: 92; Moo 2008: 200). All three appear to be true in one or another sense; nevertheless, the parallelism of the two participial phrases suggests that the first is primary.

[117] Pao 2012: 166; Dunn 1996: 158.

[118] E.g. Pao 2012: 165–166; O'Brien 1998: 117; Dunn 1996: 157.

[119] Cf. Barth and Blanke 1994: 318, 364–365.

[120] The language of putting off the body of flesh is linked with death in 1:22. The language in v. 12 of 'being buried in baptism' also suggests death. Contrary to the

Such a hard distinction may, however, be artificial, not least because 2:13 appears to suggest that the remedy for uncircumcision includes resurrection: 'And you, who were dead in your trespasses and the uncircumcision of your flesh, God made alive together with him, having forgiven us all our trespasses.'

The first half of the verse expresses the predicament of the Colossians apart from the work of Christ. Although some identify 'the uncircumcision of your flesh' as referring to the physical reality of circumcision, we have seen that the earlier reference to circumcision is a spiritual reference. In that reference too we found 'flesh' language, and that putting off the body of flesh referred to the removal of sinful flesh. We have also observed that *sarx* in the immediate context can refer to the corruption of sin (e.g. 2:23). Those ideas are confirmed here by the pairing of 'the uncircumcision of your flesh' with 'your trespasses'. But the fact that 'uncircumcision of your flesh' is described as a kind of 'death' suggests that resurrection is part of the necessary response to (spiritual) uncircumcision.

Thus Paul continues with the remedy for 'uncircumcision', which is 'he made you alive together with him' (my tr.); though that is grounded in forgiveness ('having forgiven us all our trespasses'). Throughout these chapters Paul affirms that believers have both died with Christ and been raised with Christ (2:13, 20; 3:1, 3) and while at first glance it may appear from 2:11 that circumcision refers only to death, on closer inspection it is apparent that resurrection (and indeed transformation into the image of Christ) is all part of the complex that makes up the 'circumcision made without hands'.

What is significant too is that Paul chooses to use the language of circumcision at all. As Pao rightly observes, 'The reference to circumcision here is unexpected.'[121] The result is that Paul ties the idea of sharing in the death/resurrection of the Christ with the fulfilment of the OT promise to Abraham. It is through the circumcision of Christ (his death and resurrection) that those who trust Christ are also circumcised with a circumcision made without hands. That is, they have put off the sinful body of flesh and are being transformed into the image of Christ. So although the language of blamelessness/ righteousness is not present, we still have the idea that through

suggestion of some (e.g. Salter 2010: 25; Lohse 1971: 103–104; Moo 2008: 199), baptism here does not include the idea of resurrection. As Campbell (2012: 197) notes, 'nowhere else does Paul refer to being *raised* in baptism; that image (when spiritually applied) always refers to participation in Christ's death rather than his resurrection.'

[121] Pao 2012: 164.

the sacrifice of the anointed seed of Abraham others are made blameless.

Finally, it is worth noting that there is some evidence that the circumcision the Colossians experience is deeper than a mere circumcision of the heart. Paul refers to the putting off of the '*body* of flesh'. This is not merely a circumcision that affects one organ – heart, lips, ears or genitals. It affects the whole person. That is, Paul's language in Colossians (and Philippians) suggests that the realization of circumcision *in Christ* is deeper than that experienced or called for among the OT believers. If circumcision of the heart represents the appropriation by humble faith (in the heart) of God's promises to Abraham, then the circumcision of Christ represents the transformation of the whole person through participation in his death and resurrection. That is, the circumcision of Christ represents not only radical repentance and faith and the ensuing forgiveness but also the removal by Christ of a person's sinful nature and tendency.[122]

Ephesians 2

The last NT circumcision passage we will consider in this chapter is Ephesians 2. After describing the glory of God's plan in Christ in chapter 1, in chapter 2 Paul goes on to show the depths from which the Ephesians have been plucked. They were 'dead in the trespasses and sins in which you once walked [*peripateō*]' (2:1–2). The first part of which is almost identical to Paul's statement in Colossians 2:13. The Ephesians also previously lived in the 'passions' and 'desires' of the 'flesh' (*sarx*; 2:3). Similar too is the emphasis on evil powers: 'the prince of the power of the air' (2:2; cf. Col. 2:15). But though they were dead, they have now been raised up with Christ (2:6), in order that they might 'walk' (*peripateō*) in good works prepared for them by God (2:10).

At that point, Paul turns rather unexpectedly to the topic of circumcision:

> Therefore remember that at one time you Gentiles in the flesh, called 'the uncircumcision' by what is called the circumcision, which is made in the flesh by hands – remember that you were at that time separated from Christ, alienated from the commonwealth of Israel

---

[122] My thanks go to Peter Adam for his help in formulating this observation.

and strangers to the covenants of promise, having no hope and without God in the world. (Eph. 2:11–12)

Although Paul's reference to circumcision initially seems out of place, in the light of what we have seen, particularly in Philippians and Colossians, it makes perfect sense. Circumcision symbolized God's promise of righteousness/blamelessness through the Messiah/seed of Abraham. By virtue then of not being circumcised, the Gentiles were separated from Christ, because uncircumcision implied, in general, ignorance of God's promise to Abraham. Circumcision separated the Gentiles from the Jews, but that separation was not merely social; the Gentiles were separated from Christ, from the commonwealth of Israel, they were strangers to the covenants of promise, they had no hope and were without God in the world (cf. Rom. 3:1–2; 9:1–5).

That distance, however, has been remedied by Christ. How Christ has done that is explained by what follows. First of all, he has broken down the dividing wall of hostility between Jew and Gentile 'in his flesh' (2:14). Second of all, he has done that by 'abolishing the law of commandments expressed in ordinances' (2:15). The joint purpose of these two actions was that from the two (Jew and Gentile) he might create 'one new man' (*hena kainon anthrōpon*; 2:15). The purpose was also that 'in one body' (*en heni sōmati*) he might reconcile people to God (2:16).

As in Colossians we find the emphasis on the new man, the new humanity, created in the promised Christ. But here in Ephesians the new man is not only a remedy for being dead in sin but also for the separation between Jew and Gentile. That separation has ended because in the place of the two, Jesus has created one new race or class: Christians. That is not merely a social reality, the removal of 'boundary markers', but an existential one – Christ, 'in one body', crucified their shared humanity in Adam and created a new humanity in himself. Through the Spirit the Ephesian Christians share in that (2:18, 22) and, as in Philippians, the great hope is being remade into the image of Christ.

In fact, that same emphasis on the removal of social distinctions is also present in Colossians. After having exhorted the Colossians to put on the new man, Paul notes, 'Here there is not Greek and Jew, circumcised and uncircumcised, barbarian, Scythian, slave, free; but Christ is all, and in all' (Col. 3:11).

Circumcision signified God's promise to Abraham to restore and redeem humanity through a blameless descendant of Abraham. The

Gentiles were formerly cut off from that, being ignorant of what God had promised, but now in Jesus they have been brought into the single new blameless humanity being remade in the person of Jesus Christ, Abraham's promised seed.

Summary

In this chapter we have focused particularly on the language of blamelessness. We traced three terms that are used in the LXX to translate *tāmîm*: *amōmos*, *amemptos* and *teleios*. We saw that in the NT *amōmos* carries on the sacrificial overtones present in the LXX by describing the sacrifice of Jesus as a sacrifice 'without blemish'. But it is also used to describe Jesus' presenting believers as 'without blemish' at the last day. In that role it also continues the kind of moral use seen with *tāmîm*, describing the moral perfection required for a person to be in the presence of God. The related term *amemptos* was used to describe Zechariah and Elizabeth in language deeply reminiscent of Genesis 17:1, as blameless and righteous, and walking in God's commandments. *Teleios*, too, carries the idea of moral perfection. It was also discovered that *tāmîm* was used by the Qumran community in the kind of way we would expect based on our analysis of the OT. The Qumran community linked the language of blamelessness with Genesis 17:1 but also interpreted it strongly in the light of its use within the sacrificial system.

In Philippians 3 Paul also uses the language of 'blamelessness'. Significantly he combines it with a discussion of circumcision, righteousness and faith. Paul alludes to his former 'righteousness', which was 'blameless' but moribund. Although circumcision looked for the establishment of blamelessness in sacrifice, Paul looked to the mere practice of the law rather than realizing that the ultimate solution lay in God's promise to Abraham. True righteousness and blamelessness could come only through faith in the crucified and resurrected Messiah/seed of Abraham.

In Colossians, while Paul does not use the language of 'blamelessness' or 'righteousness', many of the themes present in Philippians recur. Themes such as 'death', 'resurrection' and 'the failure of the flesh'. Paul argues that the fulfilment of God's promise to Abraham includes death and resurrection, leading to blamelessness, which comes through the death of the Messiah. In the Messiah and in his death and resurrection the Colossians have been circumcised, not merely in the heart, but in their whole person by the removal of their sinful nature and resurrection into the new humanity in Christ Jesus.

Finally, in Ephesians Paul uses similar themes as in Philippians and Colossians to reflect on circumcision. The Ephesians were 'dead' in their trespasses and sins in which they once 'walked', captive to the desires of the 'flesh'. But they have been raised up with Christ. Once they were alienated from God's promise to Abraham, signified by circumcision, to redeem and restore humanity, but now they are part of the 'new man' established in Christ. They are now recipients of all that circumcision symbolized: the new blameless humanity through the Messiah/seed of Abraham.

Chapter Five

Circumcision in Romans 2 – 4: righteousness, repentance and faith

Romans is undoubtedly Paul's magnum opus. And yet, surprisingly, it is circumcision that takes centre stage in a number of its chapters. Circumcision is woven all through Romans 2 – 4. The letter has barely begun when Paul warns his readers that because of their hard and impenitent hearts (2:5) they are storing up wrath for themselves. As will become clear, the language of hard hearts is drawn from the OT and is often found contrasted with a circumcised heart. The theme of circumcision is then expressly developed at the end of chapter 2 (2:25–29). Chapter 3, a chapter well known for its depiction of the human condition and exposition of justification, begins with the provocative question '[W]hat is the value of circumcision?' It answers that question, in part at least, by addressing the nature and relationship of righteousness and the law. Chapter 4 returns to the theme of circumcision and how it relates to righteousness, first in the life of Abraham, and then in the lives of those who share Abraham's faith. Understanding how circumcision fits into these early chapters of Romans then promises to reveal a great deal about the nature of circumcision and its relationship with righteousness and faith. In what follows, we will focus our attention on chapters 2 and 4, where the nature of circumcision is most tightly integrated into Paul's argument.

Interpretations of Romans 2

Romans 2 is a highly contested passage. Bird describes it as a '*crux interpretum* for several issues in Paul including law, works, justification and Gentiles'.[1] Yet while it is impossible to address here all the issues raised in its interpretation, we still need to come to grips with the argument in order to understand what Paul is saying about

[1] Bird 2007: 157.

circumcision. I also hope to show that by coming to this chapter armed with a better understanding of circumcision, a number of the perceived complexities are diminished.

The main source of contention between interpretations of Romans 2 lies in understanding what Paul is saying about justification. The problems arise in determining what Paul means in saying that the 'doers of the law will be justified' (*hoi poiētai nomou dikaiōthēsontai*; 2:13, my tr.), a statement that appears to be completely at odds with his assertions elsewhere, not least in 3:20, that 'from works of the law no flesh will be justified' (*ex ergōn nomou ou dikaiōthēsetai pasa sarx*, my tr.). Paul's emphasis on 'doing' the law is not restricted to 2:13. Elsewhere in chapter 2 he also notes that to 'everyone who works good' (*panti tō ergazomenō to agathon*, my tr.) God will give 'glory and honour and peace' (2:10) along with other positive affirmations of those who 'practise' (*prassō*), 'keep' (*phylassō*) and 'complete' (*teleō*) the law (2:25–27).

Yet the number of interpretations given to 'those who work good', 'doers of the law' and those who 'keep the righteous requirements of the law' (*ta dikaiōmata tou nomou phylassē*, my tr.) is manifold. The situation is further complicated by the fact that not everyone agrees that the three sections (2:1–10; 11–16; 25–29) refer to the same kind of person or mean the same thing,[2] leading to a large number of possible permutations when the options for each section are combined. Nevertheless, the possible contenders for each section have much in common and a list of the most common or most likely views of what Paul means can still be helpfully presented:[3]

1. Paul means that justification is by works. According to this view Paul is being thoroughly self-contradictory and is here asserting that people can please God by what they do.[4]
2. Paul is speaking hypothetically. In this view, phrases such as 'working good', 'doing the law' or 'keeping the righteous requirements' refer to the unobtainable standard of perfect obedience required to be justified by the law – an obedience that no one attains on account of the effects of sin.[5]

[2] For a brief survey of the differences see Schreiner 1993: 139, n. 27.

[3] See Cranfield 2004: 151–152, 155–156; Moo 1996: 140, 148; Kruse 2012: 136–140; Schreiner 1998: 114–115.

[4] E.g. Sanders 1985: 123–135; Räisänen 2010: 107–108. As Bird (2007: 158–159) notes, such a view gives Paul very little credit.

[5] E.g. Moo 1996: 140–142; Thielman 2007: 94–96. Though Moo would not describe his position as hypothetical.

3. Paul is referring to the fruit that comes from faith. In this case, although salvation is by grace through faith, God's evaluation of people on the last day is based on the good works they have done that flow from their faith. It is often expressed as the view that justification is *in accordance with works*. In this case, it may refer to either or both
   (a) Christians[6]
   (b) OT believers[7]
4. Paul is referring to faith. In this view, phrases such as 'working good', 'doing the law' or 'keeping the righteous requirements' are synonyms for faith. Again this view may be subdivided into those who see Paul as referring to the faith of one or a combination of the following groups:
   (a) Christians[8]
   (b) OT believers[9]

It is impossible to address each of the above possible views directly. Nevertheless, understanding what Paul means by phrases such as 'working good', 'doing the law' and 'keeping the righteous requirements of the law' and whether they mean the same thing is crucial for grasping how Paul understands circumcision since the one who practises, keeps and completes the law is the one who is truly circumcised (2:25–29). To flag my own view, I think there are strong reasons for believing that all three sections do in fact refer to the same kind of person: OT and Christian believers who put their faith in the Messiah promised through Abraham (views 4a and 4b). That is, the language of 'working good', 'doing the law' and 'keeping the righteous requirements of the law' are all synonyms for faith in the Messiah/ seed of Abraham. To demonstrate that, it is necessary to consider each section and its language in turn. We begin with the problem of hard-heartedness and unrepentance that Paul identifies at the beginning of chapter 2.

---

[6] E.g. Fitzmyer 1993: 297; Schreiner 1998: 114–115; Cranfield 2004: 151–152; Käsemann 1994: 75; Murray 1967: 1:86; Kruse 2012: 124–125, 142–144; Garlington 1991: 70–72.

[7] E.g. Davies 1990: 55–57, 65–67, 70–71; Snodgrass 1986: 74, 80–82.

[8] E.g. Dunn 1988: 1:85; Morris 1988: 140; Barrett 1991: 45–46, 55–58; Wright 2013: 1088–1089, 1175.

[9] E.g. Morris 1988: 140.

Hard-heartedness and repentance

Immediately before chapter 2, in 1:18–32, Paul sets out God's wrath that is being revealed against all kinds of godlessness. Chapter 2 then begins with Paul's challenge to those who judge others while failing to repent themselves. The target of Paul's comments in 2:1–5 is the person who 'practises' (*prassō*) the same things as the person in chapter 1 (see esp. 1:31). Yet this person fails to realize that God's patience and grace are intended to provide an opportunity for repentance (2:4). Such a person is storing up for himself or herself wrath on account of his or her 'hard and unrepentant heart' (*tēn sklērotēta sou kai ametanoēton kardian*, my tr.).

That phrase is reminiscent of Yahweh's condemnations of Israel in the OT (which we explored in connection with Deut. 10) for being hard-hearted (*sklērokardia/sklērokardios*; Deut. 10:16; Jer. 4:4; Ezek. 3:7), stubborn (*sklēros/sklērotēs*; Deut. 9:27; 31:27; Judg. 2:19), and stiff-necked (*sklērotrachēlos*; Exod. 33:3, 5; 34:9; Deut. 9:6, 13). Jesus too links 'hardness of heart' (*sklērokardia*) with both first-century and ancient Israel (Matt. 19:8; Mark 10:5).

The verb *sklērynō* is also used of God's hardening Pharaoh's heart (Exod. 4:21; 7:3; 9:12; 10:1, 20, 27; 11:10; 14:4, 8; cf. Rom. 9:18); of Pharaoh's heart being hardened (Exod. 7:22; 8:19; 9:35; 13:15); of God's hardening the hearts of the Egyptians (Exod. 14:17); of God's hardening the spirit of Sihon, king of Heshbon (Deut. 2:30); of God's hardening the hearts of his people so that they do not fear God (Isa. 63:17); of Zedekiah's hardening his heart and neck against Yahweh (2 Chr. 36:13); of the Israelites stiffening their necks (Jer. 7:26; 17:23; 19:15); and of people in the synagogue rejecting the gospel from Paul (Acts 19:9). In Psalm 95:8 the people are warned not to harden their hearts like their forefathers did on the way out of Egypt – a theme the writer of Hebrews picks up (Heb. 3:8, 13, 15; 4:7). The expression is also used to describe Israel's downfall and exile:

> Yet the LORD warned Israel and Judah by every prophet and every seer, saying, 'Turn from your evil ways and keep my commandments and my statutes, in accordance with all the Law that I commanded your fathers, and that I sent to you by my servants the prophets.'
> But they would not listen, but were stubborn [*esklērynan/ wayyaqšû 'et-'orpām*], as their fathers had been, who did not believe in the LORD their God. (2 Kgs 17:13–14)

Later on in Judah's history, Hezekiah appeals to the people:

Do not now be stiff-necked [*mē sklērynēte tous trachēlous hymōn*/'*al-taqšû 'orpĕkem*] as your fathers were, but yield yourselves to the LORD and come to his sanctuary, which he has consecrated for ever, and serve the LORD your God, that his fierce anger may turn away from you. For if you return to the LORD, your brothers and your children will find compassion with their captors and return to this land. For the LORD your God is gracious and merciful and will not turn away his face from you, if you return to him. (2 Chr. 30:8–9)

Hezekiah's solution is not stringent perfectionism, but humility and repentance.

In a similar way, Paul pairs hard-heartedness with unrepentance: 'your hard and unrepentant heart' (*tēn sklērotēta sou kai ametanoēton kardian*; 2:5, my tr.). Indeed, the kindness of God to his people, in contrast to the wrath being revealed against all kinds of unrighteousness in chapter 1, is not a case of overlooking sin but is 'meant to lead you to repentance [*metanoian*]' (2:4).

What is particularly significant is that, as here in Romans 2 – 4, hardness of heart often occurs alongside references to circumcised/uncircumcised hearts.[10] In Acts 7:51 Stephen accuses the Sanhedrin of being like ancient Israel: 'You stiff-necked people [*sklērotrachēloi*], uncircumcised in heart [*aperitmētoi kardiais*] and ears . . .' Notably here, 'hard' modifies 'neck' rather than 'heart', which in turn is described as 'uncircumcised'. The link between circumcision and hardness of heart is also demonstrated by the fact that in the LXX version of two significant circumcision passages, 'circumcise . . . the foreskin of your heart' in the MT is replaced with 'circumcise your hard hearts' (my tr.; Deut. 10:16; Jer. 4:4). Furthermore, we might think of the call in Leviticus 26 for the Israelites to humble their uncircumcised hearts, or Deuteronomy 9 – 10 where the remedy for Israel's stubbornness (Deut. 9:6, 27) is to '[c]ircumcise therefore the foreskin of your heart, and be no longer stubborn [*ton trachēlon hymōn ou sklēryneite*/*wĕ' orpĕkem lō' taqšû*]' (Deut. 10:16).

In other words, Paul's argument in Romans 2 – 4 regarding circumcision uses the language and theology of Deuteronomy and of the OT in general. Indeed, it will become clear that Romans 2 – 4 is full of complex references and allusions to the OT and to many

---

[10] See also Schreiner 1998: 108; Dunn 1988: 1:83–84.

passages that involve the metaphor of circumcision. But most importantly, as Paul begins his discussion of circumcision, it seems apparent that the problem he is addressing is not punctilious legalism per se but the historic problem of Israel: a conceited arrogance and self-righteousness in which a person refuses to humble himself or herself before Yahweh.[11]

To each according to works

Having raised the issue of hard-heartedness and repentance, Paul introduces the language of works, in 2:6: '[God] will give to each according to his works [*kata ta erga autou*]' (my tr.). He then proceeds to unpack that idea in verses 7–10, which are arranged in parallel:[12]

> to those who by patience in **good work** [*ergou agathou*] seek for glory and honour [*doxan kai timēn*] and immortality, he will give eternal life;
>
>> but for those who are self-seeking and do not obey the truth, but obey unrighteousness, there will be wrath and fury.
>
>> There will be tribulation and distress for every human being who **works evil** [*tou katergazomenou to kakon*], the Jew first and also the Greek,
>
>> but glory and honour [*doxa de kai timē*] and peace for everyone who **works good** [*tō ergazomenō to agathon*], the Jew first and also the Greek.[13]

To those who work good (2:7, 10) God will give glory and honour (2:10; cf. 2:7). To those who work evil (2:9) or 'obey unrighteousness' (2:8) there will be wrath (2:8) and tribulation (2:9).

As noted above, the identity of those 'working good' has been variously interpreted. But in defence of the idea that 'working good' refers to repentance and faith several points can be made.

First, the connection between 2:5 and 2:6[14] suggests that the works Paul has in mind when he says '[God] will give to each according to

---

[11] Cf. Garlington 1991: 56; Wright 2001: 140. Both think the issue is not 'legalism', but Garlington thinks the issue is exclusivism, while Wright believes it is the Jews wrongly claiming they have returned from the exile.

[12] E.g. Moo 1996: 135; Fitzmyer 1993: 303.

[13] I have modified the ESV here.

[14] The relative pronoun indicates that Paul is continuing the point (Moo 1996: 136).

his works' are works of repentance and faith.[15] That is, God will give to each according to whether he or she has a hard/unrepentant (uncircumcised) heart or a soft/repentant (circumcised) heart.

Second, Paul appears to be quoting either from Proverbs 24:12 (*apodidōsin hekastō kata ta erga autou*) or Psalm 62:12 (*apodōseis hekastō kata ta erga autou*). The wording is uncannily similar. The only difference in the case of Proverbs 24 is the change of the verb to third person and present tense. The only difference in the case of Psalm 62 is the change in the verb to the second person.[16] Either OT text supports the notion that Paul's focus in Romans 2 is on repentance and trust in contrast to hard-hearted unrepentance. Even if Paul had only a general teaching in mind rather than a specific text,[17] both texts reveal how the OT understood the notion that God will give to each according to his or her works.

Proverbs 24:12 is reflecting on God's knowledge of secrets hidden in people's hearts:

> If you say, 'Behold, we did not know this',
>   does not he who weighs the heart perceive it?
> Does not he who keeps watch over your soul know it,
>   and will he not repay man according to his work?

An attempt to divert blame by a false claim to ignorance is utter folly because God knows the secrets of our hearts. The inability to accept responsibility and the deceitful attempt to divert blame fits Paul's theme of hard-heartedness and unrepentance. So too a closer look at Psalm 62 shows that at the core of the psalm is trust in Yahweh rather than trust in one's own good deeds. A sample of verses illustrates the point:

> For God alone my soul waits in silence;
>   from him comes my salvation.
> He alone is my rock and my salvation,
>   my fortress; I shall not be greatly shaken.
>   (Ps. 62:1–2)

> On God rests my salvation and my glory;
>   my mighty rock, my refuge is God.

[15] Barrett 1991: 44–45; Morris 1988: 116–117; cf. Dunn 1988: 1:86.
[16] Schreiner 1998: 112, n. 2.
[17] Moo 1996: 136, n. 4; Morris 1988: 116.

> Trust in him at all times, O people;
> pour out your heart before him;
> God is a refuge for us.
>
> (Ps. 62:7–8)

The words of Psalm 62 are hardly the words of the self-righteous person. Nor do they point to a judgment on the basis of merit. Rather, they suggest that God saves those who trust in him.

Third, Paul's description of the 'one who works good' in verse 7 is hardly the description of perfection, or of a self-absorbed hypocrite:[18] 'to the one who by steadfastness in good work seeks glory and honour and immortality [he will give] eternal life . . .' (my tr.).

The language of 'steadfastness' and 'seeking' suggests a patient struggle, rather than a perfect or an arrogant one. As Cranfield observes, 'Paul speaks of those who seek (ζητοῦσιν) glory, honour and incorruption, not of those who deserve them.'[19]

Fourth, Paul's use of the language of 'works' throughout chapters 2–4 also supports the idea that the 'works' that matter are repentance and faith in God's promise to Abraham. There is reason to believe that in chapters 2–4 Paul is seeking to explain (or even exegete) what is meant by '[he] will give to each according to his works'. In these three chapters *ergon* and its cognates appear thirteen times.[20] In 2:15 Paul notes that the '*work* of the law' is written on the hearts of some Gentiles. In 3:20 he maintains that 'by *works* of the law no flesh will be justified'. In 3:27–28 he contrasts a 'law of *works*' with a 'law of faith'; while in 4:2 he begins a discussion of works in relation to Abraham,[21] noting that it is the one who 'does not *work* but believes' (*tō de mē ergazomenō pisteuonti*) who is justified (4:5). Paul seems to suggest there is an absolute disjunction between faith and works, not least because the law 'works' (*katergazomai*) wrath (4:15). Not only is faith reckoned as righteousness, but righteousness is reckoned *chōris*

---

[18] Davies 1990: 54.

[19] Cranfield 2004: 147.

[20] Including *katergazomai*, which appears all but indistinguishable in these chapters from *ergazomai* (Schreiner 1998: 113).

[21] Gathercole (2002b: 239) has demonstrated that the idea that Abraham was justified by what he did has some pedigree in Jewish literature of Paul's period (e.g. Sir. 44.19–20; 1 Macc. 2.52; *Jub.* 19.8–9; 23.9–10; CD 3.2–4). Moreover, the concern was not merely with respect to circumcision, Sabbath and food laws but to 'comprehensive obedience to the Torah'. Gathercole surmises, 'Paul is in dialogue with the Jewish expository tradition of an Abraham who was justified by his obedience, and Paul rejects this tradition explicitly, not implicitly, in 4:4–5' (246).

ergōn ('without reference to works'; 4:6, my tr.) such that sin is *not* counted/reckoned (4:7–8).[22]

At first glance 2:6 appears at odds with 4:6 and potentially 3:20. In 2:6 Paul asserts that God will give to each 'according to his works', while in 4:6 he speaks of the blessing wherein God reckons a person righteous 'apart from works', and in 3:20 Paul maintains that 'from works of the law' (*ex ergōn nomou*) no one will be justified. Does God then give to each according to his or her works or not?

It ought to be observed, however, that Paul himself distinguishes between two kinds of 'work' within chapters 2 and 3. In 2:15 Paul refers to the 'work of the law' written on the heart (*to ergon tou nomou grapton en tais kardiais autōn*). In contrast, in 3:20 he merely refers to the 'works of the law' (*ergōn nomou*). Although Paul does not qualify the works in 3:20 as specifically *external* 'works', that hardly matters. Chapter 2 contains a number of distinctions between the internal and external and in the cases where he wants to refer to the internal he usually makes it clear (e.g. 2:15, 28–29).

In the light of 2:15 the implication is that in 3:20 Paul is referring to the mere completion of the requirements of the law *without any inner reality*. Paul there is continuing to reflect on 2:6: God will give to each according to his or her 'work', but the work that matters is the work of the law written on the heart, not the mere completion of the various practices, procedures and commands of the law. As we will see below, that theme is also maintained in the many OT quotations running through these chapters.

Moreover, Paul's unusual reference in 2:15 to 'the work of the law' that is 'written on their hearts' also supports the idea that Paul is seeking to distinguish between two different kinds of 'work'. The similarity with Jeremiah 31 is impossible to escape.[23] What is baffling, however, is that Paul adds the word 'work' to Jeremiah's words. This strange addition has led some to reject the connection with Jeremiah 31, suggesting that it is merely the '*work* of the law', not the law itself, that is written on these Gentiles' hearts.[24] But that seems like special pleading. So why does Paul add 'work' to Jeremiah's words?

---

[22] Gathercole (2002b: 247) rightly comments, 'the New Perspective interpretation of 4:1–8 falls to the ground on this point: that David although circumcised, sabbatarian, and kosher, is described as without works because of his disobedience.'

[23] Wright (2001: 147) says, 'I find it next to impossible that Paul could have written this phrase, with its overtones of Jeremiah's new covenant promise, simply to refer to pagans who happen by accident to share some of Israel's moral teaching.'

[24] E.g. Schreiner 1998: 122; Moo 1996: 151–152; Seifrid 2000: 53.

The most obvious and satisfying answer is that Paul wishes to connect what he is saying about the fulfilment of Jeremiah 31 with his words in 2:6 about God's judging 'according to works' and about those who 'work good' versus those who 'work evil'. That is to say, in 2:15 (and 3:20–31) Paul is reflecting on which 'work' matters and which 'work' does not matter: the work that matters is the work written on the heart.

I will argue below that 'the work of the law written on the heart' is faith in the gospel. That matches the connection here between repentance and work. It is also supported by the fact that following 3:20 Paul drops the distinction between works-on-the-heart versus works-not-on-the-heart in preference for the distinction between 'faith' and 'works'. That is, after 3:20, 'works written on the heart' is spoken of under the category of faith.

In 3:27–31 Paul contrasts a 'law of works' with a 'law of faith', but the same contrasts of internal/external law and faith/works are still present. The 'law of works' is the OT law merely completed as written (*grammati*; 2:29), while the 'law of faith' is equivalent to the 'law written on the heart' – it is the original intent of the law, which was to point to faith in the blameless substitute/seed/Messiah. Hence Paul can say that by 'this faith' in the Messiah they do not overthrow the law but rather uphold it (3:31); since the Law and the Prophets always bore witness to that faith (3:21). As we have seen repeatedly, in the context of the Abrahamic covenant the law played a dual role, not only convicting people of the need for blamelessness, but also promising the provision of a blameless substitute in a descendant of Abraham.

In chapter 4 Paul's use of 'works' seems to broaden out slightly. He drops the genitive 'of the law' and refers simply to 'works', apparently countering the idea that any kind of works (whether of the law or not) is of value.[25] But once again the contrast is between faith and works: God justifies the one who does not 'work' but 'believes'.

The shift from a works-written-on-the-heart–works to a faith–works contrast supports the notion that the work of the law written on the heart refers to faith. What appears at first to be a contradiction between 2:5 and 3:20 or 4:6 then is actually a function of the fact that over three chapters Paul is attempting to explain what it means that God 'will give to each according to his works'. It may also be that Paul is countering a misunderstanding of what 'works' means. So he

---

25 Schreiner 1998: 217–218.

adopts the language of his recipients or contemporaries momentarily to show what 'works' means. Having established that the work that matters is the work written on the heart – faith – he drops the more cumbersome language of 'works written on the heart' in preference for the simpler and clearer term 'faith'.

This is further supported by chapter 7 in which the themes of 'works' (7:5, 8, 13, 15, 17–18, 20) and 'flesh' (7:5, 14, 18, 25; cf. 2:28; 3:20; 4:1) reappear together with the internal/external distinctions we discovered in chapters 2–4. Paul notes in Romans 7:5 that the reason why the law could not save was because 'while we were living in the flesh, our sinful passions, aroused by the law, were at work [enērgeito] in our members to bear fruit for death'.

The works of the law could not save because the law, rather than producing life, 'worked' sin.

So too he contrasts the internal and the external when he says:[26]

> For I delight in the law of God, in my inner being, but I see in my members another law waging war against the law of my mind and making me captive to the law of sin that dwells in my members. (Rom. 7:22–23)

And again: 'So then, I myself serve the law of God with my mind, but with my flesh I serve the law of sin' (Rom. 7:25).

Paul appears to be describing someone on whose heart the law has been written. Nevertheless, the flesh remains an obstacle to complete obedience. The central problem was that the law itself or the 'works of the law' could not rescue people from their 'body of death' (7:24) or from the 'flesh' (3:20). That rescue comes through 'Jesus Christ our Lord' (7:25). The ultimate purpose being 'that the righteous requirement of the law [to dikaiōma tou nomou] might be fulfilled in us, who walk not according to the flesh but according to the Spirit' (Rom. 8:3–4).

The remedy for the 'body of death' and the 'flesh' is neither the works of the law, nor is it repentance alone. The remedy is the blameless substitute/seed/Messiah promised through Abraham. As in Philippians and Colossians, to circumcision of the heart must be added the circumcision of the flesh/body through sharing in the death and resurrection of the Messiah by the Spirit.

In the first section of chapter 2 (2:1–10) Paul has sought to show that God gives to all 'according to works' irrespective of whether they

---

[26] For more on the internal–external distinction in chs. 7–8 see Deenick 2010.

are Jew or Gentile. The 'works' that matter are faith and repentance. And although Paul does not specifically mention circumcision, the connection is apparent through the OT language of hard-heartedness, which is intimately connected with circumcision.

Gentiles who do the law

In the next section (2:11–16) Paul continues his explanation of the works that matter, focusing now on those who 'do' (*poiētēs/poieō*) the law. Remarkably, Paul says that those who 'do' the law will be justified. As we have already noted, that statement has caused considerable debate leading to many different interpretations of what Paul means by 'the doers of the law' (*hoi poiētai nomou*) and by Gentiles who 'do the things of the law' (*ta tou nomou poiōsin*).

It should be said that not everybody views the two expressions as referring to the same people. As Moo highlights, those who think that in verses 14–16 Paul is referring to Christian Gentiles generally think the two expressions are referring to the same people.[27] While those who think verses 14–16 are referring to Gentiles who obey a kind of natural law tend to view the two expressions as referring to distinct groups.[28] But the latter drives a wedge between two almost identical phrases occurring right next to each other. As Gathercole observes, 'the parallel between οἱ ποιηταὶ νόμου (2.13) and τὰ τοῦ νόμου ποιῶσιν (2.14) is surely unmistakable on the grounds of proximity, syntactical/ logical connection, and verbal similarity'.[29] And, as we will see, the structure of the passage further suggests that the two expressions are equivalent.

The connections between 2:11–16 and 2:6–10 help to identify what Paul means by 'the doers of the law'. Paul's overarching point in 2:5–10 is that both Jew and Gentile will be treated alike: 'For God shows no partiality [*prosōpolēmpsia*]' (Rom. 2:11).

The same point is made in Deuteronomy 10:17. The people are called to circumcise their hearts because 'the LORD your God is God of gods and Lord of lords, the great, the mighty, and the awesome God, who is not partial [*ou thaumazei prosōpon*] and takes no bribe'.[30]

---

[27] E.g. Cranfield 2004: 155.

[28] Moo 1996: 149.

[29] Gathercole 2002a: 33–34; cf. Schreiner 1998: 120–122.

[30] *Prosōpolēmpsia* does not appear until the NT era and seems to be a direct translation of the Hebraism *lambanein prosōpon* (*yiśśā' pānîm*) in Deut. 10:17. See Lohse 1968.

The fact that God does not show favouritism to the fatherless, widow, sojourner (Deut. 10:18), Jew or Gentile (Rom. 2) is the motivation for the people to circumcise their hearts.

In Romans 2:12–16, in three statements that are in parallel with 2:11, each linked by 'for' (*gar*), Paul clarifies the way in which God does not show favouritism:

For [*gar*] God shows no partiality.

For [*gar*] all who have sinned without the law [*anomōs*] will also perish without the law [*anomōs*], and all who have sinned under the law [*en nomō*] will be judged by the law [*dia nomou*].

For [*gar*] it is not the hearers [*akroatai*] of the law who are righteous before God, but the doers [*poiētai*] of the law who will be justified.

For [*gar*] when Gentiles, who do not have the law, by nature do what the law requires [*ta tou nomou poiōsin*], they are a law to themselves, even though they do not have the law. They show that the work of the law is written on their hearts, while their conscience also bears witness, and their conflicting thoughts accuse or even excuse them on that day when, according to my gospel, God judges the secrets of men by Christ Jesus.

First of all, God does not show favouritism in that all who sin will be judged. Those who sin 'without the law' (*anomōs*) – that is, the Gentiles – will perish 'without the law'; while those who sin 'under the law' (*en nomō*) will be judged 'by the law' (*dia nomou*). Second, God does not show favouritism between Jews and Gentiles since it is not those who hear the law (the Jews) who are justified, but those who do the law who are justified. Third, God does not show favouritism in that Gentiles who 'do the things of the law' show that the 'work of the law' is written on their hearts.

There is no good reason to think that Paul is not continuing to employ the polarities he has been using in 2:6–10 (see Table 5.1 on p. 156).

In 2:12 Paul continues to speak about the right half of the spectrum – those who work evil (see Table 5.2 on p. 156).

If the comparison between 2:12 and 2:6–10 holds, then Paul is not speaking about those who sin *at all*, but rather those who sin in the manner of 2:8 and 2:9 – those who obey unrighteousness. Davies is

Table 5.1: Polarities in Romans 2:6–10

	Works good	Works evil
Jew	Glory and honour and peace (2:10)	Tribulation and distress (2:9)
Gentile	Glory and honour and peace (2:10)	Tribulation and distress (2:9)

Table 5.2: Polarities in Romans 2:12

	Sins
Jew/under the law	Judged 'by the law' (2:12)
Gentile/without the law	Perish 'without the law' (2:12)

probably correct then to interpret the aorist *hēmarton* (sins) as a 'complexive (constative) aorist', viewing the whole of life 'from its end'. That is, their life is characterized by sin.[31] God is impartial: Jew or Gentile will perish if their life is characterized by obedience to sin.

In 2:13 Paul shifts to the language of 'hearing' (*akroatēs*) and 'doing' (*poiētēs*). But again he appears to be working with the same contrasts as before, albeit with different language (see Table 5.3).

Table 5.3: Polarities in Romans 2:13

	Doer	Hearer only
Jew	Justified (2:13)	Not justified (2:13)
Gentile	Justified (2:13)	

What matters is not hearing the law or being a Jew but doing-the-law/ working-good. Once again justification does not fall along the Jew– Gentile axis but on the doing-not-doing axis. Verses 14–16 are then an exposition of the lower left-hand quadrant. But again it uses the same polarities (see Table 5.4 on p. 157).

The fact that Paul employs the same polarities in 2:11–16 as in 2:6–10 strongly suggests he is speaking about the same kind of person and trying to make the same point. That is, when Paul speaks of 'the doers of the law' and Gentiles who 'do the things of the law' he is referring to those who, as in 2:6–10, repent and seek God.

[31] Davies 1990: 60.

Table 5.4: Polarities in Romans 2:14–16

	Does the things of the law	[Does not do the things of the law]
Jew		
Gentile/'those not having the law'	'law to themselves' (2:14)	

That is also confirmed by the repeated reference to the 'day' of judgment occurring in both 2:16 and 2:5. In 2:5 the unrepentant and hard-hearted are storing up wrath for the 'day of wrath' (*hēmera orgēs*), while in 2:16 Paul refers to the Gentiles who will stand before God 'in the day [*en hēmera*] when God judges the secrets of men' (my tr.). Moreover, those who will be justified (*dikaiōthēsontai*; 2:13) in the 'righteous judgment of God' (*dikaiokrisias tou theou*; 2:5, my tr.) are those who 'do' the law.

So too the standard of judgment here in 2:16 reflects the standard of judgment in 2:5–10. Paul refers in 2:16 to the events

in the day when God judges the secrets of men according to my gospel through Christ Jesus. (my tr.)

en hēmera hote krinei ho theos ta krypta tōn anthrōpōn kata to euangelion mou dia Christou Iēsou.

Normally, the phrase 'according to my gospel through Christ Jesus' is understood to modify 'in the day when God judges' such that Paul's gospel announces *that* God will judge.[32] Yet it makes considerably more sense to understand it as modifying the entire preceding statement: 'in the day when God judges the secrets of men'. That is, Paul's gospel does not merely announce the *fact* that God will judge but the *manner* in which he will judge: God will judge the secrets of people's hearts according to (i.e. by the standard of) Paul's gospel through Jesus Christ.[33]

Of the eighty-four times Paul uses *euangelion* or its cognates it never *announces* judgment, though it is occasionally the *ground* of judgment. That is, one is judged by whether one 'obeys', 'perseveres in' or

---

[32] E.g. Barrett 1991: 51; Cranfield 2004: 163; Fitzmyer 1993: 312; Jewett 2006: 219; Käsemann 1994: 68; Kruse 2012: 134–135; Morris 1988: 128–129; Moo 1996: 155.

[33] Similarly, Dunn 1988: 1:103; cf. Jewett 2006: 218.

'disobeys' the gospel (e.g. Rom. 11:28; 1 Cor. 1:17–18; 15:1–2; 2 Cor. 2:12–17; 4:3–4; Col. 1:23). Even in 2 Thessalonians 1:8, which most clearly contains the threat of judgment, it is not that the gospel announces judgment, per se, but that judgment is established on the basis of whether or not one obeys the gospel. Moreover, in 1 Timothy 1:11, where Paul again uses the phrase 'according to the gospel' (*kata to euangelion*) in the context of a law–gospel contrast, Paul seems to be referring to the saving power of the gospel,[34] which is confirmed by his words in 1 Timothy 1:12–15 where we discover that Paul received mercy *in spite* of being a blasphemer.

That makes a great deal more sense of Paul's use of *euangelion* in Romans so far too. Paul has been set apart for the gospel of God (1:1), the gospel of God's Son (1:2), the gospel he is eager to preach to those in Rome (1:15), and of which he is not ashamed, 'for it is the power of God for salvation to everyone who believes, *to the Jew first and also to the Greek*' (1:16). Romans 2:16 is the first time since 1:16 that Paul returns to the *euangelion*, and he does not use that term again until 10:15. In 2:16 he has also returned to the theme of the gospel being not only for the Jew but also for the Gentile. It would be exceedingly strange in that context for Paul's reference to the 'good news' to be that Gentiles as well as Jews will be judged on the last day.

The same might be said for 'Christ' or 'Jesus'. Both remain entirely unused between 1:8 and 3:22 except for this verse. Everywhere else in Romans when Paul uses 'Jesus' or 'Christ' it is always good news. It appears then that here in 2:16 the gospel briefly makes a reappearance. So while the standard of judgment in 2:5–10 is repentance, in 2:11–16 it is faith in the gospel of Jesus Christ.

But how does that comport with Paul's statement that these Gentiles 'do the things of the law' (*ta tou nomou poiōsin*, my tr.)? A historically popular opinion has taken 'the things of the law' (*ta tou nomou*) as referring to a kind of natural law.[35] This view usually takes the *physei* (by nature) of *ta mē nomon echonta physei ta tou nomou poiōsin* (2:14) as connecting with what follows: 'doing the things of the law' (*ta tou nomou poiōsin*), thus supporting the view that the Gentiles' obedience is 'by nature'. However, *physei* could equally go with what precedes, 'those who do not have the law' (*ta mē nomon echonta*), and refer to the fact that the Gentiles (unlike the Jews) are without the law 'by nature'. Dunn argues that 'the syntax and balance of the sentence

---

34 Knight 1992: 89–91; Mounce 2000: 42–44.
35 E.g. Moo 1996: 150; Schreiner 1998: 122; Fitzmyer 1993: 306, 309–310.

require that φύσει be taken with what follows', noting that 'had Paul wanted to speak of 'those who do not have the law by nature' he would have put the φύσει *within* the phrase . . . preceding ἔχοντα'.[36] But as Kruse aptly points out, '[*physei*] is not within the following phrase either, and so neither interpretation can be supported by the position occupied by *physei*'.[37] Furthermore, Gathercole has produced additional examples where *physei* does not occur within the clause it qualifies.[38]

Taking *physei* to refer to the Gentiles 'not having the law' is supported by Paul's use of *physei* in 2:27 to describe the Gentiles who are 'by nature' uncircumcised (*hē ek physeōs akrobystia*).[39] So too Paul's use of *physei* elsewhere supports the same. In the majority of cases where Paul uses *physis* it is in the context of distinguishing between Jew and Gentile (Rom. 2:27; 11:21, 24; Gal. 2:15) or the question of identity in general (Gal. 4:8; Eph. 2:3).[40] Where the dative *physei* is specifically used, it is always used to refer to a 'state of being, never an action'.[41] Moreover, as Bird points out, Paul finished dealing with the 'natural law' in 1:18–32. His discussion now seems to be situated within the context of the Mosaic law, which is introduced in 2:12.[42]

Understanding that *physei* does not modify 'do the things of the law' clarifies that Paul is not talking about the Gentiles doing some kind of general moral good, and supports the idea that Paul is referring to faith – the very heart of what the law required. Paul's argument then is not that Gentiles who occasionally do moral things show themselves either to be justified or to be generally aware of God's

---

[36] Dunn 1988: 1:98. Maertens (2000: 511) highlights the parallel structure of vv. 14a and 14b:

ethnē	ta mē nomon echonta	physei	ta tou nomou poiōsin,
houtoi	nomon mē echontes	heautois	eisin nomos.

He argues that since *heautois* is normally taken with what follows, so also should *physei* be. But in all but one case in the NT where the dative of *heautou* follows a participle it is always taken with what precedes (Luke 12:21; John 19:17; 2 Cor. 5:19; Eph. 4:32; 5:19; Col. 3:13; 1 Tim. 6:19; Heb. 6:6; 2 Pet. 2:1; cf. Rom. 13:2).

[37] Kruse 2012: 136.

[38] Gathercole 2002a: 36. E.g. Wis. 13.1; Ign. *Eph.* 1.1; *Ant.* 8.152.

[39] Cranfield 2004: 156–157.

[40] Maertens 2000: 510. In two cases, as Maertens notes, *physis* is used to describe an action, Rom. 1:26 and 1 Cor. 11:14 (Rom. 11:24 could be added here too). Notably in all three instances *physis* does not refer to an action which is done *instinctively* but an action which defies/meets the *pattern* of nature. If that is the case, it also weakens the argument which sees these 'instinctive' actions as synonymous with the 'work of the law' written on the heart (e.g. Morris 1988: 126; Schreiner 1998: 122).

[41] Kruse 2012: 136. Rom. 2:27; Gal. 2:15; 4:8; Eph. 2:3.

[42] Bird 2007: 171.

laws. His argument runs along other lines. That is, one would never say that a Gentile (who does not have the law by nature) was justified simply by hearing the law (or turning up at the synagogue!), so why would one argue that for a Jew? Rather it is only when the Gentiles *do* the things of the law that they are justified (and that anyone considers them as such).

It appears then that 'do the things of the law' refers to faith. But before turning to the question of what it means that the law is written on their hearts, several comments ought to be made.

First, it could be argued that 'do the things of the law' refers not to faith itself but to the deeds that are the fruit of that faith.[43] However, that does not comport with the emphasis here on the 'secrets' of a person's heart. One would assume that if judgment was based on the deeds that revealed the inner character of faith, the state of a person's heart would not be so secret. It may also be that Paul is alluding to Deuteronomy 29:29, where 'The secret things [*krypta*] belong to the LORD our God, but the things that are revealed [*phanera*] belong to us and to our children for ever, that we may do all the words of this law.'

Within the context, Moses contrasts the one who says 'in his heart' 'I shall be safe, though I walk in the stubbornness of my heart' (Deut. 29:19) with the one in whose heart is the word of Yahweh (Deut. 30:14).[44] To 'do the law' is to respond with faith and repentance. Nevertheless, with Snodgrass, we must reject 'inadequate and cognitive definitions that have been given of faith'.[45] The kind of faith Paul has in mind is obedient faith (2:5) that earnestly seeks God, immortality and glory (2:7).

Second, this is not an 'anonymous faith' – a kind of faith without explicit knowledge of the Christ. It is not merely an abstract repentance that Paul is speaking of in 2:5, but an appropriation of the gospel (2:16). This will become clearer still when we consider circumcision of the heart below, which ties repentance and faith specifically with God's promises to Abraham. Similarly, as we will see in chapter 4, Paul anchors Gentile faith specifically in God's promises to Abraham.

Third, there is no need then to restrict this faith to NT believers either. As has been observed numerous times, what matters is faith in the Messiah/Christ promised through Abraham. That good news,

---

[43] Cranfield (2004: 156) notes both, but prefers the latter.
[44] The former is precisely the attitude of Paul's interlocutor in Rom. 2 (Berkley 2000: 99).
[45] Snodgrass 1986: 85; similarly, Davies 1990: 70–71.

though now revealed more fully, was announced beforehand to Abraham (Gal. 3:8) and anyone else, Jew or Gentile, who cared to listen.

The works of the law written on the heart

An examination of the meaning of the phrase 'the work of the law is written on their hearts' (*to ergon tou nomou grapton en tais kardiais autōn*; 2:15) also confirms the understanding of 'do the things of the law' as faith in the Messiah. As Paul has argued, hearing the law is not sufficient for justification: the law must be done. Paul illustrates the point by giving the example of a Gentile who 'does' the law. Such people show that the 'work of the law is written on their heart'.

I have already highlighted above the similarity between 2:15 and Jeremiah 31. I have also argued that the 'work of the law written on the heart' refers to faith. It is now possible to support that claim more fully. Several observations are useful at this point.

First, the work of the law written on the hearts of these Gentiles is clearly an imperfect work. The heart and conscience together not only defend (*apologeomai*) but also accuse (*katēgoreō*). At the very least, Paul does not envisage Gentiles being acquitted by their obedience. Nor does it seem likely that Paul could be referring to some kind of justification by the fruit of faith, since these Gentiles are also accused by their hearts.

Second, whoever these Gentiles are, they are not the same as the people in chapter 1. Gathercole is right to highlight Paul's statements about the hearts of those in chapter 1 where 'their foolish hearts were darkened' (*eskotisthē hē asynetos autōn kardia*; 1:21) and 'God gave them over to the desires of their hearts [*tais epithymiais tōn kardiōn autōn*]' (1:24, my tr.).[46] Again this speaks against viewing these Gentiles as obeying a kind of natural law since according to chapter 1 that simply does not happen.

Third, the fact that the hearts and consciences of these Gentiles defend them (*apologeomai*; 2:15) is remarkable given that Paul's interlocutor is without an excuse (*anapologētos*; 2:1), as is the person of chapter 1 (*anapologētos*; 1:20).[47] The reason why the person of chapter 1 is without an excuse is because he or she suppresses the truth of God's 'eternal power and divine nature'. What gives these Gentiles in 2:15 a defence then must be more than realizing that some things are right and other things are wrong, but must be integrally

---

[46] Gathercole 2002a: 43.
[47] Gathercole (ibid. 45) also links 2:15 to 1:20, though not to 2:1.

tied to the acknowledgment of God. The reason why the person of 2:1 is without an excuse is that he or she judges others without repenting. The defence of the Gentiles in 2:15 then presumably must also include an element of repentance.

Fourth, in contrast to the people of chapter 1 whose hearts are darkened, and the person of 2:1 who judges others, the heart and conscience of these Gentiles accuse them. Such an idea fits the theme of repentance we have found throughout. Although *katēgoreō* is not used in the NT in the sense of acknowledgment of sin, Clement uses it that way to describe Job's accusing himself before God as an act of humility (*1 Clem.* 17.4). For Clement, Job's self-accusation is of the same variety as David's words in Psalm 32 (*1 Clem.* 18).[48] Together with the preceding point then, these Gentiles, in contrast to those who suppress the truth and those who do not repent, find themselves sometimes obeying God and at other times being humbled before him on account of their disobedience.

Fifth, although Schreiner is right that Paul's description of the Gentiles who do the law as 'a law to themselves' seems like a curious description of those in whom Jeremiah 31 has been fulfilled,[49] perhaps the answer to Schreiner's objection is more obvious than it appears. While 'a law to themselves' may seem a baffling phrase, Paul goes on to explain what he means by it: 'They show that the work of the law is written on their hearts' (2:15). These Gentiles who by nature are without the law, who are not born into the law, are a law to themselves *in that* the law is written on their hearts. That is, 'a law to themselves' simply means that the law is embodied in these Gentiles – they take it to heart. In short then, 2:11–16 seems to continue the emphasis of 2:1–10 on repentance and faith in the gospel.

Keeping the law, circumcised in secret

We now turn to 2:25–29, where Paul again discusses those who are not Jewish but still in some sense practise the law:

> For circumcision indeed is of value if you obey the law [*nomon prassēs*], but if you break the law, your circumcision becomes

---

[48] Philo generally uses *katēgoreō* to refer to people being accused by others; however, on a few occasions he refers to the conscience 'accusing' people themselves (*Decal.* 86–87; *Spec.* 4.6). Similarly, *T. Jud.* 20.5 refers to a person who is 'burnt up' by the accusations of his own heart and so 'cannot raise his face to the judge' (*APOT*).

[49] Schreiner 1998: 123.

uncircumcision. So, if a man who is uncircumcised keeps the precepts of the law [*ta dikaiōmata tou nomou phylassē*], will not his uncircumcision be regarded as circumcision? Then he who is physically uncircumcised but keeps the law [*ton nomon telousa*] will condemn you who have the written code and circumcision but break the law. For no one is a Jew who is merely one outwardly, nor is circumcision outward and physical. But a Jew is one inwardly, and circumcision is a matter of the heart, by the Spirit, not by the letter. His praise is not from man but from God.

Again, whom Paul is referring to here is debated. There are three basic options: (1) the situation is hypothetical; (2) NT Gentile Christians; or (3) OT Gentile believers.

Once again, there is reason to believe that this section is connected with 2:6–10 and 2:11–16 and that the identity of the person being discussed is the same. Paul is continuing to investigate the Jew–Gentile and good–evil polarities introduced in both those earlier sections (see Table 5.5).

Table 5.5: Polarities in Romans 2:25–29

	Practise/keep/ complete the law	Break the law
Jew/'circumcised in the flesh'		Uncircumcised
Gentile/'uncircumcised (in the flesh)'	Circumcised heart	

Moreover, much of the language that Paul has used earlier can be found in this section also. For instance, Paul refers in 2:29 to 'the Jew in secret, and circumcision of the heart in the Spirit not by the law' (*ho en tō kryptō Ioudaios, kai peritomē kardias en pneumati ou grammati*, my tr.). Earlier in 2:16 Paul noted that God is the judge of the 'secrets' (*krypta*) of people's hearts. It seems likely that Paul wants us to understand that the 'secrets of men' (2:16) and being a 'secret Jew' (2:29) are related: when God judges the '*secrets* of men' what God is looking for is '*secret* Jewishness'. The pairing of that idea with 'circumcision of the heart' indicates that Paul is referring to the internalization of the very core of Judaism. I have argued above that God will judge the *secrets* of people's hearts according to (i.e. by the standard of) Paul's gospel through Jesus Christ. Thus the implication is that the '*secret* Jewishness' Paul is speaking of amounts to faith in the gospel through Jesus Christ.

This case is strengthened by considering how Paul has used *kardia* language through chapter 2.[50] Paul's interlocutor is storing up wrath for himself 'on the day of wrath' (2:5; cf. 2:16) on account of his 'hard and impenitent heart' (2:5). Similarly, the Gentiles who 'do' the law show the work of the law written on their hearts (2:15), while in 2:29 Paul explicitly links *kardia* language with circumcision when he refers to circumcision of the *heart*. We have seen already that a 'hard and impenitent' heart is the opposite in both the OT and NT of a circumcised heart. Clearly the two are connected here again. I have also argued that the idea of the law written on the heart conveys the notion of repentance and faith in God's promise to Abraham and his seed to which the law pointed. Against that background, it makes sense to understand that what Paul means to say here is that the kind of circumcision that matters is the inner circumcision of repentance.

The language of judgment also links 2:1–10, 2:11–16 and 2:25–29. The hard-hearted and unrepentant will not escape the judgment of God (2:3). God will judge the secrets of people's hearts 'on that day' (2:16). Here the emphasis shifts to the uncircumcised Gentiles who 'complete' (*teleō*) the law judging the circumcised Jews who transgress the law.

It is difficult to know, as Moo points out, whether Paul means that these righteous Gentiles 'will be appointed as judges by God' or whether their obedience to the law will of itself condemn disobedient Jews.[51] One thing, however, is certain: it cannot mean that Gentiles who occasionally obey the law will somehow by their occasional obedience judge Jews who also occasionally obey the law. Whatever 'keeping', 'practising' and 'completing' the law means here, it is more than occasional. Moreover, in 1 Corinthians 6:2 when Paul expresses a similar view, it is the 'saints' who will judge the world.[52] That supports the idea that the Gentiles Paul has in mind here are believers (rather than hypothetical ones). Despite the shift from *God's* judging, to God's judging in some sense *through* Gentile believers, the point remains that judgment links all three sections. And more importantly,

---

[50] Also Rom. 1:21, 24–25.

[51] Moo 1996: 172.

[52] So too when Jesus refers to the people of Nineveh and the queen of Sheba judging 'this generation', they attain that prerogative on account of their repentance (Matt. 12:41–42).

the standard of judgment remains the same: a soft, repentant, law-written-on, circumcised heart.

So too Paul uses three phrases here that like 'working good' (2:9) and 'do the things of the law' (2:14) at first glance appear to suggest wholesale obedience to the law:[53] 'practise the law' (*nomon prassēs*), 'keep the righteous requirements of the law' (*ta dikaiōmata tou nomou phylassē*) and 'complete the law' (*ton nomon telousa*).[54] We are now in a position to consider precisely what Paul means by these phrases.

First of all, the parallelism between these three phrases suggests that whatever they mean, they each refer to the same thing. As Rosner notes, 'Looking for distinctions among the three verbs is to indulge in overinterpretation. In Romans 2:25–27 Paul uses them in such close proximity, suggesting that the change of verbs may be put down to stylistic variation.'[55]

Second, as Barrett astutely observes, whatever it means to keep or do the law it cannot include keeping the circumcision command. He notes, regarding 2:16, that whatever it is that these Gentiles do it is

> clearly not the detailed precepts of the Mosaic code: in *vv.* 26f. Paul says that the 'uncircumcision' (which in the nature of the case does not observe the ritual law) may keep the righteous requirements of the law, and fulfil it.[56]

Third, 'keep[ing] the righteous requirements of the law' (*ta dikaiōmata tou nomou phylassē*) can hardly be hypothetical or impossible since God says that Abraham did it: 'and he kept my ordinances and my commands and my righteous requirements and my laws' (*kai ephylaxen ta prostagmata mou kai tas entolas mou kai ta dikaiōmata mou kai ta nomima mou*; Gen. 26:5, my tr.). So too, as we have seen before, a very similar thing is predicated of Zechariah and Elizabeth: 'And they were both righteous before God, walking blamelessly in all the commandments [*dikaiōmasin*] and statutes of the Lord' (Luke 1:6). For Paul to speak about 'keeping' and 'doing' the law is, in that sense, no different from the numerous phrases we have seen in the OT that speak about being blameless – in the context of repentance and faith in the blameless Messiah to come, those claims were true. Paul's

---

[53] The following are my translations.
[54] E.g. Moo 1996: 168–171.
[55] Rosner 2013: 95.
[56] Barrett 1991: 49.

particular concern here is to show that it is true not only of Jews but also of Gentiles.[57]

Paul's point is hardly novel. One need only think of the many Gentiles in the OT who came to faith in the God of Abraham. Job was blameless (Job 1:1). Nebuchadnezzar was humbled by God after 'walking' in pride (Dan. 4:37). Ruth proclaimed her allegiance to Yahweh (Ruth 2:16–17). The people of Nineveh repented (Jon. 3:5–10). Naaman declared his allegiance to Yahweh (2 Kgs 5:15–19).[58] In contrast to these OT examples of Gentiles being included in God's promises to Abraham by their faith, there are no examples of Gentiles being included in God's promises to Abraham by their perfect obedience, nor is there any suggestion in the OT that if that were attainable they would be. The condition for their inclusion was always repentance and trust in Yahweh and identification with what God was doing through Abraham.

Fourth, the language of 'keep[ing] the righteous requirements of the law' is present in many significant OT contexts. It is used first of all in contexts referring to the law of Moses. Rosner notes:

> The two words *phylassō* (keep) and *dikaiōmata* (righteous requirements) appear together more than seventy times in the LXX. Almost uniformly these verses refer to keeping the *dikaiōmata* of the Lord . . . , meaning doing the Law of Moses.[59]

But the same language is also used in many contexts that speak of either circumcision of the heart or a new heart/spirit. In Deuteronomy 10 after calling the people 'to keep [*phylassesthai*] the commandments of the Lord your God and his righteous requirements [*dikaiōmata*]' (Deut. 10:13, my tr.), Yahweh calls on the people to circumcise their

---

[57] Paul also says in Rom. 8:4 that in Jesus God condemned sin 'in the flesh', 'in order that the righteous requirements of the law might be fulfilled [*to dikaiōma tou nomou plērōthē*] in us who do not walk [*peripatousin*] according to the flesh but according to the Spirit' (my tr.). The shift from 'do' to 'fulfil' may be significant. For instance, Rosner (2013: 96–97), following Betz (1979: 275), observes that for Paul, Christians do not 'do' the Torah but 'fulfil' it. To be sure, there is a difference between Abraham's 'keeping' the *dikaiōmata* and Christians 'fulfilling' them. Abraham kept the *dikaiōmata* (and was blameless) as he looked forward in faith to what God would do through the blameless Messiah, while the *dikaiōmata* (and blamelessness) are fulfilled *in* Christians through the work of the Messiah who has come. Moo (1996: 170, n. 21) rightly notes, 'Paul reserves this language for the eschatological "filling up" of the basic demand of the law that has been made possible with the coming of Christ.'

[58] Davies 1990: 56.

[59] Rosner 2013: 96.

hearts and no longer be stiff-necked (Deut. 10:16). In Deuteronomy 30 Yahweh promises to circumcise his people's hearts so that they will 'keep and to do [*phylassesthai kai poiein*] all his commandments and his righteous requirements [*dikaiōmata*]' (30:10, my tr.). In Ezekiel 36:25–27, Yahweh promises to cleanse his people, to give them a new heart and a new spirit, to give them a heart of flesh in the place of a heart of stone, to put his Spirit within them so that they will 'walk in my righteous requirements [*dikaiōmasin*] and keep and do [*phylaxēsthe kai poiēsēte*] my judgments' (my tr.).[60]

Most striking of all, however, is Ezekiel 18:

> If a man is righteous and does what is just and right – if he does not eat upon the mountains or lift up his eyes to the idols of the house of Israel, does not defile his neighbour's wife or approach a woman in her time of menstrual impurity, does not oppress anyone, but restores to the debtor his pledge, commits no robbery, gives his bread to the hungry and covers the naked with a garment, does not lend at interest or take any profit, withholds his hand from injustice, executes true justice between man and man, walks in my statutes, and keeps my rules by acting faithfully [LXX: *kai ta dikaiōmata mou pephylaktai tou poiēsai auta*] – he is righteous [*dikaios houtos estin*]; he shall surely live, declares the Lord GOD. (Ezek. 18:5–9)

The context also speaks about the *anomos* (lawless) who turns from his *anomiōn* (lawlessness) in order to 'do' (*poieō*) and 'keep' (*phylassō*) the commandments and 'do' righteousness (*dikaiosynē*; 18:5, 17, 21, 27). That person will live. Indeed, that person is righteous (*dikaios*). The term *anomos* and its cognates occur a total of eleven times in Ezekiel 18, but it is also a term that has considerable significance in Romans 2 where those who sin *anomōs* will perish *anomōs*, and in 4:7 where the blessed person's *anomiai* (lawless deeds) are forgiven. In Ezekiel *anomos* is remedied by repentance, while in Romans 2 and 4, it is remedied by faith.

Ezekiel 18 ends with a call for the people to repent and make a new heart and new spirit: 'Repent and turn from all your transgressions, lest iniquity be your ruin. Cast away from you all the transgressions that you have committed, and make yourselves a new heart and a new spirit!' (Ezek. 18:30–31).

---

[60] Berkley 2000: 93. See also Ezek. 11:19–20.

Although Ezekiel 18 does not use the language of circumcision, it nevertheless highlights the need for repentance and a new heart/spirit. Within the context of Ezekiel and within the broader context of the Abrahamic covenant and Deuteronomy 10 and 30 and Leviticus 26, the means by which that new heart/spirit is appropriated is through faith in God's promise to Abraham.

Fifth, the result of 'keep[ing] the righteous requirements of the law' is that 'his uncircumcision will be regarded as circumcision' (*hē akrobystia autou eis peritomēn logisthēsetai*). The language of 'reckoning' (*logizomai*) links Paul's thought here with chapter 4.[61] In chapter 4 Paul uses *logizomai* eleven times, all as part of his argument that God reckons faith as righteousness. Admittedly, Paul twice uses *logizomai* in chapters 2–4 not referring to God's 'reckoning righteousness' (2:3; 3:28). But Paul's use in 2:26 shares a similarity with chapter 4 in that a transaction of sorts is in view: just as faith is reckoned as righteousness, uncircumcision is reckoned as circumcision.

The point of comparison between 2:26–29 and chapter 4 is not immediately clear. Not least because in 4:4 Paul envisages two ways that something may be reckoned: either 'according to grace' (*kata charin*, my tr.) or 'according to an obligation' (*kata opheilēma*, my tr.). The mere use of *logizomai* in 2:26 then does not help us to determine whether here Paul means that happens 'by grace' or 'by obligation'. The situation is not helped by the fact that in chapter 2 it is *uncircumcision* that is reckoned as *circumcision*, whereas in chapter 4 it is *faith* that is reckoned as *righteousness*. What is the relationship between the pairings of uncircumcision–faith and circumcision–righteousness? These dissimilarities raise the question as to whether anything meaningful can be discerned from the comparison.

There are, however, good reasons for believing that a connection between 2:26–29 and chapter 4 is intended. To be reckoned as circumcised clearly means to be considered in some sense a genuine descendant of Abraham and heir with him of God's promise. That same theme dominates chapter 4. In chapter 4 the uncircumcised share in God's promise to Abraham and his 'offspring'. Abraham is the father of all who believe, circumcised or uncircumcised (4:11–12). And it is those who share Abraham's faith, irrespective of their physical descent, who are heirs with him of God's promise (4:13–16).

---

[61] Dunn 1988: 1:122; Schreiner 1998: 141; Cranfield 2004: 173, n. 4; cf. Moo 1996: 169, n. 17.

Thematically then the two chapters are almost identical: they speak of the uncircumcised being included in God's promise to Abraham. In chapter 2 that takes place 'if a man who is uncircumcised keeps the precepts of the law'. In chapter 4 that takes place 'by faith'. The similarity of Paul's argument in 2:26–29 and chapter 4 suggests that the slightly longer construction 'if a man who is uncircumcised keeps the precepts of the law, will not his uncircumcision be regarded as circumcision?' (*ean oun hē akrobystia ta dikaiōmata tou nomou phylassē, ouch hē akrobystia autou eis peritomēn logisthēsetai?*; 2:26) is roughly equivalent to 'his faith is counted as righteousness' (*logizetai hē pistis autou eis dikaiosynēn*; 4:5). That is, it is not uncircumcision that is equivalent to faith, but 'keeping the righteous requirements of the law'.

Sixth, that seems to be confirmed by Paul's reference to 'he who is physically uncircumcised but keeps the law' (*hē ek physeōs akrobystia ton nomon telousa*; 2:27) who will judge the Jew who is a transgressor. The use of *teleō* is curious. Its meaning is generally 'complete'. It is a verb Paul uses only five times and never in relation to the law.[62] Notably it is derived from the same *tel-* root as *teleioō* and *teleios*. To find the idea of completion/perfection in close connection with circumcision is by now hardly surprising. This is not to suggest that the two verbs, *teleō* and *teleioō*, mean the same thing. Schippers notes regarding the Greek background to the terms that *teleō* means 'to bring to a *telos*, to complete' and 'anything that has reached its *telos* is *teleios*'.[63] Of particular interest is Paul's comment in Romans 10:4: 'Christ is the end of the law for righteousness for all who believe' (*telos gar nomou Christos eis dikaiosynēn panti tō pisteuonti*, my tr.). In the light of the earlier study of *teleios* language it seems unlikely that Paul means that Christ is simply the end/finish of the law but rather that Christ is the purpose/goal of all that the law embodied.[64] So too the fact that Christ is the *telos* of the law makes it unlikely that 'completing' the law refers simply to obeying the totality of it.[65] Rather, the Gentile who 'completes' the law is the one who appropriates by faith the blameless substitute/seed/Messiah foreshadowed in the law, and hence the one who is brought to perfection/

---

[62] Rosner 2013: 96.

[63] Schippers 1986: 59.

[64] Of course, we do not have to decide absolutely between 'end' and 'goal', since now that Christ (the goal of the law) has come, the law is at an end in a salvation-historical sense (Moo 1996: 641).

[65] E.g. Räisänen 2010: 103.

completion in him.[66] That is, *circumcision* of the heart does not refer to general obedience to the law but specifically to an appropriation of God's promises to Abraham of blamelessness/righteousness through a blameless seed/Messiah.

It is now possible to summarize Paul's view of circumcision in chapter 2. Paul argues that the appropriation of the Abrahamic covenant that matters is not the appropriation in the flesh, through physical circumcision (or physical descent), but the appropriation in the heart. Those who repented and believed God's promise to Abraham were the true descendants of Abraham and the true co-heirs with him. Physical circumcision alone without a commensurate trust in God who raises the dead and in his Messiah Jesus leaves a person with the obligation to be blameless/righteous but without the means to achieve it. This is not to say that circumcision and the law were useless. On the contrary, the 'advantage' of circumcision and the law, according to Paul, was that they preached the gospel. They were the 'words of God', they bore witness to the righteousness of God, but they did not accomplish it. In the words of Calvin, 'the gospel did not so supplant the entire law as to bring forward a different way of salvation. Rather, it confirmed and satisfied whatever the law had promised, and gave substance to the shadows.'[67]

Romans 2 and the problem of Israel

This emphasis on repentance and faith is confirmed by looking at 2:17–24 and 3:1–20. In that section Paul alludes to an enormous range of OT texts, many of which refer to circumcision. Indeed, it is striking that so much has been written on the situation within first-century Judaism as the background to what Paul is saying, when Paul seems much more interested in anchoring his analysis in the OT. To be sure, the two are not mutually exclusive. Yet, as we will see, the problem Paul identifies did not originate in the first century, nor is it merely the result of the coming of Christ. It had its roots in the OT.

---

[66] Wright (2001: 137) also notes the connection between 2:25–29 and 10:4–11 and says of the latter, 'Paul is using Deuteronomy 30 . . . as his basis for saying that when someone believes the Christian gospel, that person is thereby "keeping the law", whether or not they have heard it, and despite the fact that in several points such as circumcision they are not doing what the law apparently required.'

[67] Calvin 2006: 2.9.4.

Jeremiah 9

In verses 17–18 Paul alludes to Jeremiah 9: 'But if you call yourself a Jew and rely on the law and boast [*kauchasai*] in God and know his will [*ginōskeis to thelēma*] and approve what is excellent, because you are instructed from the law . . .'[68]

The similarities with Jeremiah 9 are apparent:

> Thus says the LORD: 'Let not the wise man boast [*kauchasthō*] in his wisdom, let not the mighty man boast [*kauchasthō*] in his might, let not the rich man boast [*kauchasthō*] in his riches, but let him who boasts [*kauchōmenos*] boast [*kauchasthō*] in this, that he understands and knows me, that I am the LORD who practises steadfast love, justice, and righteousness in the earth. For in these things I delight [*thelēma*], declares the LORD.
>
> 'Behold, the days are coming, declares the LORD, when I will punish all those who are circumcised merely in the flesh – Egypt, Judah, Edom, the sons of Ammon, Moab, and all who dwell in the desert who cut the corners of their hair, for all these nations are uncircumcised, and all the house of Israel are uncircumcised in heart.' (Jer. 9:23–26)

The theme and vocabulary of boasting dominates Jeremiah 9.[69] The object of the boast is also the same in both Jeremiah 9 and Romans 2. In Romans 2 the person boasts in God. In Jeremiah 9 God calls his people to boast that they understand and know him. In Romans 2 the person boasts in knowing God's will (*ginōskeis to thelēma*). In Jeremiah 9 God calls his people to boast that they know his delight/ will (*thelēma*)[70] in mercy, justice and righteousness. But Jeremiah 9 also shares with Romans 2 an interest in circumcision and, more particularly, circumcision of the heart.

What is unexpected, however, is that Paul's interlocutor in Romans 2 fulfils the positive half of Jeremiah 9 – the boast in knowing God. Paul does not accuse his opponent of boasting in his wisdom or might or riches but in knowing God and knowing God's delight/will. Yet the implication in Romans 2 is that the boast is empty. Paul says as

---

[68] Berkley 2000: 87–90; Dunn 1988: 110; Fitzmyer 1993: 316; Käsemann 1994: 69.

[69] On the links between these two passages see Berkley 2000: 87–89.

[70] The MT has *ḥpṣ* which generally means 'delight'. The LXX translates this as *thelēma*, which aligns with Paul's statement in 2:18 and which means 'will', or perhaps 'wish', more than 'delight'.

much in verse 23: 'You who boast in the law dishonour God by breaking the law.'

Verse 23 represents a subtle but significant shift from boasting 'in God' (*en theō*) to boasting 'in the law' (*en nomō*). It appears that the ground of the boast of Paul's interlocutor that he knows God is his possession of the law. That is confirmed by a closer look at verses 17–18:

> But if you **call yourself a Jew** and **rely on the law** and **boast in God** and **know his will** and **approve what is excellent**, because you are instructed from the law . . .

> *Ei de sy **Ioudaios eponomazē** kai **epanapauē nomō** kai **kauchasai en theō** kai **ginōskeis to thelēma** kai **dokimazeis ta diapheronta** katēchoumenos ek tou nomou . . .*

Paul strings together five present indicatives that express his interlocutor's confidence. Those five are followed by the participial phrase 'because you are instructed from the law' (*katēchoumenos ek tou nomou*). While it is possible to connect that phrase with only the last of the five present indicatives, it makes more sense to connect it with the whole sentence: Paul's interlocutor calls himself a Jew, rests in the law, boasts in God, knows the will of God, discerns what is superior *because* he is instructed in the law.[71] But as both Paul and Jeremiah argue, circumcision of the heart in repentance and faith, not possession of the law, is the sign that a person knows God.

Isaiah 42

Next Paul appears to draw on Isaiah 42 when he says in 2:19–20:[72]

---

[71] Curiously Moo (1996: 161) connects the participial phrase with the two indicatives in v. 18 but does not extend it back to the three indicatives in v. 17 (similarly, Schreiner 1998: 130; Cranfield 2004: 166; Fitzmyer 1993: 317). But all five are strung together by *kai*. Dunn (1988: 1:108–109, 111) observes that vv. 17–18 and 19–20 share a common structure, both climaxing in participial statements about the law. Yet he still links only the participial phrase in v. 18 with the two indicatives in v. 18.

[72] Jewett 2006: 225; Schreiner 1998: 130–131. Berkley (2000: 74–77) does not think Paul is using Isa. 42 in the construction of his argument but merely 'echoing' it. Berkley has a number of criteria for assessing intertextuality. Isa. 42 meets all but two. It shares common vocabulary, clustered vocabulary, links with other OT texts present in Romans 2, and shared themes. However, Isa. 42 does not meet Berkley's criterion that a reference to Isa. 42 should appear elsewhere in Paul. But it seems unfair that Paul should not be allowed to use a text only once. Additionally, according to Berkley, Isa. 42 also does not help explain Paul's exegetical path. I would suggest that Isa. 42 *does* help explain Rom. 2.

and if you are sure that you yourself are a guide to the blind [*typhlōn*], a light [*phōs*] to those who are in darkness [*skotei*], an instructor of the foolish, a teacher of children, having in the law the embodiment of knowledge and truth . . .

In Isaiah 42 God is speaking of his servant in whom his soul delights, upon whom he has put his Spirit and through whom he will bring forth justice for the nations. This servant has been called in righteousness and Yahweh will give him as

> a covenant for the people,
>   a light [*phōs*] for the nations,
>   to open the eyes that are blind [*typhlōn*],
>   to bring out the prisoners from the dungeon,
>   from the prison those who sit in darkness [*skotei*].
>   (Isa. 42:6–7)

The vocabulary links between Isaiah 42 and Romans 2 are strong with the triad of 'blind . . . darkness . . . light' occurring in the OT only in Isaiah 42.[73] Also linking the two passages is Isaiah's emphasis on Yahweh's establishing righteousness and justice, together with Yahweh's covenant purpose to bless the nations, not just Israel. Moreover, as in Romans 2, Isaiah 42 ends with accusations against God's own people.

After promising that his servant will open the eyes of the blind, in Isaiah 42:18–25 Yahweh goes on to accuse his 'servant' Israel of being deaf and blind. The problem, as in Romans 2, is bound up with the law:

> The LORD was pleased, for his righteousness' sake,
>   to magnify his law and make it glorious.
> But this is a people plundered and looted;
>   they are all of them trapped in holes
>   and hidden in prisons;
> they have become plunder with none to rescue,
>   spoil with none to say, 'Restore!'
> Who among you will give ear to this,
>   will attend and listen for the time to come?

---

[73] Berkley 2000: 75. Clearly the language of teaching (*didaskalos*, *paideutēs*, etc.) is missing in Isa. 42, but the notion of instruction is very much present.

Who gave up Jacob to the looter,
and Israel to the plunderers?
Was it not the LORD, against whom we have sinned,
in whose ways they would not walk,
and whose law they would not obey?

(Isa. 42:21–24)

The implication of Paul's argument seems to be that the Jews of his day had assumed to themselves the honour of being God's servant and fulfilling God's promise to Abraham – opening the eyes of the blind and being a light to the nations – but just as in Isaiah's day, the people were trapped in sin.

Jeremiah 7

Paul goes on to make the same point with a series of questions drawn from Jeremiah 7. Paul asks, 'you then who teach others, do you not teach yourself? While you preach against stealing, do you steal? You who say that one must not commit adultery, do you commit adultery? You who abhor idols, do you rob temples?' (2:21–22).

Berkley has successfully shown how Paul depends here on Jeremiah 7.[74] The two share a common triad of sins: stealing (*kleptō*), committing adultery (*moicheuō*) and temple robbery (*hierosyleō*). The first two appear obviously in Jeremiah 7:8:

But if you trust in deceptive words, whereby you will not benefit, and murder and commit adultery [*moichasthe*] and steal [*kleptete*] and swear wrongly and offer incense to the goddess Baal and go after foreign gods that you do not know . . . (NETS)

The third term in Romans 2 (*hierosyleō*) is more unusual.[75] Its literal meaning appears to be 'temple robbery', but it seems also to have developed the more general meaning of 'commit sacrilege'[76] or 'religious transgression generally'.[77]

[74] Ibid. 82–87. Barrett (1991: 54) notes a similarity but takes it no further.
[75] Stealing and adultery occur together relatively frequently (e.g. Ps. 50:18; Matt. 19:18; Mark 10:19; Luke 18:20; Rom. 13:9; *1 Clem.* 35.8; *Did.* 2.2; *Post.* 82; *Conf.* 163; *Ios.* 84; *Decal.* 36; *Spec.* 4.1), often directly reflecting the Ten Commandments. However, the two rarely occur with *hierosyleō*. The three do occur together in Philo (*Conf.* 163; cf. *Ios.* 84), while *Pss Sol.* 8.8–13 speaks of both adultery and 'plunder[ing] the sanctuary of God' but stealing is missing, and *T. Levi* 14.4–8 refers to plundering and stealing offerings and adultery (Berkley 2000: 83–84).
[76] BDAG 471.
[77] Schrenk 1965: 255.

What Paul means by *hierosyleō* in Romans 2 is not immediately clear.[78] Most peculiar of all is that Paul's use of *hierosyleō* seems to break the pattern established by the preceding three questions. A table of 2:21–22 highlights the problem (see Table 5.6).

Table 5.6: Word pairings in Romans 2:21–22

	Pairing
ho oun didaskōn heteron seauton ou didaskeis?	teach/teach
ho kēryssōn mē kleptein klepteis?	steal/steal
ho legōn mē moicheuein moicheueis?	commit adultery/commit adultery
ho bdelyssomenos ta eidōla hierosyleis?	abhor idols/rob temples?

In the three preceding questions the last word matches the earlier part of the question. Not so with the last question. Instead, we have 'temple robbery' matched with idolatry. While on the surface it may appear that Paul is straightforwardly condemning those who say they abhor idols but then steal idols from other temples, Jeremiah 7 suggests Paul has something else in mind.

Although the precise term *hierosyleō* does not appear in the LXX of Jeremiah 7, the parallels are significant.[79] Idolatry is clearly in focus in 7:9 when Jeremiah accuses the people of making offerings to Baal and going after other gods. But in addition, this duplicitous practice of claiming to know God but stealing, committing adultery and worshipping other gods is described in Jeremiah 7:11 as turning God's house into 'a den of robbers'.

So while Paul is using a term not present in Jeremiah 7 it seems clear that it forms the background to what he is saying. Moreover, in the three other questions in Romans 2:21–22, Paul uses a single word to convey the indictment: *didaskō*, *kleptō* and *moicheuō*. This raises the question 'What other single word could Paul have employed that would be more precisely suited to summarize the condemnation of Jeremiah 7?'

Perhaps most compelling of all is that Jeremiah 7 also shares with Romans 2 the denunciation of Israel's stiffening their neck (Jer. 7:26; cf. Rom. 2:5). Rather than continuing in sin and trusting in the temple

[78] Numerous proposals have been made (see the brief survey in Kruse 2012: 149–151). Establishing the background of *hierosyleis* in Jer. 7 helps solve the riddle.

[79] 'Teaching' does not occur in Jer. 7 either. But Berkley (2000: 84) is right to point out that Paul is not here quoting from Jeremiah; rather, 'his text is laced with the language of the originating text'.

cult, the people of Jeremiah's day needed to turn from their sin to God. Yahweh says to them:

> For in the day that I brought them out of the land of Egypt, I did not speak to your fathers or command them concerning burnt offerings and sacrifices. But this command I gave them: 'Obey my voice, and I will be your God, and you shall be my people. And walk in all the way that I command you, that it may be well with you.' But they did not obey or incline their ear, but walked in their own counsels and the stubbornness of their evil hearts, and went backwards and not forwards. (Jer. 7:22–24)

What Jeremiah is countering is a belief that the practice of the sacrificial/legal cult could compensate for a lack of repentance and trust in Yahweh. In the same vein, what Paul is countering is not so much punctilious observance of the law, nor a national elitism that excludes Gentiles, but a belief that the practice of the sacrificial/legal cult could compensate for a lack of repentance and trust in the Messiah/seed promised through Abraham. In the words of 2:4, 'God's kindness is meant to lead you to repentance'.

Isaiah 52 and Ezekiel 36

This leads to Paul's final indictment in verses 23–24:

> You who boast in the law dishonour God by breaking the law. For, as it is written, 'The name of God is blasphemed among the Gentiles because of you [to gar onoma tou theou di' hymas blasphēmeitai en tois ethnesin].'

In this last example, Paul's use of the phrase 'as it is written' (kathōs gegraptai) demonstrates that he is quoting directly from the OT. The quotation appears to come from the LXX of Isaiah 52:5: 'Because of you my name is always blasphemed among the nations [to onoma mou blasphēmeitai en tois ethnesin]' (my tr.).

We have already seen in chapter 3 that the context of Isaiah 52:5 contains a reference to circumcision:

> Awake, awake,
>   put on your strength, O Zion;
>   put on your beautiful garments,
>   O Jerusalem, the holy city;

176

> for there shall no more come into you
>   the uncircumcised and the unclean.
> Shake yourself from the dust and arise;
>   be seated, O Jerusalem;
> loose the bonds from your neck,
>   O captive daughter of Zion.

For thus says the LORD: 'You were sold for nothing, and you shall be redeemed without money.' (Isa. 52:1–3)

The redemption spoken of in Isaiah 52:3 will be by Yahweh's servant (Isa. 52:13 – 53:12), who will bear his people's sorrows and be wounded for their transgressions (53:4–5), whose life will be an offering for sin (53:10), and who by his righteousness will 'make many to be accounted righteous' (53:11). Isaiah 53 then highlights many of the themes we have seen bound up with circumcision; in particular, the promise of a blameless seed of Abraham through whom blamelessness would come to God's people.

As Berkley argues, there are also echoes in Romans 2:24 of Ezekiel 36, which is seen particularly in the repeated references to Israel's profaning (*bebēloō*) God's name among the nations (Ezek. 36:20–23).[80] The remedy for that comes in Ezekiel 36:24–27:

> I will take you from the nations and gather you from all the countries and bring you into your own land. I will sprinkle clean water on you, and you shall be clean from all your uncleannesses, and from all your idols I will cleanse you. And I will give you a new heart, and a new spirit I will put within you. And I will remove the heart of stone from your flesh and give you a heart of flesh. And I will put my Spirit within you, and cause you to walk in my statutes and be careful to obey my rules.

This promise shares the language of heart and spirit with Romans 2 as well as the notion of an interior spirituality.[81] Similarly, Paul speaks of the one who 'keeps the precepts of the law' (*ta dikaiōmata tou nomou phylassē*; 2:26), while in Ezekiel Yahweh promises that they will 'walk in my statutes [*en tois dikaiōmasin*] and be careful to obey

---

[80] Ibid. 90–94, 137–140; similarly, Dunn 1988: 1:115; Morris 1988: 138; cf. Moo 1996: 166, n. 49; Schreiner 1998: 134–135.
[81] Berkley 2000: 92–93.

[*phylaxesthe*] my rules'.[82] That is not an impossible goal. We have already observed that 'walking blamelessly' in Yahweh's 'statutes' (*dikaiōma*) is precisely what Zechariah and Elizabeth did.

Psalm 51

Before turning to Paul's discussion of circumcision in chapter 4 and drawing all these threads together, we will consider several other OT citations in 3:1–20, but particularly Paul's quotation from Psalm 51. At the beginning of chapter 3 Paul asks the question 'Then what advantage has the Jew? Or what is the value of circumcision?' (3:1). The perhaps surprising answer is 'Much in every way.'

In 3:4 Paul discusses the benefits that existed for the people of God. If circumcision itself was not a benefit (*ipso facto*) then what advantage was there in being a Jew? Paul's answer is their advantage consisted in being 'entrusted' (*episteuthēsan*) with the 'oracles/words of God' (*ta logia tou theou*). Yet the 'unfaithfulness' (*apisteō*) of some may seem to call into question the 'faithfulness' (*pistis*) of God and his words. But far from being undermined by the unfaithfulness of Israel, God's words are in fact justified by the unfaithfulness of Israel.

Paul proves that point with a quotation from Psalm 51:4:

> That you may be justified in your words,
> and prevail when you are judged.
> (Rom. 3:4)[83]

The context of the original quotation is astonishing: it is not only some who are unfaithful, but even David himself, the great king, suffers from this affliction that justifies God's words in the law. In Psalm 51 David is appealing for God's mercy to 'blot out' his transgressions and cleanse him from sin. His sin is ever before him. He was

> brought forth in iniquity,
> and in sin did my mother conceive me.
> (Ps. 51:5)

Paul's reference to David sets up perfectly his string of quotes from the OT in 3:10–18 which likewise establish that 'all, both Jews and Greeks, are under [the power of] sin' (Rom. 3:9). God's 'words'

---

[82] Ibid. 93.
[83] The difference between *logia* (3:2) and *logois* (3:4) is probably no more than stylistic, the latter reflecting the original quotation.

establish the unfaithfulness of all. Indeed, the unfaithfulness of Israel proves the truth of those 'words'.[84]

In that light, the unfaithfulness of Israel did not catch God by surprise; rather, the spectre of judgment and the offer of salvation bound up within the 'words' God entrusted to Israel presuppose such unfaithfulness. Moreover, the unfaithfulness of some, including David, does not undermine God's faithfulness but serves to highlight it all the more, since God has mercy not on the righteous but on the unrighteous.

In Psalm 51 David makes two other pleas that help to underpin Paul's argument in Romans 2 – 3. First, David appeals to God to purge him with hyssop. It becomes clear that David is seeking Yahweh to do an *inner* work – 'create in me a clean heart, O God' (Ps. 51:10) – though he uses the *language* of the law.

Second, David pleads for forgiveness, though not through the mechanism of the sacrificial system. David says:

> For you will not delight in sacrifice, or I would give it;
> you will not be pleased with a burnt offering.
> The sacrifices of God are a broken spirit;
> a broken and contrite heart, O God, you will not despise.
> (Ps. 51:16–17)

Again we find ourselves within the realm of repentance. David recognizes that the mechanisms of the law were inadequate and even pointed beyond themselves: he is using the language of the sacrificial system but using it to refer to an inner reality. The point is that the dutiful exercise of the sacrifices was insufficient – repentance was required. But repentance too is inadequate. A deeper spiritual cleansing of the heart was also needed – a cleansing that water and hyssop could not effect. In both cases David looks beyond the provision of the law to Yahweh himself.

---

[84] The significance of v. 4b is contested. Schreiner (1998: 151–152) notes two possibilities: (1) the quotation is being used to refer to the 'eschatological triumph of God in the justification of the ungodly' (e.g. Käsemann 1994: 81–82; Jewett 2006: 246–247; Dunn 1988: 1:134); or (2) it refers to the righteousness of God exercised in judgment (e.g. Schreiner; Moo 1996: 187–188; Murray 1967: 195–196). The problem with the first is that it ignores the original context of the quotation (so Schreiner). The problem with the second is that the justification of God's words here appears to be in the present, not at the final judgment. V. 7 suggests that Paul's lie *presently* abounds to God's glory because it already demonstrates the truth of God's words that all were bound over to sin (3:9–18).

Paul's quotation from Psalm 51 sets up his conclusion in 3:20: 'For by works of the law no human being will be justified in his sight, since through the law comes knowledge of sin.'

As David himself recognized, the law highlighted the need for a deeper level of cleansing and transformation, but the law itself could not provide it.

The OT problem that Israel faced was that they were hardened in sin and often refused to repent. They frequently assumed that stepping through the motions of the law's requirements would give them what they needed to make them right with God. However, some, such as David himself, saw that the law pointed to something deeper, to a remedy for sin beyond the power of the law itself to deliver. God promised a day when he would bring his stiff-necked nation to repentance and trust in him and his promised Messiah.

Circumcision and righteousness in Romans 4

We have seen in Romans 2 that the person who is truly circumcised (in the heart) is the one who repents and trusts in God's promise to Abraham. We now turn to Romans 4 where Paul links circumcision and righteousness even more explicitly. Romans 4 confirms the same view of circumcision and the same emphasis on the gospel promise as we observed in Romans 2, while emphasizing in an even stronger way the emblematic significance of circumcision with respect to righteousness and faith.

Paul returns to his discussion of circumcision by considering Abraham himself. Abraham was counted righteous on the basis of faith, not works. The same polarities are found in chapter 4 as in chapter 2. For example in 4:9–12 (see Table 5.7).[85]

Table 5.7: Polarities in Romans 4:9–12

	Faith	Circumcised only
Jew/circumcised	Righteous	(Not righteous)
Gentile/uncircumcised	Righteous	

Indeed, Abraham was counted righteous while he was still uncircumcised. His righteousness then had nothing to do with his

---

[85] So too the same polarities can be found in 3:30 (see Table 5.8 on p. 181). The implication is that a single thread is being woven by Paul throughout chs. 2–4.

Table 5.8: Polarities in Romans 3:30

	Faith	Works of the law
Jew/circumcised	Justified	
Gentile/uncircumcised	Justified	

circumcision. Rather, says Paul, 'He received the sign of circumcision as a seal of the righteousness that he had by faith while he was still uncircumcised' (Rom. 4:11).

By calling circumcision a 'sign' Paul is relativizing it from being something essential to being something that communicated a deeper truth. What circumcision signified is explained by the second half of the sentence: circumcision 'sealed' (*sphragis*) the righteousness-by-faith that Abraham had while he was uncircumcised.[86]

A *sphragis* could be used to indicate ownership, such as of a slave or animal, or to certify integrity or authenticity, such as of a document.[87] The latter is almost undoubtedly in view here since *sphragis* is qualified by what follows: 'the righteousness that he had by faith while he was still uncircumcised'. Moreover, Paul's use of *sphragis* elsewhere suggests that he has in mind attestation or confirmation.[88] As Morris notes, 'God gave the sign of circumcision and by doing so set his seal on the righteousness imputed to the patriarch.'[89]

Wright has noted the similarity and dissimilarity between Paul's words in 4:11 and Yahweh's words in Genesis 17:11. In Romans 4 circumcision is a 'sign' of Abraham's righteousness by faith, while in Genesis 17:11 it is a sign of 'the covenant between me and you'.[90] Wright deduces from this that righteousness is about covenant status.[91] But as we have seen, righteousness is tied strongly to the concept of blamelessness, which is a moral category. Moreover, while

---

[86] Some early Jewish literature refers to circumcision as a seal (*b. Shabb.* 137b; *Exod. Rab.* 19 (81c); *Tg. Ket.* Cant. 3:8; cf. *Barn.* 9.6); however, 'their late date makes it uncertain whether the description was known in Paul's day' (Moo 1996: 269; cf. Cranfield 2004: 236; Dunn 1988: 1:209). The fact that Paul qualifies more precisely what he means by 'seal' in the rest of the phrase suggests that he was either newly defining the term or redefining an existing one.

[87] Morris 1988: 202–203; Jewett 2006: 319; Schramm 1990.

[88] E.g. 1 Cor. 9:2; 2 Cor. 1:22; Eph. 1:13; 4:30; 2 Tim. 2:19. The one exceptional use is Rom. 15:28. See Kruse 2012: 209.

[89] Morris 1988: 203; similarly, Jewett 2006: 319; Cranfield 2004: 236.

[90] Wright 2009: 77.

[91] Ibid. 195; Wright 2002: 494–495.

Paul seems studiously to avoid any reference to 'covenant' in chapter 4, the word that stands in for it is not 'righteousness' but 'promise' (4:13–14, 16, 20–21).[92] In fact, 4:13 suggests that righteousness is a middle term between faith and promise/covenant. Paul says, 'For the promise to Abraham and his offspring that he would be heir of the world did not come through the law but through the righteousness of faith.'

The progression of events in Genesis 15 suggests the same. There Abraham believes God, God counts his faith for righteousness, and *then* God makes a covenant with him to give him the land. It is only later in Genesis 17 that Abraham receives circumcision as a sign, not only of the covenant, but also of the righteousness-by-faith on the basis of which the promise/covenant was given (4:13).

Thus Dunn is not quite right to say that Paul is reworking the ideas of circumcision and covenant to show 'circumcision [was] not so much a direct sign of the covenant, but a sign of the righteousness Abraham received through faith'.[93] Circumcision *was* a sign of the covenant, but that covenant was received on the basis of righteousness-by-faith. Paul is not so much reworking circumcision and covenant, but refuting misunderstandings of them.

That is seen especially in Paul's point that circumcision was not a seal in general of those who were circumcised, but a seal of *Abraham's* righteousness-by-faith.[94] Abraham's circumcision was unique. His circumcision sealed/guaranteed that righteousness was by faith. Further acts of circumcision were intended to commemorate that fact, rather than to demarcate who was 'in' and who was 'out'. The uniqueness of Abraham's role with respect to the signifying value of circumcision is confirmed by Paul's emphasis on Abraham's role as 'father'. The *reason* that circumcision was given as a seal of Abraham's righteousness-by-faith was

---

[92] As in Galatians (e.g. 3:14, 16–19, 21–22, 29; 4:23, 28). It is probably right to suggest that the language of covenant was too strongly tied among Paul's Jewish contemporaries to the *Mosaic* covenant so that he avoids the term (Fitzmyer 1993: 380–381; Kruse 2012: 209). Moreover, 'promise' more directly indicates the dependence on grace, since one cannot 'work' to make someone else's promise a reality (e.g. Rom. 4:14, 16; Gal. 3:18).

[93] Dunn 1988: 1:209.

[94] As Salter (2010: 20) notes, 'this verse is speaking descriptively about *Abraham* and not prescriptively about his seed'. In contrast to Abraham's righteousness which was sealed by circumcision, NT believers are sealed by the Holy Spirit (2 Cor. 1:22; Eph. 1:13; 4:30), not by baptism (e.g. Käsemann 1994: 115). The view of baptism as a seal appears only in the second century (e.g. Herm. *Sim.* 8.6.3; 9.16.3–4; *2 Clem.* 7.6; 8.6; so Dunn 1988: 1:210).

to make him the **father** of all who believe without being circumcised, so that righteousness would be counted to them as well,

and to make him the **father** of the circumcised who are not merely circumcised but who also walk in the footsteps of the faith that our father Abraham had before he was circumcised. (Rom. 4:11–12)

Abraham's circumcision gave him the unique role as 'father' of all those who also believed and were uncircumcised, together with those Jews who are not merely circumcised but who also share Abraham's faith.[95]

The unique function and meaning of Abraham's circumcision is also supported by the fact that his circumcision sealed not only his righteousness-by-faith but his righteousness-by-faith-while-uncircumcised. Three times in verses 11 and 12 Paul draws attention to 'faith-while-uncircumcised':

- Circumcision sealed Abraham's 'righteousness of faith in uncircumcision' (*tēs dikaiosynēs tēs pisteōs tēs en tē akrobystia*, my tr.).
- He is the father of 'all who believe though uncircumcised' (*pantōn tōn pisteuontōn di' akrobystias*, my tr.).
- And he is the father also of those Jews who share 'the faith-while-uncircumcised of our father Abraham' (*tēs en akrobystia pisteōs tou patros hēmōn Abraam*, my tr.).

Controversially then circumcision was not simply a sign of the special significance of the Jews but also a sign of the fact that the uncircumcised can be justified by faith, just as Abraham was. Abraham's circumcision sealed or guaranteed that. As O'Brien comments, 'Circumcision cannot be seen as a badge denoting the status enjoyed exclusively by Jews. Instead, it points beyond itself to the righteousness of faith that is universally available.'[96]

Finally, the *object* of Abraham's faith is described in chapter 4 as 'him who justifies the ungodly' (4:5), but it is also the fact that God could bring life – the life of a son – from Abraham's dead body (4:19). Abraham believed God 'who gives life to the dead and calls into

---

[95] Kruse 2012: 209–210; Cranfield 2004: 236–238.
[96] O'Brien 2004: 383.

existence the things that do not exist' (4:17).[97] So also when Paul describes the faith of 'us who believe' it is faith in 'him who raised from the dead Jesus our Lord, who was delivered up for our trespasses and raised for our justification' (4:24–25). The two strands of faith woven through the chapter are faith in God's power to bring life from death and to justify the ungodly.

Summary

Romans 2 – 4 confirms what we have seen with respect to circumcision and righteousness in other places. First, it confirms that righteousness is bound up with God's promise to Abraham. Second, it confirms that righteousness remedies not only the relational and forensic categories, but it remedies the ongoing reality of sin as well. Third, it confirms that righteousness came to Abraham by faith in God's promise. Fourth, it confirms that circumcision was an emblem and confirmation of the fact that all who share the humble repentance and faith of Abraham, whether Jew or Gentile, also share in that same righteousness that God promised through the seed of Abraham.

---

[97] As Seifrid (2000: 68) notes, 'justification is necessarily a *creation ex nihilo* . . . The divine reckoning alone makes us righteous, not by transforming us, but by recreating our persons in God's sight.'

Chapter Six

Circumcision in Galatians: righteousness by faith in the promised seed

Nowhere are the connections between circumcision and righteousness worked out at greater length than in Galatians. Circumcision first appears in chapter 2 when Paul defends his ministry. The gospel he preached among the uncircumcised was confirmed by the other apostles (2:2, 7–10). There was a division of labours: Paul would go to the uncircumcised and Peter to the circumcised. Not only that, the apostles agreed that Paul's ministry companion Titus need not be circumcised (2:3), which in itself was an acknowledgment of the fact that circumcision was now a matter of indifference. However, at the end of chapter 2 it becomes apparent that a division had arisen between the circumcised and the uncircumcised. Peter and others had stopped eating with the uncircumcised Gentiles (2:12), a matter that for Paul struck at the very heart of the gospel. Such a move risked suggesting that justification was not by faith but by 'works' (2:16). Paul then begins to argue that the law cannot justify, but that rather justification and righteousness are to be found through faith in God's promise to Abraham and his 'seed'.

Circumcision itself, however, then disappears and does not resurface until the beginning of chapter 5 when Paul says, 'Look: I, Paul, say to you that if you accept circumcision, Christ will be of no advantage to you' (Gal. 5:2).

Yet, although circumcision is not mentioned in chapters 3 and 4, the way Paul suddenly reintroduces circumcision in chapter 5 suggests that his arguments in chapters 3 and 4 form the basis for what he is saying about circumcision. So too, although circumcision is not mentioned in chapters 3 and 4 the thread of circumcision is carried through those chapters by the focus on Abraham and God's promise to him and later by the focus on Isaac and Ishmael – two other central characters in the establishment of circumcision. In short, Galatians presents us with a rich resource for coming to terms with circumcision and its relationship with righteousness and faith.

The problem of the law

Before we can fully understand what Paul is saying about circumcision we need to wrestle with the vexed issue of what he is saying about the law. Briefly, the problem with the law was both that the law itself was unable to effect righteousness, and also that despite that, those 'from the law' are cursed by it if they do not continue to do it. We will consider both those problems in turn.

Unable to make righteous

First, the law itself was unable to effect righteousness. In 2:16 Paul makes exactly the same remark about the law as he makes in Romans 3:20:

> from works of the law no flesh will be justified. (my tr.)

> *ex ergōn nomou ou dikaiōthēsetai pasa sarx.*

The wording is identical to Romans 3:20: *ex ergōn nomou ou dikaiōthēsetai pasa sarx enōpion autou.* Despite the addition of a few words in Romans, it seems likely that Paul is making the same point about 'works of the law' here as there.[1] That in turn implies that what Paul means by the 'works of the law' is identical in both Romans and Galatians.[2] We saw in Romans that by 'works of the law' Paul meant the mechanics of law obedience apart from faith in Christ. Certainly the context of Galatians 2:16 seems to support that notion.

Paul is recounting the occasion when he confronted Peter who, out of fear of the 'circumcision party',[3] had stopped eating with Gentiles. The problem was that Peter was implying by his actions that the Gentiles needed to live like Jews (2:14). Although what it means to

---

[1] Bruce 1982: 140; Dunn 1988: 1:158; Matera 2007: 94; cf. Martyn 2008: 252–253.

[2] If there is a difference it is the focus. In Romans Paul is seeking to demonstrate that the real intent of the law was to point to Christ, while in Galatians Paul is seeking to show why Christians who do not continue to practise the law are not cursed.

[3] The identity of the 'circumcision party' is disputed (see Schreiner 2010: 143–144; R. N. Longenecker 1998: 73–75), but solving those issues is unnecessary for our purposes.

'live like a Jew' (*ioudaizō*) has been variously interpreted,[4] the most obvious target in the context is circumcision.[5] While food laws are never explicitly raised in Galatians, the issue of receiving circumcision has been raised by Paul already (2:3) and will be raised again in 5:2–12 and 6:12–15. The circumcision party was putting pressure on Peter to eat only with the circumcised.[6] Nevertheless, whatever the precise issue at stake, the fact that Paul goes on to speak about 'works of the law' immediately after speaking of 'living like a Jew' implies that 'living like a Jew' involves adopting practices from the law, whether it be circumcision alone, food laws or even moral or other ceremonial practices.

Paul then contrasts the failure of the 'works of the law' to effect righteousness with the power of the Spirit in a series of questions that begin chapter 3. He asks the Galatians, 'Did you receive the Spirit by works of the law or by hearing with faith? Are you so foolish? Having begun by the Spirit, are you now being perfected by the flesh?' (Gal. 3:2–3).

The 'works of the law' are bound up with the flesh. It is the Spirit received by faith that brings 'perfection' (*epiteleō*), not the flesh and the 'works of the law'. As in Philippians, Colossians and Romans, the law is unable to bring perfection.

Paul's emphasis is on the *power of God* through the Spirit that comes by faith versus the *powerlessness* of the 'works of the law'. That is evident from his second set of questions in verse 5: 'Does he who supplies the Spirit to you and works miracles among you do so by works of the law, or by hearing with faith . . . ?'

Paul makes a very similar contrast in 5:4–5, where he notes, 'you who would be justified by the law; you have fallen away from grace. For through the Spirit, by faith, we ourselves eagerly wait for the hope of righteousness.'

---

[4] For Dunn (1993: 129) it refers to adopting a 'Jewish way of life'; Schreiner (2010: 147), 'boundary markers' of food laws, circumcision and Sabbath; Fung (1988: 110–111), dietary laws, but ultimately leading to circumcision; R. N. Longenecker (1998: 78), wholesale conversion to Judaism; or Betz (1979: 112), 'forcing one to become a Jewish convert obliged to keep the whole Torah'.

[5] Dunn (1993: 129) rejects the suggestion that the issue is circumcision, partly because it seems unlikely that Peter would have reneged on the central point of the Jerusalem agreement and pressured Gentiles to be circumcised. However, it seems likely that Paul's accusation is not that Peter *directly* pressured Gentiles to be circumcised, but he did so *indirectly* by choosing to eat only with Jews (Moo 2013: 151; Fung 1988: 110).

[6] Though circumcision may have been emblematic for other issues such as food laws and the Sabbath.

Those who seek justification/righteousness through the law have fallen away from grace. In contrast, Paul and those with him wait for righteousness through the Spirit by faith. It is those who live by the Spirit who conquer the flesh (5:16), not those who live by the law or circumcision. Indeed, as in Philippians, even emasculation is ineffective in the battle against sin (5:12; cf. Phil. 3:2).

So too in 4:1–12 Paul highlights the failure of the law. Paul says that before the coming of Christ the Jews were enslaved to the law. We will see in a moment that slavery to the law meant that the law had to be done or practised. However, Paul also shows that those practices which the law compelled them to do were ineffective in making them children of God and heirs of the Spirit.

In 4:3 Paul says that those under the law were 'enslaved to the elementary principles of the world' (*hypo ta stoicheia tou kosmou ēmetha dedoulōmenoi*). The background of the phrase 'elementary principles of the world' is contested.[7] Nevertheless two things are clear. First, before the Galatians had come to know God they too were 'enslaved', but to 'those that by nature are not gods' (4:8). Yet by seeking to embrace the law the Galatians are returning 'again' to slavery under the 'elementary principles of the world' (4:9). Remarkably then Paul considers the Galatians embracing the law to be equivalent (in some sense) to their returning to their pagan past![8] Second, the 'elementary principles' Paul has in mind are made clear in 4:10:[9] 'You observe days and months and seasons and years!'

The ambiguity of those terms has led some to suggest that Paul had pagan practices in mind.[10] The truth is more complex. As Moo points out, 'Since it is the law of Moses that the Galatians are being urged to adopt, the language undoubtedly has some reference to Jewish religious observances.'[11] Hence, it is right to see a reference here to Sabbaths, festival days or new moon festivals in a similar

---

[7] De Boer (2007) following BAGD lists four possibilities: (1) 'elements (of learning), fundamental principles'; (2) 'the four elements of the world (earth, air, fire, water)'; (3) 'the *elemental spirits*'; (4) '*heavenly bodies*'. De Boer suggests that option 2 is the only legitimate starting point. Schreiner (2010: 267–269) is less certain, but agrees at least that option 2 is the most common meaning in Greek literature. Others are not so sure (R. N. Longenecker 1998: 165–166; Moo 2013: 260–261).

[8] Barrett 1985: 61.

[9] De Boer (2007: 216–217) convincingly links 'the elementary principles of the world' in Paul's argument with calendrical observances.

[10] T. Martin 1996.

[11] Moo 2013: 278.

fashion to Colossians 2:16. Nevertheless, Paul's point is that taking up these Jewish celebrations of days and months is just as ineffective as the celebration of days and months that they pursued in their paganism.[12]

The specific problem, however, with these practices ('works'?) of the law is that they are 'weak' (*asthenēs*) and 'worthless' (*ptōchos*). The weakness and impotence of these 'elementary principles' ought to be understood in terms of Paul's initial contrast in 3:3–5 (and the later contrast in 5:4–5) between the power of God through the Spirit by faith and the 'works of the law'. The weakness of these elementary principles or 'works of the law', as in Colossians and Philippians, is that they are incapable of bringing perfection or incapable of giving life (3:21).[13] Paul's point is that the power of God came not through the works of the law but through faith.

That also seems to be the import of Paul's comment in 3:11. Leaving aside the much debated reference to Habakkuk 2:4 in the second half of the verse, the first half at least is clear that righteousness could not be obtained by the law: 'Now it is evident that no one is justified before God by the law . . .' Indeed, if justification were possible through the law, says Paul, then Christ died for no purpose (2:21). The failure of the law lay not in the inherent weakness of people but in the inherent weakness of the law: even where the law was done scrupulously the law did not make people righteous – it did not restore the world or people to the condition before the fall.

The curse of the law

The first problem with the law was that, of itself, it was unable to effect righteousness. We now turn to the second problem, which was that despite the inability of the law to effect righteousness, those 'from the law' were bound to do it and cursed if they did not.

In 3:10 Paul makes the radical claim that the law cursed rather than blessed:

For as many as are from works of the law are under a curse. (my tr.)

hosoi gar ex ergōn nomou eisin, hypo kataran eisin.

---

[12] Betz 1979: 218; de Boer 2007: 216–217. The law, of course, in contrast to paganism, was given by God and foreshadowed the gospel. Nevertheless, from Paul's present point of view, now that the Messiah has come both the law and paganism share the same nature: they are weak and worthless.

[13] Martyn 2008: 412.

In contrast to those who by faith along with Abraham are *blessed*, those under the law are *cursed*.[14] Paul gives the proof for that in the form of a quotation from Deuteronomy 27:26: 'for it is written, "Cursed be everyone who does not abide by all things written in the Book of the Law, and do them"' (Gal. 3:10).

As has often been noted, however, Paul's supporting evidence seems to contradict his point. Luther wrote:

> Now these two sentences of Paul and Moses seem clean contrary. Paul saith, whosoever shall do the works of the law is accursed. Moses saith, whosoever shall not do the works of the law [is] accursed. How shall these two sayings be reconciled together?[15]

There are a number of ways of understanding the connection between 10a and 10b. The following five are especially prominent.[16]

First, there are those who see Paul's highlighting the law's demand for perfect obedience.[17]

1. Those who fail to do the whole law are cursed (v. 10a).
2. No one does everything written in the law.
3. Therefore all who are from the law are cursed (v. 10b).

Second, there are those who see the issue as those seeking to establish a claim on God by their obedience.[18]

1. Living 'from the law' means being committed to earning one's salvation (v. 10a).
2. Such a process is an arrogant attempt to establish a claim on God.
3. Therefore all who are 'from the law' are under a curse (v. 10b).[19]

---

[14] The Abrahamic covenant also included a curse, but the curse rested on those who *rejected* Abraham and the covenant (Gen. 12:3; 17:14). The law, however, uttered curses on those *within* the covenant; those who did not continue to practise the law (e.g. Deut. 27 – 29).

[15] Luther 1810: 271.

[16] For an extended treatment see Das 2010: 145–170; and more briefly, Thielman 2007: 66–67; Wright 1993: 144–147. I follow Wright in expressing the views as syllogisms.

[17] Schreiner 2010: 204; Moo 2013: 202–205; Fung 1988: 142; R. N. Longenecker 1998: 118; Matera 2007: 123; Das 2010: 146.

[18] Fuller 1975: 31–33; Bultmann 1952: 1:263–264.

[19] This syllogism is taken from Wright 1993: 145.

Third, some see Paul's highlighting the curse that has fallen on Israel as a whole because of the people's national disobedience. As Wright notes:[20]

1. All who embrace Torah are thereby embracing Israel's national way of life (v. 10a).
2. Israel as a nation has suffered, historically, the curse that the Torah held out for her if she did not keep it.
3. Therefore all who embrace Torah are now under this curse (v. 10b).

Fourth, some identify ethnic exclusivity as the problem. To summarize Dunn's approach:[21]

1. All who fail to do the whole law are cursed (v. 10a).
2. Those who exclude Gentiles by their practice of Jewish 'boundary markers' fail to do the law.
3. Therefore those who practise such ethnic exclusivity are cursed (v. 10b).

Fifth, some see the problem as bound up with the new epoch of salvation history. Dumbrell's view may be represented as follows:

1. All who fail to do the whole law are cursed (v. 10a).
2. The provisions within the Mosaic covenant for atonement have now ended with the cross.[22]
3. Therefore those who resort to the Mosaic covenant as a source of forgiveness and atonement are under a curse (v. 10b).

The problem with all these approaches is that each assumes a different unexpressed premise: the first, that no one does or can do the law; the second, that to seek to earn one's salvation is arrogant; the third, that Israel is under a curse for failing to keep the covenant; the fourth, that excluding Gentiles by focusing on 'boundary markers' amounts to a failure to keep the law; and the fifth, that the provisions within the Mosaic covenant for atonement have now been brought to

---

[20] Ibid. 147. Problematic for this view is that the curse Paul quotes from Deut. 27:26 comes at the end of a list that highlights individual, rather than national, sins (Stanley 1990: 484). Moreover, the quotation itself focuses on individuals: *pas hos* (Moo 2013: 204).

[21] Dunn 1993: 172–173.

[22] Dumbrell 2000: 23–25, 27–28.

an end by the cross. These may or may not be perfectly valid premises. Indeed, all five may simultaneously be true. The question then becomes 'How do we determine which of these five premises Paul means us to understand here?'

Yet a solution exists that requires no unexpressed premise and makes better sense of the original context of Paul's quotation. The curse Paul quotes from Deuteronomy 27 is found at the end of a long list that threatens curses for disobedience, and it precedes a list that offers blessings and threatens curses for those who do or do not do 'all' the commandments of Yahweh. In Deuteronomy 27 threatened curses were read out to all the people gathered, at the end of which they were to respond by way of acceptance, saying, 'Amen.' Deuteronomy 27:26 then is not in the first place speaking of a curse that has been actuated in history, but rather is threatening a *potential* curse for those who do not keep doing the law.[23] That the curse has in fact been actuated both in the history of the nation, through exile, and in the lives of individuals, through various punishments including death, is largely immaterial for Paul at this point. It is far more natural to understand that Paul is making the straightforward observation that the law *threatened* a curse on all those who were under it. Paul's problem is not first of all with the sinfulness of the people but with the fact that the law pronounced curses to which the people had said, 'Amen.'

Such a reading also explains why Paul does not say that those 'from the law' (*ex ergōn nomou*) are *epikataratos* (cursed), as the quotation from Deuteronomy 27:26 (LXX) insists, but *hypo kataran* (under a curse).[24] Elsewhere in Galatians when Paul uses *hypo* in connection with the law the dominant note is slavery.[25] Those under the law were 'imprisoned' (3:22–23), 'held captive' (3:23), 'under a guardian' (3:25), 'under guardians and managers' (4:2), 'enslaved under the elementary principles of the world' (4:3), and they needed to be 'redeemed' (4:5).[26] Indeed, whether *hypo* is present or not, Paul's dominant view of the law is that it enslaved/imprisoned. For example:

But the Scripture imprisoned [*synkleiō*] everything under sin, so that the promise by faith in Jesus Christ might be given to those who believe. (Gal. 3:22)

[23] Stanley 1990: 500; Braswell 1991: 76; cf. Das 2010: 147–148.
[24] Stanley 1990: 498; Braswell 1991.
[25] Also Hübner 1984: 33.
[26] *Exagorazō* refers to release of those from slavery through the payment of a price (Büchsel 1964: 126–128).

Now before faith came, we were held captive [*phroureō*] under the law, imprisoned [*synkleiō*] until the coming faith would be revealed. (Gal. 3:23)

So then, the law was our guardian [*paidagōgos*] until Christ came, in order that we might be justified by faith. (Gal. 3:24)

In the same way we also, when we were children, were enslaved [*douloō*] to the elementary principles of the world. (Gal. 4:3)

Now Hagar is Mount Sinai in Arabia; she corresponds to the present Jerusalem, for she is in slavery [*douleuō*] with her children. (Gal. 4:25)

For freedom Christ has set us free; stand firm therefore, and do not submit again to a yoke of slavery [*douleia*]. (Gal. 5:1)

Paul uses a wide variety of language to make the same essential observation. So although after 3:10–13 Paul never returns to the language of 'curse', throughout 3:21 – 5:2 he repeatedly makes only one point about the law: it imprisons/enslaves.

Together then with the connection evinced by the use of *hypo*, it makes sense to think that what Paul means by the 'curse' of the law is taken up in his discussion of the imprisonment/enslavement of the law.[27] The alternative is to believe that Paul identified two problems with the law – that it brought a curse and that it enslaved people – and that while going to great lengths to explain the former, he left the latter largely unexplained. But Paul does explain that those 'from the law' were enslaved by the law, not primarily in the sense that they were condemned for not doing it all (though that is an implication of what Paul is saying), but in the sense that they were compelled to keep doing all of it by the ongoing threat of a curse. That, after all, is the nature of slavery: being under compulsion to obey a master (or guardian or pedagogue).

Indeed, the significance of the term *emmenō* (persist in) in 3:10 seems to have been underappreciated. As already noted, that Paul should use the quotation he does from Deuteronomy 27:26 is remarkable. Consider that Paul is seeking to explain why the Gentiles (and Jews) no longer need to keep the law, but Deuteronomy 27:26

---

[27] Also Braswell 1991: 76.

suggests that it is not those who continue in the law who are cursed but those who do not continue who are under a curse! Paul is here taking the bull by the horns. He is dealing with the fundamental question that surrounds the gospel: 'Why, if the law pronounced a curse on those who do not continue to do it, are Christians not cursed?' If Paul cannot answer that question, his salvation-apart-from-the-law gospel is untenable.

But Paul is also escalating the debate. The law demanded not simply that some of it be done, but that *all* of it be done. Paul's point is not that those who fail to live up to the law's demands are cursed; rather, his point seems to be that those who are 'from the law' (Jews, and Gentiles who have obligated themselves to it) are under the threat of a curse if they do not continue to do *all* the law, including not only its 'moral' components but also its rituals. From the perspective of the law, one cannot simply pick which parts matter and which parts do not.

In 5:3 Paul makes the same point again when he observes that the one who accepts circumcision is 'obligated' (*opheiletēs*) to keep the 'whole' law. Those who embrace circumcision therefore are not *cursed* by their decision but *obligated* by it.[28] The language of obligation matches the broader language of slavery and imprisonment. Paul's argument in 5:1–5 is that those who embrace circumcision are enslaved by the law and obligated to do all of it.[29]

Yet, as has rightly been pointed out, that the law had to keep being done would not have seemed like much of a 'curse' to Paul's contemporary Jews, since guilt for sin could be atoned for through the law's sacrifices.[30] But according to Paul, the curse of the law on those who do not continue to do it is only half the story. The other problem is that the law is ineffective in bringing about the righteousness promised to Abraham. Instead, Paul waits for righteousness through the Spirit and by faith (5:5).

That the law's enslavement *and* powerlessness are both aspects of the curse is demonstrated by Paul's hotly contested words in 3:9–14. The connection between verse 10 and verses 11–12 is complex, but the fact that Paul returns to the theme of curse in 3:13 suggests that all of 3:10–12 (not merely 3:10 itself) is taken up with explaining the

[28] On this see below, pp. 204–208.
[29] Livesey 2010: 87–91.
[30] E.g. Sanders 1985: 28–29; Dunn 2008: 319; Moo 2013: 324; Westerholm 2004: 420; cf. B. W. Longenecker 1998: 139–142.

law's curse. The underlined words in the following text highlight the connections:[31]

10   For all who rely on works of the law are under a **curse** [*kataran*]; for it is written, '**Cursed** [*epikataratos*] be everyone who does not abide by all things written in the Book of the Law, and do them.'

11   Now it is evident that no one is justified before God by the <u>law</u> [*nomō*], for 'The righteous <u>shall live</u> [*zēsetai*] <u>by faith</u> [*ek pisteōs*].'

12   But the <u>law</u> [*nomos*] is not <u>of faith</u> [*ek pisteōs*], rather 'The one who does them <u>shall live</u> [*zēsetai*] by them.'

13   Christ redeemed us from the **curse** [*kataras*] of the law by becoming a **curse** [*katara*] for us – for it is written, '**Cursed** [*epikataratos*] is everyone who is hanged on a tree.'

Verses 10 and 13 both deal with the curse of the law, while verses 11 and 12 contrast faith and the law. But the key observation is that verses 11 and 12 are caught up within Paul's argument about the curse of the law. In the light of these connections and what we have seen above, Paul's argument in these verses progresses as follows:

1. Those 'from the law' are under the threat of a curse if they do not continue to do the law.
2. But the law cannot effect righteousness (since that comes through faith).
3. And the law ought not to be confused with faith (since the law required doing).
4. But Christ has redeemed Israel (and the Gentiles, v. 14) from the curse threatened on those who do not continue to do all the law (and who have not done all the law).[32]

The curse of the law is that it needed to be done though it does not justify.[33] But Jesus Christ has redeemed those 'from the law' from this

---

[31] Verses 9 and 14 are also paired, sharing the common themes of 'blessing' and 'Abraham'.

[32] Cf. Wright (1993: 151–153), who thinks that Christ has redeemed only Israel from the curse, which he identifies as exile. The removal of which has brought blessings (only indirectly) for the Gentiles.

[33] It is crucial to distinguish between '*the* curse' (i.e. the curse following the fall of Adam and Eve) and 'the curse of the law'. The first precedes the second, which is, of course, Paul's point in Rom. 5: people were condemned by their disobedience long

curse of having to continue in the law since he became a curse for us. The law imprisoned people under sin in that it showed sin to be sin, but did not provide the means for sin to be conquered (though it did provide the means for sin to be forgiven, albeit proleptically). Those under the law were 'enslaved to the elementary principles of the world' – principles which themselves ultimately achieved nothing, though God had commanded them to be done.

The heart of Paul's argument is not merely that humanity's sinful condition makes people unable to keep the law (although that is true); rather, it is that their sinful condition makes them unrighteous and the law does nothing to rectify the situation – it cannot bring about the righteousness God requires and worse, it simply serves to bring down curses on them for their continuing disobedience. To express the problem eschatologically, as Paul does in Philippians and Colossians: the problem with the law was that while it could (at times) restrain people's sinful impulses it could not inaugurate the new creation. That remedy is found in the death and resurrection of Jesus.

God's promise to Abraham

Alongside his argument about the limitations of the law Paul also demonstrates that what the law could not do (and was never intended to do) God did through his promise to Abraham. In contrast to the law, which could not effect righteousness, Paul shows that God's promise to Abraham included righteousness.

Galatians 3 begins with a dual Spirit–flesh and law–faith contrast, similar to Philippians 3. We begin with the Spirit–flesh contrast before turning to the law–faith contrast in the next section. Paul asks:

> Are you so foolish? Having begun by the Spirit, are you now being perfected [*epileteō*] by the flesh? . . . Does he who supplies the Spirit to you and works miracles among you do so by works of the law, or by hearing with faith . . . ? (Gal. 3:3–5)

Once again we find the language of perfection/completion.[34] Perfection/completion does not come through the flesh, but through

(note 33 *cont.*) before the law came through Moses. The law merely brought the reality of that curse to light. In a sense, then, not only the promise precedes the law (Gal. 3), but so does the condemnation (Rom. 5). In Galatians, Paul primarily has the 'curse of the law' in view.

[34] *Epileteō* is based on *teleō*, which comes from the same *tel-* root as *teleioō* and *teleios*. As noted above, the completion/end that is in view is perfection/righteousness.

196

the Spirit. The Spirit, in turn, does not come through the 'works of the law' but by 'hearing with faith' (3:5).

The connection between 3:5 and 3:6 suggests that the work of the Spirit is bound up with righteousness. Paul asks in 3:5, 'Therefore, does the one who gives the Spirit to you and works wonders among you do so by the works of the law or by the hearing of faith?' (my tr.).

His answer is supplied in verse 6,[35] 'Just as Abraham believed God, and it was reckoned [*logizomai*] to him as righteousness' (my tr.).

In verse 5 the *Spirit* comes by faith, while in verse 6 *righteousness* is 'reckoned' by faith. The parallelism indicates that the righteousness that comes by faith is somehow connected with the Spirit, who comes by faith.[36] Fung perceptively writes:

Paul takes it for granted that Abraham's being justified by faith *proves* that the Galatians must have received the Spirit by faith also; and this argument from Scripture falls to the ground *unless* the reception of the Spirit is in some sense equated with justification. For if this were not so, it could be objected that even though Abraham was indeed justified by faith, it does not necessarily follow that reception of the Spirit also has to be dependent on faith; conceivably while justification is by faith the gift of the Spirit could be conditioned on works. We may take it, then, that Paul conceives of receiving the Spirit in such close connection with justification that the two can be regarded in some sense as synonymous, so that in the Galatians' receiving the Spirit their justification was also involved.[37]

---

[35] The connection between 3:5 and 3:6 is contested. V. 6 may either conclude 3:1–5 (e.g. Moo 2013: 187; Fung 1988: 135; Martyn 2008: 296–297; Matera 2007: 113) or begin what follows in 3:7–9 (e.g. Betz 1979: 137, 140). Bruce (1982: 152–153; also Lee 2013: 35) opts for both. Regardless, some who see v. 6 as beginning the section 3:7–9 still see a strong connection with v. 5 (e.g. R. N. Longenecker 1998: 108–109, 112; Dunn 1993: 159–161). Longenecker points out that the connection between vv. 5 and 6 is supplied by *pistis* and also by the fact that 3:1–5 and 3:6–14 are connected by the return to a focus on the Spirit in 3:14.

[36] S. K. Williams 1987: 92–93; Moo 2013: 188. Schreiner (2010: 190–191) rejects the connection between 3:5 and 3:6 chiefly on the grounds that the Spirit is a gift of the eschaton and that although the Spirit was active in the OT 'we do not find the claim that Abraham had the Spirit'. But that overlooks the distinction between promise and reality. Bruce (1982: 152) astutely comments, 'True, Abraham could not be said to have received the Spirit through faith, for he lived in the age of promise, not of fulfilment . . . The Galatians, who lived in the age of fulfilment, had received the Spirit as well as a righteous standing before God – alike by faith.'

[37] Fung 1988: 136 (emphasis his).

It is also apparent that for Paul the gift of the Spirit is a key part of God's promise to Abraham. In verse 14 Paul notes that Christ redeemed us from the curse of the law,

> so that [*hina*] in Christ Jesus **the blessing of Abraham** [*hē eulogia tou Abraam*] might come to the Gentiles,

> so that [*hina*] we might receive **the promised Spirit** [*tēn epangelian tou pneumatos*] through faith.

The parallelism between these two lines suggests 'the blessing of Abraham' (or the blessing promised to Abraham) is 'the promise of the Spirit'. That the two are synonymous,[38] rather than the second being the result of the first[39] or merely related in some way,[40] can be seen in that elsewhere in Galatians 'promise' (*epangelia*) always refers to the promise to Abraham (3:16–19, 22, 29; 4:23, 28).[41] Williams observes that Paul might easily have left out 'promise' and said, 'that we might receive the Spirit'. But by including 'promise' Paul introduces and defines the content of the promise that he goes on to expound.[42] The implication then is that the '*promise* of the Spirit' is the Spirit promised to Abraham – the Spirit who comes through Jesus Christ by faith.[43]

Moreover, Paul has earlier linked the 'blessing (*eulogia*) of Abraham' with justification when he says,[44] 'And the Scripture, foreseeing that God would justify [*dikaioō*] the Gentiles by faith, preached the gospel beforehand to Abraham, saying, "In you shall all the nations be blessed (*eneulogeō*)"' (Gal. 3:8).

The rubric of promise helps us to hold together both Abraham's justification and the promise of the Spirit. God's promise to Abraham preached the gospel beforehand, saying that through Abraham's seed,

---

[38] E.g. Schreiner 2010: 218; Bruce 1982: 167–168; Dunn 1993: 179; Fung 1988: 151–152; Martyn 2008: 322; Matera 2007: 120. As Schreiner rightly observes, 'there is no need to claim that the gift of the Spirit exhausts all that is involved in the promise given to Abraham, but the gift of the Spirit represents one aspect or dimension of the Abrahamic promise'.

[39] Lightfoot 1874: 140.

[40] E.g. Lee 2013: 53–59; Moo 2013: 216.

[41] R. N. Longenecker 1998: 123–125; Burton 1962: 176–177; cf. Kwon 2004: 107–111.

[42] S. K. Williams 1988: 712–713.

[43] To say that the Spirit was promised to Abraham does not mean that Abraham must have understood it as such. Paul's point seems to be the promise of the Spirit was included, albeit obliquely, in God's promise to Abraham of 'righteousness' and his promise to put the world right through his 'seed'.

[44] S. K. Williams 1987: 92.

righteousness and the Spirit would come to those who believe. Although Abraham did not possess the Spirit or righteousness/blamelessness in their fullest sense, nevertheless, in receiving God's promise by faith, Abraham was reckoned already to have what God had promised. In the same way as Abraham then, the Galatians were reckoned righteous by faith. That is, they were reckoned to possess what they had been promised in Christ but did not yet fully have. Like Abraham, they awaited the fulfilment of the fully realized righteousness promised in Christ. But unlike Abraham, through the coming of the Christ they possessed the Spirit and Spirit-wrought righteousness in a unique and greater way than Abraham.

The same ideas are taken up later in chapter 5, but explicitly in the context of circumcision. In 5:2–4 Paul implies that those who receive circumcision are seeking to be justified by the law.[45] He says to those who are considering being circumcised, 'You are severed from Christ, you who would be justified by the law; you have fallen away from grace' (Gal. 5:4).

In contrast:

> **For** [*gar*] through the Spirit, by faith, we ourselves eagerly wait for the hope of righteousness.

> **For** [*gar*] in Christ Jesus neither circumcision nor uncircumcision counts for anything, but only faith working through love. (Gal. 5:5–6)

Several points are worth noting. First, by referring to the 'hope of righteousness' and by speaking of 'waiting' for that hope, Paul implies that righteousness is in some sense something he does not yet fully possess. Second, the hope of righteousness for which Paul waits comes through faith in Christ Jesus, not through circumcision. Third, the parallelism between verses 5 and 6 implies that the hope of righteousness is somehow bound up with 'faith working through love'. Fourth, the hope of righteousness for which Paul waits comes by the Spirit through faith in Christ Jesus. What Paul has in mind here is not the 'legal verdict' of righteous but the transforming work of the Spirit, through whom (as we have seen elsewhere) people are transformed into the image of Christ.[46]

---

[45] The verb *dikaiousthe* should be taken as conative ('seeking to be justified') rather than durative ('are being justified') (Wallace 1996: 535; Moo 2013: 325).

[46] Or according to Thielman (2007: 53, n. 32), 'not *merely* "forensic" but "ethical" as well' (emphasis mine).

That is supported by Paul's last reference to circumcision in Galatians, which is of the same form as his statement here in 5:6. In 5:6 Paul writes:

For in Christ Jesus **neither circumcision** [*oute peritomē*] **nor un-circumcision** [*oute akrobystia*] counts for anything,

> **but** [*alla*] only faith working through love.

While in 6:15 he says:

For **neither circumcision** [*oute gar peritomē*] counts for anything, **nor uncircumcision** [*oute akrobystia*],

> **but** [*alla*] a new creation.

The first half of both statements contains almost identical words, expressing indifference to circumcision or uncircumcision. So too the second half of both statements is introduced by *alla*, but what follows is distinct. This parallelism suggests that 'faith working through love' is synonymous with (or the outworking of) the 'new creation' and, in turn, that the 'hope of righteousness' for which Paul waits is the new creation in which God's new people live out the commandment of love that fulfils the law (5:13–14).[47] In other words, those whose faith is in Christ fulfil the law through the Spirit. In contrast, those who by circumcision seek to be justified by the law are obligated to a law that cannot bring righteousness. Circumcision (and the law) are unable to bring about the new creation in Christ Jesus. Once again we have the theme of the 'new' (*kainos*) creation, as in Colossians, where Paul urges his readers to put on the 'new' (*neos*) man, and Ephesians 2, where Jesus has made one 'new' (*kainos*) man out of two.

Moreover, as in Philippians 3, Colossians 2 and Ephesians 2 the need for this new creation/humanity is anchored in the failure of the flesh. Galatians 6:12 demonstrates that the background to Galatians is that some wanted the Galatian Christians to be circumcised: 'It is

---

[47] Paul makes a very similar statement in 1 Cor. 7:19: 'neither circumcision counts for anything nor uncircumcision, but keeping the commandments of God [*tērēsis entolōn theou*]'. As in Rom. 2:26, whatever 'keeping the commandments of God' means, it is indifferent to circumcision! In 1 Cor. 7:19, as in Rom. 2 and here, what matters is not the mechanics of law obedience but repentance and faith in Christ that work out in love and obedience to Christ (Rosner 2013: 33–39, 128–133; Schreiner 2010: 317–318).

those who want to make a good showing in the flesh who would force you to be circumcised, and only in order that they may not be persecuted for the cross of Christ.'

The motivation is so that they may avoid persecution. But in addition they also want to 'make a good showing in the flesh'. The same is reiterated in verse 13: 'For even those who are circumcised do not themselves keep the law [*nomon phylassousin*], but they desire to have you circumcised that they may boast in your flesh.'

These references to the flesh in chapter 6 follow the flesh–Spirit contrast that runs through 5:16 – 6:8. The flesh and the Spirit are utterly opposed to one another:

> But I say, walk by the Spirit, and you will not gratify the desires of the flesh. For the desires of the flesh are against the Spirit, and the desires of the Spirit are against the flesh, for these are opposed to each other, to keep you from doing the things you want to do. (Gal. 5:16–17)

The flesh is the source of sin (5:19), while the Spirit is the source of love, joy, peace, patience, and so on (5:22–23). Paul's point then in 6:12 and 13 is that circumcision itself is of no value since, unlike the Spirit, it fails to tame the flesh. That takes us back to Paul's initial question in 3:3: 'Are you so foolish? Having begun by the Spirit, are you now being perfected by the flesh?' (Gal. 3:3).

Perfection does not come through the flesh or the law but through the Spirit promised through the Christ. That was the essence of God's promise to Abraham, albeit oblique at the time, but filled out through the unfolding of redemptive history.

The seed of Abraham: circumcision or faith in the Christ?

We have seen that Paul argues that the law could not effect righteousness; instead, that gift comes through God's promise to Abraham. Paul demonstrates that the promise to Abraham was righteousness, both as a present reality and as a future hope. But Paul not only spells out *what* God promised to Abraham; he also shows *who* are the heirs of God's promise to Abraham. That brings us to consideration of circumcision itself.

Along with its emphasis on righteousness and the Spirit, Galatians 3 is intimately concerned with who are the legitimate 'seed' of

Abraham.[48] That can be seen by the way the chapter begins and ends. In 3:7 Paul says, 'Know then that it is those of faith who are the sons of Abraham.' And in 3:29 he concludes, 'And if you are Christ's, then you are Abraham's offspring [*sperma*], heirs according to promise.'

What lies between is an exposition of that fact. Paul argues that Jesus is the true 'seed' (*sperma*) of Abraham to whom the promise was made, but that those of faith are heirs of that same promise by virtue of their inclusion in Christ.

In 3:16 Paul asserts that God's promise was to Abraham and his 'seed' (singular). That is, it was to one descendant: Christ. Paul says, 'Now the promises were made to Abraham and to his offspring [*spermati*]. It does not say, "And to offsprings [*spermasin*]", referring to many, but referring to one, "And to your offspring [*spermati*]", who is Christ' (Gal. 3:16).

This is not a mere Pauline fancy. Paul most probably has Genesis 17 in mind. The exact expression 'and to your seed' occurs only in Genesis 13:15, 17:8 and 24:7 (LXX).[49] But Genesis 17:8 also shares the focus on *sperma* and *diathēkē* present in Galatians 3, with the two terms occurring frequently in Genesis 17.[50] We have seen that right from the beginning of Genesis God had promised a 'seed'. We have also seen in Genesis 17 that a careful distinction is made between Isaac and everyone else in Abraham's household, a distinction that continues to be made throughout the OT, particularly in the language that distinguishes the line of 'Abraham, Isaac and Jacob'. The 'seed' who is in view, according to Paul, is Christ (3:16).

In turn, those who are Christ's are Abraham's offspring and heirs together with him of the promise (3:29). They are heirs, not by virtue of their own status or descent – there is neither Jew or Greek, slave or free, male or female – but by being united with Christ.[51] Paul makes that same point in several ways:

in Christ Jesus you are all sons of God, through faith. (3:26)

---

[48] Ch. 4 also begins and ends with references to sonship (4:1–7, 21–31). Hahn (2009: 244–245) convincingly argues that sonship is the theme of both chs. 3 and 4.

[49] The expression 'to your offspring' (*tō spermati*) occurs elsewhere (Gen. 12:7; 15:18; 22:18; 24:7), but as Schreiner (2010: 228) notes, 'the inclusion of the word "and" (καὶ) within the quotation "and to your offspring" (καὶ τῷ σπέρματι αὐτοῦ) must hearken back to an OT text where the word "and" (καὶ) is used'.

[50] Moo 2013: 228–229.

[51] S. K. Williams 1987: 96.

For as many of you as were baptized into Christ have put on Christ. (3:27)

for you are all one in Christ Jesus. (3:28)

But not only is inclusion in God's promise to Abraham only through inclusion in Christ; that inclusion is *by faith* and not *through the law*. Paul maintains, 'Know then that it is those of faith [*ek pisteōs*] who are the sons of Abraham' (Gal. 3:7). And, 'for in Christ Jesus you are all sons of God, through faith [*dia tēs pisteōs*]' (Gal. 3:26).

According to Paul, a promise is received by faith *by definition*, since if it comes by the law it no longer comes by promise (3:18). Moreover, the law came 430 years after the promise and cannot overturn the earlier promise (3:17). Finally, while God spoke directly and personally with Abraham when making that covenant, he used intermediaries in instituting the covenant through Moses (3:19). That means that the law which came later had another purpose. That purpose Paul explains in verse 19: 'Why then the law? It was added because of transgressions, until the offspring [*sperma*] should come to whom the promise had been made . . .'

In contrast to the promise that was made to Abraham and his 'seed', the law was given to the nation as a whole. The law served not to turn the promise into reality but to lock things up and serve as a pedagogue until the coming of the seed of Abraham to whom God had made the promise (3:22–24). For that reason, justification could never be by the law since that was not the law's purpose. As such, the law was not opposed to the promise, since its purpose was quite distinct. The law did not bring righteousness, but simply served as a guide and teacher until the coming of the seed of Abraham, who makes righteousness a reality.

Paul returns to the themes of law, promise, faith and offspring/seed in a rather enigmatic way in 4:21–31. He notes that Abraham did not have one son, but two. Ishmael was the child of a slave woman, whereas Isaac was the child that God had promised to Sarah (4:22–23). Only Isaac was an heir of God's promise to Abraham. Ishmael was not, despite the fact that he was a son of Abraham and, though Paul does not mention it, despite the fact that Ishmael was circumcised in accordance with the promise to Abraham. In a similar way, Paul argues that those who are merely 'of the law' are like Ishmael: sons of Abraham according to the flesh and (implicitly) recipients of circumcision, but not heirs of the promise. As Muller observes:

It is precisely this distinction that Paul exploits to disinherit, as it were, circumcision Jews who reject Christ. Abraham's true offspring belong to the covenant made with Abraham and that covenant was constituted by faith in God, not by fleshy descent. If the Jews do not manifest faith then they are outside the community of Israel (see Gal. 6:16). Ishmael, who can claim fleshy descent and who was circumcised (Gen. 17:23), does not share in the covenant![52]

At that point Paul returns to the topic of circumcision: 'Look: I, Paul, say to you that if you accept circumcision, Christ will be of no advantage to you' (Gal. 5:2).

The fact that Paul returns to the topic of circumcision immediately after discussing Isaac and Ishmael suggests that he means for the Galatians to understand that receiving circumcision does not make one a recipient of the blessings promised to Abraham in the covenant, just as being a physical descendant of Abraham does not make one a recipient of the blessings promised to Abraham. According to 5:2 (and the whole preceding argument beginning in chapter 2), what matters is not descent or circumcision but faith in the Christ, or, more particularly, faith in the seed of Abraham to whom circumcision pointed.

In fact, Paul presents an absolute disjunction between Christ and circumcision. For the Galatians to accept circumcision would sever them from Christ: 'I testify again to every man who accepts circumcision that he is obligated to keep the whole law. You are severed from Christ, you who would be justified by the law; you have fallen away from grace' (Gal. 5:3–4).

Confusingly, Paul also says that circumcision is a matter of indifference (Gal. 5:6; 6:15). The issue here, however, is those who embrace circumcision as a way of seeking righteousness from the law. It is those 'who would be justified by the law' who have 'fallen away from grace' (5:4). In contrast, the hope of righteousness does not come through the law, but Paul waits for it from the Spirit who comes by faith in Christ (5:5). The one who accepts circumcision is both severed from Christ and obligated to 'do the whole law'.

Several options exist for what Paul is warning against in saying that these Gentiles must 'do the whole law'.[53] Many of the views are similar to those noted above in relation to 3:10 since understanding what Paul means depends to some degree on understanding the

---

[52] Muller 1990: 83.
[53] For a brief survey see Moo 2013: 323–325.

problem Paul identifies with the law. So some suggest that the Galatians were unaware until Paul pointed it out here that embracing circumcision meant also doing everything else in the law.[54] Moo suggests that the issue is that now that Christ has come the OT sacrifices are invalid and hence there is no means of atonement in doing the law – the only option then is perfect doing, which is impossible.[55] Dunn suggests that the issue was the Galatians shifting their allegiance from Christ to membership of a people and the resulting loss of their own Gentile identity.[56] But there is another way of understanding what Paul means which is more compelling, both in terms of fitting with the understanding of 3:10 given above and in terms of fitting with the immediate context of chapter 5.

The apparent play on words between verses 2 and 3 suggests that being severed from Christ and being obligated to the law are two sides of the same coin.[57] Paul says:

> Look: I, Paul, say to you that if you **accept circumcision**, Christ will be of no advantage to you [*ouden ōphelēsei*].

> I testify again to every man who **accepts circumcision** that he is obligated to keep the whole law [*opheiletēs estin holon ton nomon poiēsai*]. (Gal. 5:2–3)

The wordplay suggests that Paul's emphasis falls not on 'doing the whole law' but on the contrast between 'benefit' (*ōphelēsei*) and 'obligation' (*opheiletēs*). Moreover, the fact that *opheiletēs* stands at the beginning of the clause suggests that the emphasis falls on 'obligation' more than on 'all' or 'do'.[58] By embracing circumcision the Galatians are rejecting Christ and the help that comes from him. And by rejecting Christ the Galatians are obligating themselves to the law (enslaving themselves again to it).[59] The import of that is seen in the contrast between verses 4 and 5:

---

[54] E.g. Bruce 1982: 230; R. N. Longenecker 1998: 226–227.
[55] Moo 2013: 324–325.
[56] Dunn 2008: 320.
[57] Lührmann 1992: 96; Dunn 1993: 265. Some maintain that with *palin* in v. 3 Paul is referring to his earlier point in 3:10 that 'all who rely on works of the law are under a curse' (e.g. Schreiner 2010: 314; Gundry 1985: 25–26). But the play on words with v. 2 suggests otherwise (Moo 2013: 322; de Boer 2011: 312–313). Moo also points out that in other similar places where Paul uses *palin* he 'almost always draws a connection with an immediately preceding point' (e.g. Rom. 15:10–12; 1 Cor. 3:20; 12:21; Phil. 4:4).
[58] So also Howard 1990: 16.
[59] Cf. Bruce 1982: 231.

You are severed from Christ, you who would be **justified** [*dikaiousthe*] by the law; you have fallen away from grace.

For through the Spirit, by faith, we ourselves eagerly wait for the hope of **righteousness** [*dikaiosynēs*]. (Gal. 5:4–5)

While those who embrace circumcision seek justification and righteousness in the law, Paul waits for the righteousness that comes through the Spirit by faith in Christ. By embracing circumcision the Galatians are simultaneously rejecting the Christ and the righteousness ('benefit') that comes through him and obligating themselves to a law which is of no advantage in obtaining righteousness.[60]

Indeed, Paul later implies that Christians do in fact fulfil the 'whole law'. In 5:14 Paul says, 'For the whole law is fulfilled in one word [*ho gar pas nomos en heni logō peplērōtai*]: "You shall love your neighbour as yourself"' (Gal. 5:14).

Although Paul has shifted from *holos ho nomos* (5:3) to *ho pas nomos* (5:14), the shift seems hardly significant.[61] More significant is the move from *poieō* to *plēroō*.[62] Although it is possible to see the two as more or less synonymous,[63] Moo argues convincingly that *plēroō* is 'often used in the NT to denote the "fulfilment" of the OT in Christ' and hence carries the sense of eschatological completion.[64] Such a distinction neatly fits Paul's contrast between the law and the Spirit that we have already observed: 'doing the law' could not bring

---

[60] Das (2010: 168) is mistaken that 'the only way 5:3 can function as a technique of *dissuasion* is if obeying the whole law is difficult or impossible' (emphasis his). The other option for which I have argued is that keeping the law is *futile*: to be circumcised is to reject Christ and to be obligated to futility.

[61] Thielman 2007: 52; Moo 2013: 346, 350. Bruce (1982: 241) makes a distinction between the two: 'ὅλος ὁ νόμος in v 3 is the sum-total of the precepts of the law, ὁ πᾶς νόμος here is the law as a whole – the spirit and intention of the law.' Bruce follows Hübner (1984: 37), who establishes this distinction on the basis that in 5:3 *holos* is in the predicate position, while in 5:14 *pas* is in attributive position. By way of counterexample, Moo notes Paul's use of *holō tō kosmō* in Rom. 1:8 compared with *pas ho kosmos* in Rom. 3:19, and *holon to sōma* in 1 Cor. 12:17 with *pan to sōma* in Eph. 4:17.

[62] Betz (1979: 275) notes that 'the Jew is obliged to do the Torah . . . while the Christian fulfils the Torah through the act of love, to which he has been freed by Christ . . . [T]he "doing" of the Jewish Torah is not required for Christians, but the "fulfilling" is'.

[63] Thielman 1994: 140.

[64] Moo 2013: 347. It is often used in fulfilment formulas (e.g. Matt. 1:22; 2:15, 17, 23; 3:15; 4:14; 5:17; 8:17; 12:17; 13:35; 21:4; 26:54, 56; 27:9). Martyn (2008: 488) ascribes to it the double meaning of prophetic fulfilment and something being brought to perfection.

righteousness, though it guided and taught people. The fulfilment of righteousness instead comes through the Spirit received by faith in the Christ.

Paul makes a similar point again about Christians 'fulfilling' the law in 6:2: 'Bear one another's burdens, and so fulfil the law [*anaplērōsete ton nomon*] of Christ.'

Again Paul uses yet another term to refer to carrying out the law: *anaplēroō*. More significantly, he refers to fulfilling the 'law of Christ'. We encountered a similar concept in Romans 2 – 4, where Paul distinguished between a 'law of works' and a 'law of faith'. There the 'law of faith' referred to the appropriation of Jesus as the fulfilment of the law (Rom. 3:21–22, 27–31). Here too Paul seems to envisage that the law that Christians fulfil is somehow different from the law that the Galatians are being persuaded to 'do'. It seems entirely plausible, given what we have seen in Galatians so far, that here too Paul means to distinguish between the law as 'works' (the mechanics of the law) versus the fulfilment of righteousness in Christ to which the law pointed.[65]

It must be noted that what Paul means by 'doing the law' here seems to be different from what he means by it in Romans 2:13–14. In Romans 2:12–16 it is the '*doers* of the law' (*hoi poiētai nomou*) who are justified. Likewise, it is the uncircumcised who '*keep* the righteous requirements of the law' (*ta dikaiōmata tou nomou phylassē*, my tr.) who show that the law is written on their hearts (Rom. 2:26). In both cases I argued that Paul was referring to those who repent and believe in the Messiah. Yet here in Galatians Paul says that those who accept circumcision are obligated to 'do the whole law' (*holon ton nomon poiēsai*, my tr.) and are cut off from Christ, which on the surface seems to be quite the opposite point. In Romans 'doing' the law involves appropriating Christ; here in Galatians 'doing' the law is set in stark contrast to Christ. Several comments can be made.

First, we cannot expect a word as commonplace as 'do' always to carry the same connotation. We must allow the context to determine its meaning, and there are significant differences in the way Paul employs it here and in Romans 2. First, Paul's use of the phrase 'the whole law' (*holon ton nomon*) suggests that he has something different in mind than in Romans 2. In Romans 2 the Gentiles do the slightly

---

[65] The meaning of 'the law of Christ' is heavily contested and a full investigation of the options is beyond the scope of this book (e.g. Moo 2013: 376–377; Schreiner 2010: 359–360; B. W. Longenecker 1998: 85–87). I am simply offering what I hope is a plausible reconstruction on the basis of our earlier study of Galatians and Romans.

ambiguous '*things* of the law' without knowing all the law itself. There also, the Gentiles who 'keep' the law do so without even being circumcised. In contrast, here Paul suggests that those who are circumcised need to keep the 'whole law'. Second, in Romans 2 Paul is deliberately making a contrast between inner spirituality and external conformity, as I have argued. There 'doing' and 'keeping' were explicitly in reference to internal spirituality. Here, 'doing' simply refers to the external mechanics of the law. Third, in Galatians the function of 'inner doing' (as we might call it) is served by the concept of 'fulfilment'. Fourth, regardless of the word 'do' being used differently, Paul is still making the same point both here and in Galatians: it is not the bare doing of the mechanics of the law that matters but faith in Christ to whom the law pointed and the righteousness that comes from him through the Spirit.

To embrace circumcision then is to reject Christ (5:2). But to reject Christ is to obligate oneself to keep doing the law – to keep doing a law that cannot effect righteousness. It is not the physical act of circumcision that matters; after all, neither circumcision nor uncircumcision really matters (5:6; 6:15). Rather, receiving circumcision as a means of pursuing righteousness is deeply problematic. To receive circumcision as a pathway to righteousness is to deny that the promised 'seed' of Abraham, through whom righteousness comes, has finally appeared – it is to be severed from Christ. One can choose either circumcision (and implicitly other kinds of elementary principles that achieve nothing) or the Christ through whom comes the promised Spirit and righteousness.[66] The key point for our purposes is that once again circumcision is bound up with faith in God's promise to Abraham, and more particularly faith in the Messiah/seed of Abraham through whom those promises have come to fruition.

Circumcision in Galatians

In Galatians Paul demonstrates that God's promise to Abraham, signified in circumcision, was not about fleshly descent, but about faith in the promised 'seed'. The content of what was promised was righteousness through the Spirit, who comes through that promised righteous seed. To embrace circumcision, or other elementary

---

[66] In that way Paul's view of circumcision here coheres with his view of other ritual practices in other places (e.g. Rom. 14; Col. 2:16–19): if one knows and trusts Christ, they are a matter of complete indifference; yet if embraced as a path to righteousness, they are positively damaging.

principles or works of the law, as a means of obtaining righteousness is to miss the point. Those things could not bring about the righteousness that comes by faith in Christ. Now that the promised seed and the Spirit have come, circumcision is at best irrelevant, and, at worst, takes a person away from Christ. Circumcision without the Messiah leaves one obligated to the whole law, but the law is of no help in bringing about righteousness, blamelessness and love. Because of their commitment to the law they are alienated from Christ and the Spirit who do bring about righteousness, blamelessness and love. What matters is faith in the Messiah through whom the promised righteousness, Spirit and new creation come.

A test case: Acts 7

So far we have focused largely on Paul's view of circumcision. But before concluding this chapter it is helpful to turn to Stephen's speech to the Sanhedrin in Acts 7. Although we could consider numerous other circumcision passages in Acts, such as Acts 10 and 15, we will focus on Acts 7 since that passage presents a useful test case of everything I have argued, drawing together all the themes of circumcision, righteousness and faith in Abraham's seed.

Stephen's speech seems almost to be an exposition of the Abrahamic covenant. He starts with the promise to Abraham and circumcision and ends with the condemnation that the hearts of his hearers are uncircumcised. In his speech Stephen recounts the history of Israel, beginning with God's appearance to Abraham (Acts 7:2). God promised to give him and his 'offspring' the land (7:5). Stephen recalls how God gave Abraham the covenant of circumcision and how Abraham circumcised Isaac (7:8). Isaac became the father of Jacob, and Jacob of the twelve patriarchs (7:8).

In the remainder of the speech Stephen focuses on individual characters, both how God used them and how the people rejected them. So God raised up Joseph, but his brothers were jealous of him (7:9–10). He raised up Moses, but the people also rejected him (7:20–43). He used Joshua to bring the people into the land (7:45). David found favour in the eyes of God (7:45–46). Solomon built the temple (7:47). Acts 7 is the history of the seed (singular) of Abraham – Isaac, Jacob, Joseph, Moses, Joshua, David, Solomon – and also of their rejection.

Stephen summarizes the import of this telescoped account in verses 51–53:

You stiff-necked people [*sklērotrachēloi*], uncircumcised in heart and ears, you always resist the Holy Spirit. As your fathers did, so do you. Which of the prophets did your fathers not persecute? And they killed those who announced beforehand the coming of the Righteous One, whom you have now betrayed and murdered, you who received the law as delivered by angels and did not keep it. (Acts 7:51–53)

Several points are worth noting. First, Stephen accuses the people of being 'stiff-necked' and being 'uncircumcised in heart and ears'. The connection of uncircumcision of the heart and stubbornness is one that we have seen many times before. Second, he links uncircumcision of heart and stubbornness with the rejection of the prophets, especially those whose history he has just narrated. Third, he sees the rejection of the prophets in Israel's earlier history as symptomatic of their rejection of the promised 'Righteous One'. Although Stephen does not use the language of Abraham's 'seed', the connection with 'uncircumcision' and the way his history has been told, beginning as it does with Abraham and tracing through specific descendants, suggests that he has Abraham's 'seed' in view. Continually the people rejected Abraham's seed, and ultimately they rejected Jesus, the final 'seed' around whom God's community would be formed. Fourth, he mentions righteousness in the same breath as circumcision/ uncircumcision. I have argued that those two concepts were always intimately related, and that righteousness would ultimately find fulfilment in the coming of the promised seed of Abraham. Fifth, he combines rejection of the 'Righteous One' and uncircumcision of the heart with receiving the law but not keeping it. That is, at the heart of keeping the law, and at the heart of circumcision, is receiving the promised 'Righteous One', the seed of Abraham, through whom righteousness comes.

Chapter Seven

Conclusion: circumcision, righteousness and faith

We began this study by asking whether or not righteousness and faith were always connected with circumcision, and if so how. The diverse portrayal of circumcision within the Bible does not immediately suggest that righteousness and faith lie at the very heart of its meaning. Not only so, but the *nature* of the righteousness communicated by circumcision is somewhat uncertain. The 'justification' language often connected with circumcision in the NT is typically thought of in quite a different category from the 'circumcision of the heart' language connected with circumcision in the OT; both of which seem quite distinct from references to physical circumcision and the promise of land and descendants. So too circumcision often occurs in contexts in both Testaments that seem to suggest that complete obedience is expected or demanded.

My argument here has been that right from the institution of circumcision, righteousness and blamelessness have been at the very heart. That righteousness/blamelessness is both a present status but also a future promise that is appropriated by humble trust in God's promise to Abraham of a blameless 'seed'.

Righteous by promise

Circumcision is unavoidably bound up with both the demand and the promise of righteousness/blamelessness. I have tried to show that the opening verse of Genesis 17 is crucial to understanding circumcision. There Yahweh called Abraham to 'walk before me and be blameless'. The fulfilment of Yahweh's promise to Abraham was dependent on the realization of that kind of blameless life before Yahweh. However, such a demand is no ordinary accomplishment, since blamelessness represents the perfections of God himself.

But the idea of blamelessness is intimately connected with righteousness, both in Genesis, in the person of Noah, and the wider OT and NT. In that light, it is clear that even before Yahweh called

211

Abraham to be blameless/righteous in Genesis 17, Yahweh had reckoned him to be that in Genesis 15. Moreover, the link between the covenant ceremonies of those two chapters suggests that circumcision was a sign of the covenant already established in Genesis 15 on the basis of Abraham's faith. In other words, although the ultimate fulfilment of all that God promised Abraham lay in the realization of truly blameless people, the fulfilment of the demand for Abraham and others to be blameless/righteous lies irrevocably within the promise of God.

The promissory nature of righteousness/blamelessness is supported by the sacrificial system's use of blameless substitutes. The OT people of God were continually to offer to God 'blameless' sacrifices to atone for their not-blameless lives. In that way, the disjunction between the ideal of blamelessness and the sinful reality of people's lives was held together – through the hope of a blameless substitute which could atone for the moral incompleteness of the offerer. Thus the sacrificial system, received in faith, afforded the people a status that did not comport with the reality of their present lives.

The legitimacy of reading God's call to Abraham to be blameless through the lens of the sacrificial system is supported by the use of blamelessness language both within the NT and within other contemporaneous documents. The Qumran community, for example, understood blamelessness to be a moral category, while simultaneously linking it with the OT sacrificial system, and, as in Genesis 17, often using it in conjunction with the language of walking. So too the *Testament of Benjamin* presents the curious example of the blameless one who would die on behalf of lawless men. More particularly, within the NT, blamelessness is understood to represent the perfections of God himself. But believers will be presented blameless by Christ before the Father at the eschaton, by virtue of Christ's own blameless sacrifice for their sins.

By tying righteousness with blamelessness it becomes clear that righteousness is not merely a status but a moral quality. Still less is righteousness merely the attribute of being 'in the covenant'. From the outset righteousness was tied to God's demand for a perfect people – people who are perfect as he is perfect. Yet that demand was never separated from God's remarkable provision of grace. That grace came in the form of a promise to Abraham, that through one of his descendants God would bless the world. It came in the form of a promise embodied in the sacrificial provision of the law that one day God's people would walk before him blamelessly.

That is not to deny that righteousness is a present status. Nor is it to claim that 'justification' means to 'make righteous'. Rather, the present verdict of righteous/blameless is anchored in God's promise to effect righteousness through the sacrifice and life of his beloved Son. The category of promise enables us to hold together both the demand for righteousness and the reality of God's present grace without ironing out the contours of redemptive history. What God promised, Abraham did not have in full, and yet God reckoned him to have it (Gen. 15:6). Abraham possessed forgiveness long before the blameless sacrifice laid down his life. He was justified long before the resurrection of Jesus from the dead. And he had the sure and certain hope of his own resurrection long before, through the Spirit, being united with Jesus' historic bodily resurrection from the dead.

Moreover, the full-orbed notion of blamelessness/righteousness suggests that the promise/fulfilment lies not only in forgiveness but also in a positively righteous character. That is essentially what the doctrine of the 'imputed righteousness' of Christ has always been trying to affirm – that it is not enough to be 'not guilty': we must also be reckoned to be perfectly obedient and holy.[1] But imputation alone is merely one side of the coin of blamelessness. Being reckoned to possess what we will possess is a wonderful present reality that gives us confidence before God, but it is still only a part of God's larger programme of remaking us in the image of his majestic Son. And although Paul strives to take hold of that greater reality, such striving is firmly anchored in the promise of God and the person and work of Christ.

Which is not to say that over time we become more justified; rather, it is to say that over time we become more and more what God has promised to make us and what he has already declared us to be. As Bavinck writes:

> A person is ungodly in an ethical sense, but on account of the righteousness of Christ that person becomes righteous in a juridical sense . . . [They are like] a child who, having been graciously adopted by a wealthy man, can as a future heir be called rich even though at the moment he or she does not yet own a penny. God declares sinners righteous, adopts them as children, promises them Christ and all his benefits; for that reason they are called righteous and will one day gain possession of all the treasures of grace.[2]

---

[1] Grudem 2004: 724–726.
[2] Bavinck 2008: 213.

Righteous by faith

The idea of promise almost immediately demands the notion of faith. A promise cannot be earned but only received. And the faith-based reception of the promise held out in circumcision is repeatedly demonstrated through the OT and NT.

In Leviticus 26 circumcision is tied to humility. The remedy for the judgment that was inevitably coming on Israel on account of their sin was to be found in humility and repentance, together with making amends for sin. In the case of the people of Israel, amends would be made by the exile. But again, within the context of the sacrificial system established within Leviticus, the ultimate hope lay in atonement of the kind foreshadowed on the Day of Atonement, where the ark containing the tablets of the Mosaic covenant would be sprinkled with blood, offering the hope of forgiveness for breaking the very covenant itself. In Deuteronomy the people are again called to absolute obedience. Yet in the context of assured *dis*obedience, the hope of obedience is found through humility and repentance centred on Yahweh's promise to Abraham. Trust in Yahweh's promise to Abraham is metaphorized in the language of circumcision of the heart. In Deuteronomy 10 the people themselves are called to come in trust and repentance. Yet in Deuteronomy 30 it becomes clear that even that move towards God is an act of his initiative and grace.

With remarkable constancy that theme of righteousness through humble repentance and faith is connected with circumcision in a host of OT passages. Not least in Joshua 5, where standing on the edge of the Promised Land after forty years in the wilderness the people are commanded by Yahweh to begin circumcision again. Circumcision was stopped after Yahweh had handed down his judgment on the people for their unbelief – their disbelieving he could really bring them into the Promised Land. On the edge of the Promised Land the people began circumcision again as a reminder of how Yahweh had 'rolled away' the reproach of their unbelief. In that way uncircumcision was tied even more strongly with unbelief, and circumcision with faith and trust in Yahweh.

Similarly, in Romans 2 – 4 Paul explicitly explains the significance of circumcision with respect to righteousness and faith. The 'works' that matter are the works of humility, repentance and faith in God's promise to Abraham. It is not those who hear the law or those promises, but those who appropriate them through faith and repentance whose hearts are circumcised. That was evident even in Abraham's own circumcision. His circumcision was a seal, or confirmation, of the by-faith-righteousness that he had already received while he was uncircumcised.

Righteous through the promised seed

But circumcision not only pointed to the hope of righteousness; it also revealed the means through which that righteousness would come. The language of 'walking before Yahweh' commanded of Abraham is taken up through the remainder of the OT almost exclusively in connection with the Davidic king. The hope for fulfilment of Yahweh's promise to Abraham lay somehow in the arrival of the promised son of David, who would walk before Yahweh and do all that is in his heart and mind – a faithful messiah for whom God would build a faithful house (1 Sam. 2:35). That hope of a single 'seed' through whom the promise would be established is already hinted at throughout Genesis, but it takes definite shape as the OT and NT unfold.

In Exodus and Isaiah 52 the hope of the promised 'seed' returns explicitly in connection with circumcision. In Exodus the threat to Moses' son, together with the genealogy tracing Moses back to Abraham, Isaac and Jacob, reaffirmed the importance of the solitary figure through whom the covenant promises would be realized. In Isaiah 52 Yahweh's promise of a Zion without the uncircumcised and unclean ultimately finds its fulfilment in the suffering servant of Isaiah 53, whose 'seed' will prosper, and through whose sacrifice many will be accounted righteous.

In Philippians 3 Paul eschews his former blamelessness/righteousness in preference for the righteousness that comes through the death and resurrection of the Messiah. The 'circumcision' are those who receive that righteousness through Christ, not those who mutilate the flesh. The same theme is found in Colossians 2, where it is through the circumcision of Christ (his death and resurrection) that believers are transformed into the image of Christ; while in Ephesians 2, those who used to 'walk' in sins and transgressions, who used to be called the 'uncircumcised', have now been brought into the one new humanity established in Christ Jesus.

In Galatians Paul explains why circumcision has come to an end and now remains largely a matter of indifference: circumcision pointed to the 'seed' of Abraham who was to come. It is faith in the promised seed, Jesus, that brings righteousness and justification, not the mechanics of the law or circumcision. Those who hang on to circumcision, and so miss Jesus, miss out on the righteousness God promised to Abraham.

Circumcision as a sign of righteousness by faith in the promised seed

Circumcision was a sign of God's covenant with Abraham. That covenant promised righteousness and the Spirit who comes through the 'seed' of Abraham – Jesus Christ. The reason that *circumcision* was the sign was because it was focused not on the nation as a whole but on the one descendant of Abraham through whom the promises would become a reality. Moreover, participation in that promise and sharing in the inheritance come not through *physical* circumcision or the law in general, but through faith in God's promise to Abraham, and ultimately through faith in the Messiah/seed descended from Abraham. To trust in that promise humbly and repentantly is to have a 'circumcised heart'. That promise, received by faith, results in people who are transformed into the image of God's beloved Son, the seed of Abraham. But faith in God's promise of a 'seed' also results in people who are reckoned to possess already the righteousness and blamelessness God has promised but not yet brought to complete fulfilment.

Before the arrival of the promised 'seed of Abraham' circumcision was, in a sense, indispensable. It was Yahweh's mandated sign pointing to the promise. It could not be lightly thrown aside; not because it achieved something of itself, but because it communicated the nature of the promise. In that sense, it preserved the gospel promise. Nevertheless, to trust in the sign itself was to miss the point. Likewise, to embrace circumcision, now that the Messiah/seed of Abraham has come, fundamentally misses the point. As Rupert Tuitiensis, the twelfth-century theologian wrote:

> Now see how great a sacrilege it would be, after the arrival of [Abraham's] seed, to still impose on one's flesh a sign of his circumcision. No, in fact according to the truth written beforehand, undertaking circumcision is the profession that his seed is being expected. Whoever is circumcised professes that he is expecting that the seed that was promised to Abraham would come, even if not by knowledge, but nevertheless by that sign. But he, namely Christ, has already come, has already been born, and since he has been given as a blessing to all nations the truth of God has been

216

fulfilled. Therefore whoever is still circumcised denies that he has come, the one he pronounces by such a sign that he is expecting to come, and for this reason he denies that the one who has already come is the Christ. Rightly and truly therefore the Apostle says: if you are circumcised, Christ will be of no benefit to you.[3]

Despite the diversity within the presentations of circumcision within the OT and the NT, it is clear that the themes of righteousness and faith are not peripheral but are of central importance. The two are brought together in the promise of a blameless/righteous seed of Abraham through whom righteousness/blamelessness will come to those who receive the promise by faith. It is for that reason that circumcision is often so closely associated with debates about righteousness and the nature of the gospel in the NT and with the great promises of the gospel in the OT – it was because circumcision was a sign of the gospel of righteousness by faith in the promised blameless seed of Abraham.

---

[3] Rupert Tuitiensis, *De Trinitate* 5.31 (PL 167:395, my tr.).

Bibliography

Alexander, T. Desmond (1983), 'Genesis 22 and the Covenant of Circumcision', *JSOT* 25: 17–22.

———— (1993), 'Genealogies, Seed and the Compositional Unity of Genesis', *TynBul* 44: 255–270.

———— (1995), 'Messianic Ideology in the Book of Genesis', in Philip E. Satterthwaite, Richard S. Hess and Gordon J. Wenham (eds.), *The Lord's Anointed: Interpretation of Old Testament Messianic Texts*, Grand Rapids: Baker, 19–39.

———— (1997), 'Further Observations on the Term "Seed" in Genesis', *TynBul* 48: 363–367.

———— (2012), *From Paradise to the Promised Land: An Introduction to the Pentateuch*, 3rd edn, Grand Rapids: Baker.

Allen, Leslie C. (1990), *Ezekiel 20–48*, WBC 29, Dallas: Word.

———— (2008), *Jeremiah: A Commentary*, OTL, Louisville: Westminster John Knox.

Allen, Ronald B. (1996), 'The "Bloody Bridegroom" in Exodus 4:24–26', *BSac* 153: 259–269.

Andersen, Francis I. (2001), *Habakkuk: A New Translation with Introduction and Commentary*, AB 25, New York: Doubleday.

Anderson, A. A. (1972), *The Book of Psalms*, 2 vols., NCB, London: Marshall, Morgan & Scott.

Arnold, Bill T. (2009), *Genesis*, NCBC, Cambridge: Cambridge University Press.

Auld, A. Graeme (2004), *Joshua: Jesus Son of Naue in Codex Vaticanus*, Septuagint Commentary Series, Leiden: Brill.

Averbeck, Richard E. (1997), 'רצה', in *NIDOTTE* 3: 1186–1188.

Barker, Paul A. (2004), *The Triumph of Grace in Deuteronomy: Faithless Israel, Faithful Yahweh in Deuteronomy*, PBM, Milton Keynes: Paternoster.

Barr, James (1992), '"Thou Art the Cherub": Ezekiel 28.14 and the Post-Ezekiel Understanding of Genesis 2–3', *Priests, Prophets and Scribes: Essays on the Formation and Heritage of Second Temple*

Judaism in Honour of Joseph Blenkinsopp, JSOTSup 149, Sheffield: Sheffield Academic Press, 213–223.

Barrett, C. K. (1985), *Freedom and Obligation: A Study of the Epistle to the Galatians*, London: SPCK.

—— (1991), *The Epistle to the Romans*, rev. edn, BNTC, London: Continuum.

Barstad, H. M. (2004), 'רצה', in *TDOT* 13: 618–630.

Barth, Markus, and Helmut Blanke (1994), *Colossians: A New Translation with Introduction and Commentary*, tr. Astrid B. Beck, AB 34B, New Haven: Yale University Press.

Bavinck, Herman (2008), *Holy Spirit, Church, and New Creation*, ed. John Bolt, tr. John Vriend, vol. 4 of *Reformed Dogmatics*, Grand Rapids: Baker Academic.

Beale, G. K. (1999), *The Book of Revelation: A Commentary on the Greek Text*, NIGTC, Grand Rapids: Eerdmans.

Beentjes, Pancratius C. (ed.) (1997), *The Book of Ben Sira in Hebrew: A Text Edition of All Extant Hebrew Manuscripts and a Synopsis of All Parallel Hebrew Ben Sira Texts*, VTSup 68, Leiden: Brill.

Berkley, Timothy W. (2000), *From a Broken Covenant to Circumcision of the Heart: Pauline Intertextual Exegesis in Romans 2:17–29*, SBLDS 175, Atlanta: Society of Biblical Literature.

Bernat, David A. (2009), *Sign of the Covenant: Circumcision in the Priestly Tradition*, AIL 3, Atlanta: Society of Biblical Literature.

Best, Ernest (1955), *One Body in Christ: A Study in the Relationship of the Church to Christ in the Epistles of the Apostle Paul*, London: SPCK.

Betz, Hans Dieter (1979), *Galatians: A Commentary on Paul's Letter to the Churches in Galatia*, Hermeneia, Philadelphia: Fortress.

Bird, Michael F. (2007), *The Saving Righteousness of God: Studies on Paul, Justification and the New Perspective*, PBM, Eugene: Wipf & Stock.

Blaschke, Andreas (1998), *Beschneidung: Zeugnisse der Bibel und verwandter Texte*, TANZ, Tübingen: Francke.

Blenkinsopp, Joseph (2002), *Isaiah 40–55: A New Translation with Introduction and Commentary*, AB 19A, New Haven: Yale University Press.

Block, Daniel I. (1997), *The Book of Ezekiel: Chapters 1–24*, NICOT, Grand Rapids: Eerdmans.

—— (1998), *The Book of Ezekiel: Chapters 25–48*, NICOT, Grand Rapids: Eerdmans.

Bockmuehl, Markus (1997), *The Epistle to the Philippians*, BNTC, London: Continuum.

Boling, Robert G. (1982), *Joshua: A New Translation with Notes and Commentary*, AB 6, Garden City: Doubleday.

Braswell, Joseph P. (1991), '"The Blessing of Abraham" Versus "The Curse of the Law": Another Look at Gal 3:10–13', *WTJ* 53: 73–91.

Bruce, F. F. (1982), *The Epistle to the Galatians: A Commentary on the Greek Text*, NIGTC, Grand Rapids: Eerdmans.

—— (1984), *The Epistles to the Colossians, to Philemon, and to the Ephesians*, NICNT, Grand Rapids: Eerdmans.

—— (2009), 'Habakkuk', in Thomas E. McComiskey (ed.), *The Minor Prophets: An Exegetical and Expository Commentary*, Grand Rapids: Baker Academic, 831–896.

Büchsel, Friedrich (1964), 'Ἀγοράζω, Ἐξαγοράζω', in *TDNT* 1: 124–128.

—— (1965), 'Εἰλικρινής', in *TDNT* 2: 397–398.

Bultmann, Rudolf (1952), *Theology of the New Testament*, tr. Kendrick Grobel, 2 vols., London: SCM.

Burton, Ernest de Witt (1962), *A Critical and Exegetical Commentary on the Epistle to the Galatians*, ICC, 1921, repr., Edinburgh: T&T Clark.

Butler, Trent C. (2014), *Joshua*, 2nd edn, 2 vols., WBC 7, Grand Rapids: Zondervan.

Calvin, John (2006), *Institutes of the Christian Religion*, ed. John T. McNeill, tr. Ford Lewis Battles, 2 vols., LCC, Louisville: Westminster John Knox.

Campbell, Constantine R. (2012), *Paul and Union with Christ: An Exegetical and Theological Study*, Grand Rapids: Zondervan.

Carson, D. A. (2000), 'Systematic Theology and Biblical Theology', in *NDBT*, 89–104.

—— (2010), 'Matthew', in *EBC* 9: 23–670.

Christensen, Duane L. (2002), *Deuteronomy 21:10–34:12*, WBC 6B, Dallas: Word.

Coats, George W. (1983), *Genesis: With an Introduction to Narrative Literature*, FOTL 1, Grand Rapids: Eerdmans.

Cohen, Shaye J. D. (2005), *Why Aren't Jewish Women Circumcised? Gender and Covenant in Judaism*, Berkeley: University of California Press.

Collange, Jean François (1979), *The Epistle of Saint Paul to the Philippians*, tr. A. W. Heathcote, London: Epworth.

Collins, C. John (1997), 'A Syntactical Note (Genesis 3:15): Is the Woman's Seed Singular or Plural?', *TynBul* 48: 139–148.

Cooke, G. A. (1951), *A Critical and Exegetical Commentary on the Book of Ezekiel*, ICC, Edinburgh: T&T Clark.

Cooper Sr, Lamar Eugene (2001), *Ezekiel*, NAC 17, Nashville: Broadman & Holman.

Cotter, David W. (2003), *Genesis*, Berit Olam, Collegeville: Liturgical Press.

Coxhead, Steven R. (2006), 'Deuteronomy 30:11–14 as a Prophecy of the New Covenant in Christ', *WTJ* 68: 305–320.

Craigie, Peter C. (1976), *The Book of Deuteronomy*, NICOT, Grand Rapids: Eerdmans.

Craigie, Peter C., Page H. Kelley and Joel F. Drinkard Jr (1991), *Jeremiah 1–25*, WBC 26, Dallas: Word.

Cranfield, C. E. B. (2004), *A Critical and Exegetical Commentary on the Epistle to the Romans*, vol. 1, ICC, 1975, repr., London: T&T Clark.

Creach, Jerome F. D. (2003), *Joshua*, IBC, Louisville: John Knox.

Cross, Frank Moore (1973), *Canaanite Myth and Hebrew Epic: Essays in the History of the Religion of Israel*, Cambridge: Harvard University Press.

Das, A. Andrew (2010), *Paul, the Law, and the Covenant*, 2001, repr., Grand Rapids: Baker.

Davies, Glenn (1990), *Faith and Obedience in Romans: A Study in Romans 1–4*, JSNTSup 39, Sheffield: JSOT Press.

De Boer, Martinus C. (2007), 'The Meaning of the Phrase τὰ στοιχεῖα τοῦ κόσμου in Galatians', *NTS* 53: 204–224.

——— (2011), *Galatians: A Commentary*, NTL, Louisville: Westminster John Knox.

Deenick, Karl (2010), 'Who Is the "I" in Romans 7:14–25?', *RTR* 69: 119–130.

——— (2011), 'Priest and King or Priest-King in 1 Samuel 2:35', *WTJ* 73: 325–339.

Deidun, Tom (1986), '"Having His Cake and Eating It": Paul on the Law', *HeyJ* 27: 43–52.

DeRouchie, Jason S. (2004), 'Circumcision in the Hebrew Bible and Targums: Theology, Rhetoric, and the Handling of Metaphor', *BBR* 14: 175–203.

Duguid, Iain M. (1999), *Ezekiel*, NIVAC, Grand Rapids: Zondervan.

Dumbrell, William J. (2000), 'Abraham and the Abrahamic Covenant in Galatians 3:1–14', in Peter Bolt and Mark Thompson (eds.), *The*

Gospel to the Nations: Perspectives on Paul's Mission, London: Apollos, 19–31.

—— (2009), *Covenant and Creation: A Theology of Old Testament Covenants*, 1984, repr., Eugene: Wipf & Stock.

Dunn, James D. G. (1988), *Romans*, 2 vols., WBC 38, Dallas: Word.

—— (1993), *The Epistle to the Galatians*, BNTC, London: Continuum.

—— (1996), *The Epistles to the Colossians and to Philemon: A Commentary on the Greek Text*, NIGTC, Grand Rapids: Eerdmans.

—— (2008), *The New Perspective on Paul*, rev. edn, Grand Rapids: Eerdmans.

Durham, John I. (1987), *Exodus*, WBC 3, Dallas: Word.

Ebel, G. (1986), 'Walk, Run, Way, Conduct', in *NIDNTT* 3: 933–947.

Eichrodt, Walter (1970), *Ezekiel: A Commentary*, tr. Cosslett Quin, OTL, London: SCM.

Embry, Bradley (2010), 'The Endangerment of Moses: Towards a New Reading of Exodus 4:24–26', *VT* 60: 177–196.

Fee, Gordon D. (1995), *Paul's Letter to the Philippians*, NICNT, Grand Rapids: Eerdmans.

Fitzmyer, Joseph A. (1993), *Romans: A New Translation with Introduction and Commentary*, AB 33, New York: Yale University Press.

Fox, Michael V. (1974), 'Sign of the Covenant: Circumcision in the Light of the Priestly 'Ôt Etiologies', *RB* 81: 557–596.

Freedman, H., and Maurice Simon (eds.) (1939), *Midrash Rabbah*, tr. H. Freedman, 10 vols., London: Soncino.

Fretheim, Terence E. (1991), *Exodus*, IBC, Louisville: Westminster John Knox.

Fuller, Daniel P. (1975), 'Paul and the Works of the Law', *WTJ* 38: 28–42.

Fung, Ronald Y. K. (1988), *The Epistle to the Galatians*, NICNT, Grand Rapids: Eerdmans.

García Martínez, Florentino, and Eibert J. C. Tigchelaar (eds.) (1997–8), *The Dead Sea Scrolls Study Edition*, 2 vols., Leiden: Brill.

Garlington, D. B. (1991), 'The Obedience of Faith in the Letter to the Romans (Part 2)', *WTJ* 53: 47–72.

Gathercole, Simon J. (2002a), 'A Law Unto Themselves: The Gentiles in Romans 2.14–15 Revisited', *JSNT* 85: 27–49.

—— (2002b), *Where Is Boasting? Early Jewish Soteriology and Paul's Response in Romans 1–5*, Grand Rapids: Eerdmans.

Gentry, Peter J., and Stephen J. Wellum (2012), *Kingdom Through Covenant: A Biblical-Theological Understanding of the Covenants*, Wheaton: Crossway.

Greenberg, Moshe (1997), *Ezekiel 21–37: A New Translation with Introduction and Commentary*, AB 22A, 1983, repr., New Haven: Yale University Press.

Grudem, Wayne (2004), *Systematic Theology: An Introduction to Biblical Doctrine*, Grand Rapids: Zondervan.

Gundry, Robert H. (1985), 'Grace, Works, and Staying Saved in Paul', *Bib* 66: 1–38.

Gunkel, Hermann (1997), *Genesis*, tr. Mark E. Biddle, Macon: Mercer University Press.

Hahn, Scott W. (2009), *Kinship by Covenant: A Canonical Approach to the Fulfillment of God's Saving Promises*, New Haven: Yale University Press.

Hamilton Jr, James M. (2006), *God's Indwelling Presence: The Holy Spirit in the Old and New Testaments*, NACSBT, Nashville: B&H Academic.

———— (2007), 'The Seed of the Woman and the Blessing of Abraham', *TynBul* 58: 253–273.

Hamilton, Victor P. (1990), *The Book of Genesis: Chapters 1–17*, NICOT, Grand Rapids: Eerdmans.

———— (2011), *Exodus: An Exegetical Commentary*, Grand Rapids: Baker Academic.

Hamlin, John E. (1983), *Inheriting the Land: A Commentary on the Book of Joshua*, ITC, Grand Rapids: Eerdmans.

Hansen, G. Walter (2009), *The Letter to the Philippians*, PNTC, Grand Rapids: Eerdmans.

Harris, Murray J. (2010), *Colossians and Philemon*, rev. edn, EGGNT, Nashville: B&H Academic.

Harstad, Adolph L. (2004), *Joshua*, ConcC, Saint Louis: Concordia.

Hasel, Gerhard F. (1981), 'The Meaning of the Animal Rite in Genesis 15', *JSOT* 19: 61–78.

Hauck, Friedrich (1967), 'Ἄμωμος', in *TDNT* 4: 830–831.

Hawk, L. Daniel (2000), *Joshua*, Berit Olam, Collegeville: Liturgical Press.

Hawthorne, Gerald F., and Ralph P. Martin (2004), *Philippians*, rev. edn, WBC 43, Dallas: Word.

Hays, Christopher (2007), '"Lest Ye Perish in the Way": Ritual and Kinship in Exodus 4:24–26', *HS* 48: 39–54.

Helfmeyer, F. J. (1978), 'הָלַךְ', in *TDOT* 3: 388–403.

Hengel, Martin (2004), 'The Effective History of Isaiah 53 in the Pre-Christian Period', in Bernd Janowski and Peter Stuhlmacher (eds.), Daniel P. Bailey (tr.), *The Suffering Servant: Isaiah 53 in Jewish and Christian Sources*, Grand Rapids: Eerdmans, 75–146.

Holladay, William L. (1986), *Jeremiah 1: A Commentary on the Book of the Prophet Jeremiah, Chapters 1–25*, Hermeneia, Philadelphia: Fortress.

Horton, Michael (2011), *The Christian Faith: A Systematic Theology for Pilgrims on the Way*, Grand Rapids: Zondervan.

Howard, George (1974), 'Faith of Christ', *ExpTim* 85: 212–214.

——— (1990), *Paul: Crisis in Galatia: A Study in Early Christian Theology*, 2nd edn, SNTSMS 35, Cambridge: Cambridge University Press.

Hübner, Hans (1984), *Law in Paul's Thought*, SNTW, Edinburgh: T&T Clark.

Jewett, Robert (2006), *Romans: A Commentary*, ed. Eldon J. Epp, Hermeneia, Minneapolis: Fortress.

Joyce, Paul M. (2007), *Ezekiel: A Commentary*, LHBOTS 482, New York and London: T&T Clark/Continuum.

Kaiser Jr, Walter C. (1978), *Toward an Old Testament Theology*, Grand Rapids: Zondervan.

Käsemann, Ernst (1994), *Commentary on Romans*, tr. Geoffrey W. Bromiley, 1980, repr., Grand Rapids: Eerdmans.

Kedar-Kopfstein, Benjamin (2006), 'תָּמַם', in *TDOT* 15: 699–711.

Keil, Carl Friedrich, and Franz Delitzsch (1996), *Commentary on the Old Testament*, 10 vols., Peabody: Hendrickson.

Kidner, Derek (1967), *Genesis: An Introduction and Commentary*, TOTC, Leicester: Inter-Varsity Press; Downers Grove: InterVarsity Press.

——— (1973), *Psalms 1–72: An Introduction and Commentary on Books I and II of the Psalms*, TOTC, Leicester: Inter-Varsity Press.

Kiuchi, Nobuyoshi (2007), *Leviticus*, AOTC 3, Nottingham: Apollos; Downers Grove: InterVarsity Press.

Klijn, A. F. J. (1965), 'Paul's Opponents in Philippians 3', *NovT* 7: 278–284.

Kline, Meredith G. (1968), *By Oath Consigned: A Reinterpretation of the Covenant Signs of Circumcision and Baptism*, Grand Rapids: Eerdmans.

——— (2006), *Kingdom Prologue: Genesis Foundations for a Covenantal Worldview*, Eugene: Wipf & Stock.

Knight, George W. (1992), *The Pastoral Epistles: A Commentary on the Greek Text*, NIGTC, Grand Rapids: Eerdmans.

Konkel, A. H. (1997), 'גלל', in *NIDOTTE* 1: 867–868.

Koperski, Veronica (1993), 'The Meaning of *Pistis Christou* in Philippians 3:9', *LS* 18: 198–216.

—— (1996), *The Knowledge of Christ Jesus My Lord: The High Christology of Philippians 3:7–11*, CBET 16, Kampen: Kok Pharos.

Kosmala, Hans (1962), 'The "Bloody Husband"', *VT* 12: 14–28.

Kruse, Colin G. (2012), *Paul's Letter to the Romans*, PNTC, Grand Rapids: Eerdmans.

Kwon, Yon-Gyong (2004), *Eschatology in Galatians: Rethinking Paul's Response to the Crisis in Galatia*, WUNT 2.183, Tübingen: Mohr Siebeck.

Lambdin, T. O. (1973), *Introduction to Biblical Hebrew*, London: Darton, Longman and Todd.

Lee, Chee-Chiew (2013), *Blessing of Abraham, the Spirit, and Justification in Galatians: Their Relationship and Significance for Understanding Paul's Theology*, Eugene: Wipf & Stock.

Lemke, Werner E. (2003), 'Circumcision of the Heart: The Journey of a Biblical Metaphor', in Brent A. Strawn and Nancy R. Bowen (eds.), *A God So Near: Essays on Old Testament Theology in Honor of Patrick D. Miller*, Winona Lake: Eisenbrauns, 299–319.

Lightfoot, J. B. (1874), *Saint Paul's Epistle to the Galatians: A Revised Text with Introduction, Notes, and Dissertations*, 10th edn, CCGNT, London: Macmillan.

Livesey, Nina E. (2010), *Circumcision as a Malleable Symbol*, WUNT 2.295, Tübingen: Mohr Siebeck.

Lohse, Eduard (1968), 'Προσωπολημψία, Προσωπολήμπτης, Προσωπολημπτέω, Ἀπροσωπολήμπτως', in *TDNT* 6: 779–780.

—— (1971), *Colossians and Philemon: A Commentary on the Epistles to the Colossians and to Philemon*, tr. William R. Poehlmann and Robert J. Karris, Hermeneia, Philadelphia: Fortress.

Longenecker, Bruce W. (1998), *The Triumph of Abraham's God: The Transformation of Identity in Galatians*, Nashville: Abingdon.

Longenecker, Richard N. (1998), *Galatians*, WBC 41, Dallas: Word.

Lührmann, Dieter (1992), *Galatians*, tr. O. C. Dean Jr, CC, Minneapolis: Fortress.

Lundbom, Jack R. (1999), *Jeremiah 1–20: A New Translation with Introduction and Commentary*, AB 21A, New York: Doubleday.

Luther, Martin (1810), *A Commentary on St. Paul's Epistles to the Galatians*, London: Mathews and Leigh.

Luz, Ulrich (2007), *Matthew 1–7: A Commentary on Matthew 1–7*, ed. Helmut Koester, tr. James E. Crouch, rev. edn, Hermeneia, Minneapolis: Fortress.

McComiskey, Thomas E. (1985), *The Covenants of Promise: A Theology of the Old Testament Covenants*, Leicester: Inter-Varsity Press.

McConville, J. Gordon (2002), *Deuteronomy*, AOTC 5, Leicester: Apollos; Downers Grove: InterVarsity Press.

McKane, William (1986), *A Critical and Exegetical Commentary on Jeremiah*, 2 vols., ICC, Edinburgh: T&T Clark.

McKenzie, John L. (2008), *Second Isaiah: Introduction, Translation, and Notes*, AB 20, 1968, repr., New Haven: Yale University Press.

Maertens, P. (2000), 'Une Étude de Rm 2.12–16', *NTS* 46: 504–519.

Martin, Raymond Albert (1965), 'Earliest Messianic Interpretation of Genesis 3:15', *JBL* 84: 425–427.

Martin, Troy (1996), 'Pagan and Judeo-Christian Time-Keeping Schemes in Gal 4.10 and Col 2.16', *NTS* 42: 105–119.

Martyn, J. Louis (2008), *Galatians: A New Translation with Introduction and Commentary*, AB 33A, 1974, repr., New Haven: Yale University Press.

Matera, Frank J. (2007), *Galatians*, rev. edn, SP 9, Collegeville: Liturgical Press.

Matlock, R. Barry (2009), 'Saving Faith: The Rhetoric and Semantics of Πίστις in Paul', in Michael F. Bird and Preston M. Sprinkle (eds.), *The Faith of Jesus Christ*, Milton Keynes: Paternoster, 73–89.

Meade, John D. (2014), 'Circumcision of the Heart in Leviticus and Deuteronomy: Divine Means for Resolving Curse and Bringing Blessing', *SBJT* 18.3: 59–85.

Melick, Richard R. (2001), *Philippians, Colossians, Philemon*, NAC 32, Nashville: Broadman & Holman.

Melugin, Roy F. (1976), *The Formation of Isaiah 40–55*, BZAW 141, Berlin: de Gruyter.

Merrill, Eugene H. (1994), *Deuteronomy*, NAC 4, Nashville: Broadman & Holman.

——— (1997), 'הלך', in *NIDOTTE* 1: 1032–1035.

Metzger, Bruce M. (1994), *A Textual Commentary on the Greek New Testament*, 2nd edn, New York: United Bible Societies.

Milgrom, Jacob (2001), *Leviticus 23–27: A New Translation with Introduction and Commentary*, AB 3B, New York: Doubleday.

Miller Jr, Patrick D. (1982), *Sin and Judgement in the Prophets: A Stylistic Analysis*, SBLMS 27, Chico: Scholars.

Moo, Douglas J. (1996), *The Epistle to the Romans*, NICNT, Grand Rapids: Eerdmans.

—— (2008), *The Letters to the Colossians and to Philemon*, PNTC, Grand Rapids: Eerdmans.

—— (2013), *Galatians*, BECNT, Grand Rapids: Baker.

Morris, Leon (1988), *The Epistle to the Romans*, PNTC, Grand Rapids: Eerdmans.

Motyer, J. A. (1993), *The Prophecy of Isaiah: An Introduction and Commentary*, Leicester: Inter-Varsity Press; Downers Grove: InterVarsity Press.

Mounce, William D. (2000), *Pastoral Epistles*, WBC 46, Dallas: Word.

Muller, Earl C. (1990), *Trinity and Marriage in Paul: The Establishment of a Communitarian Analogy of the Trinity Grounded in the Theological Shape of Pauline Thought*, AUS 60, New York: Peter Lang.

Murray, John (1967), *The Epistle to the Romans: The English Text with Introduction, Exposition and Notes*, NLCNT, London: Marshall, Morgan & Scott.

Nelson, Richard D. (1997), *Joshua: A Commentary*, OTL, Louisville: Westminster John Knox.

Nolland, John (2005), *The Gospel of Matthew: A Commentary on the Greek Text*, NIGTC, Grand Rapids: Eerdmans.

Noort, Edward (2005), 'The Disgrace of Egypt: Joshua 5.9a and Its Context', in Anthony Hilhorst and George H. van Kooten (eds.), *The Wisdom of Egypt: Jewish, Early Christian, and Gnostic Essays in Honour of Gerard P. Luttikhuizen*, Ancient Christianity and Early Judaism 59, Leiden: Brill, 3–19.

O'Brien, Peter T. (1991), *The Epistle to the Philippians: A Commentary on the Greek Text*, NIGTC, Grand Rapids: Eerdmans.

—— (1998), *Colossians, Philemon*, WBC 44, Dallas: Word.

—— (2004), 'Was Paul Converted?', *The Paradoxes of Paul*, vol. 2 of *Justification and Variegated Nomism*, Grand Rapids: Baker, 361–391.

Ortlund, Dane C. (2012), *Zeal Without Knowledge: The Concept of Zeal in Romans 10, Galatians 1 and Philippians 3*, LNTS 472, London: T&T Clark.

Oswalt, John N. (1998), *The Book of Isaiah: Chapters 40–66*, NICOT, Grand Rapids: Eerdmans.

Pao, David W. (2012), *Colossians and Philemon*, ZECNT 12, Grand Rapids: Zondervan.

Peterson, David (2005), *Hebrews and Perfection: An Examination of the Concept of Perfection in the 'Epistle to the Hebrews'*, SNTSMS 47, Cambridge: Cambridge University Press.

Propp, William H. C. (1993), 'That Bloody Bridegroom (Exodus IV 24–6)', *VT* 43: 495–518.

—— (1999), *Exodus 1–18: A New Translation with Introduction and Commentary*, AB 2, New Haven: Yale University Press.

Rad, Gerhard von (1972), *Genesis: A Commentary*, rev. edn, OTL, London: SCM.

Räisänen, Heikki (2010), *Paul and the Law*, 2nd edn, WUNT 29, 1983, repr., Eugene: Wipf & Stock.

Reis, Pamela Tamarkin (1991), 'The Bridegroom of Blood: A New Reading', *Judaism* 40: 324–331.

Reumann, John (2008), *Philippians: A New Translation with Introduction and Commentary*, AB 33B, New Haven: Yale University Press.

Reymond, Robert L. (2002), *A New Systematic Theology of the Christian Faith*, 2nd edn, Nashville: Thomas Nelson.

Roberts, J. J. M. (1991), *Nahum, Habakkuk, and Zephaniah: A Commentary*, OTL, Louisville: Westminster John Knox.

Robertson, O. Palmer (1990), *The Books of Nahum, Habakkuk, and Zephaniah*, NICOT, Grand Rapids: Eerdmans.

Robinson, Bernard P. (1986), 'Zipporah to the Rescue: A Contextual Study of Exodus 4:24–6', *VT* 36: 447–461.

Rogers Jr, Cleon L. (1970), 'The Covenant with Abraham and Its Historical Setting', *BSac* 127: 241–256.

Rosner, Brian S. (2013), *Paul and the Law: Keeping the Commandments of God*, NSBT 31, Nottingham: Inter-Varsity Press.

Sabourin, Léopold (1980), 'Why Is God Called "Perfect" in Mt 5:48?', *BZ* 24: 266–268.

Sailhamer, John H. (1992), *The Pentateuch as Narrative: A Biblical-Theological Commentary*, Library of Biblical Interpretation, Grand Rapids: Zondervan.

—— (2009), *The Meaning of the Pentateuch: Revelation, Composition and Interpretation*, Downers Grove: IVP Academic.

Salter, Martin (2010), 'Does Baptism Replace Circumcision? An Examination of the Relationship Between Circumcision and Baptism in Colossians 2:11–12', *Them* 35: 15–29.

Sanders, E. P. (1985), *Paul, the Law, and the Jewish People*, Minneapolis: Fortress.

Sarna, Nahum M. (1989), *Genesis: The Traditional Hebrew Text with the New JPS Translation*, JPSTC, Philadelphia: Jewish Publication Society.

———— (1991), *Exodus: The Traditional Hebrew Text with the New JPS Translation*, JPSTC, Philadelphia: Jewish Publication Society.

Sasson, Jack M. (1966), 'Circumcision in the Ancient Near East', *JBL* 85: 473–476.

Schenk, Wolfgang (1984), *Die Philipperbriefe des Paulus*, Stuttgart: Kohlhammer.

Schippers, R. (1986), 'Τέλος', in *NIDNTT* 2: 59–66.

Schmithals, Walter (1972), *Paul and the Gnostics*, tr. John E. Steely, Nashville: Abingdon.

Schramm, T. (1990), 'Σφραγίς', in *EDNT* 3: 316–317.

Schreiner, Thomas R. (1983), 'Circumcision: An Entree into "Newness" in Pauline Thought', PhD diss., Fuller Theological Seminary.

———— (1985), 'Paul and Perfect Obedience to the Law: An Evaluation of the View of E. P. Sanders', *WTJ* 47: 245–278.

———— (1993), 'Did Paul Believe in Justification by Works? Another Look at Romans 2', *BBR* 3: 131–155.

———— (1998), *Romans*, BECNT, Grand Rapids: Baker.

———— (2010), *Galatians*, ZECNT 9, Grand Rapids: Zondervan.

Schrenk, Gotlob (1965), 'Ἱεροσυλέω', in *TDNT* 3: 255–256.

Seifrid, Mark A. (1992), *Justification by Faith: The Origin and Development of a Central Pauline Theme*, NovTSup 68, Leiden: Brill.

———— (2000), *Christ, Our Righteousness: Paul's Theology of Justification*, NSBT 9, Leicester: Apollos; Downers Grove: InterVarsity Press.

Silva, Moisés (2005), *Philippians*, 2nd edn, BECNT, Grand Rapids: Baker.

Skinner, John (1930), *A Critical and Exegetical Commentary on Genesis*, 2nd edn, ICC, Edinburgh: T&T Clark.

Smith, Ralph L. (1998), *Micah–Malachi*, WBC 32, Dallas: Word.

Snodgrass, Klyne (1986), 'Justification by Grace – to the Doers: An Analysis of the Place of Romans 2 in the Theology of Paul', *NTS* 32: 72–93.

Stählin, G. (1968), 'Ἀπρόσκοπος', in *TDNT* 6: 747–748.

Stanley, Christopher D. (1990), '"Under a Curse": A Fresh Reading of Galatians 3.10–14', *NTS* 36: 481–511.

Stott, John R. W. (1994), *The Message of Romans: God's Good News for the World*, BST, Leicester: Inter-Varsity Press.

Stuart, Douglas K. (2007), *Exodus*, NAC 2, Nashville: Broadman & Holman.

Thielman, Frank (1994), *Paul and the Law: A Contextual Approach*, Downers Grove: InterVarsity Press.

——— (2007), *From Plight to Solution: A Jewish Framework for Understanding Paul's View of the Law in Galatians and Romans*, NovTSup 61, 1989, repr., Eugene: Wipf & Stock.

Thiessen, Matthew (2011), *Contesting Conversion: Genealogy, Circumcision, and Identity in Ancient Judaism and Christianity*, New York: Oxford University Press.

Thompson, J. A. (1974), *Deuteronomy: An Introduction and Commentary*, TOTC 5, Leicester: Inter-Varsity Press; Downers Grove: InterVarsity Press.

——— (1980), *The Book of Jeremiah*, NICOT, Grand Rapids: Eerdmans.

Tigay, Jeffrey H. (1996), *Deuteronomy: The Traditional Hebrew Text with the New JPS Translation*, JPSTC, Philadelphia: Jewish Publication Society.

Wallace, Daniel B. (1996), *Greek Grammar Beyond the Basics: An Exegetical Syntax of the New Testament*, Grand Rapids: Zondervan.

Walters, Joseph A. (2002), 'Moses at the Lodging Place: The Devil in the Ambiguities', *Encounter* 63: 407–425.

Walton, John H. (1994), *Covenant: God's Purpose, God's Plan*, Grand Rapids: Zondervan.

Ward, William H. (1911), 'Habakkuk', *A Critical and Exegetical Commentary on Micah, Zephaniah, Nahum, Habakkuk, Obadiah and Joel*, ICC, Edinburgh: T&T Clark.

Weinfeld, Moshe (1970), 'The Covenant of Grant in the Old Testament and in the Ancient Near East', *JAOS* 90: 184–203.

Wenham, Gordon J. (1979), *The Book of Leviticus*, NICOT, Grand Rapids: Eerdmans.

——— (1987), *Genesis 1–15*, WBC 1, Nashville: Thomas Nelson.

——— (1994), *Genesis 16–50*, WBC 2, Nashville: Thomas Nelson.

Westerholm, Stephen (2004), *Perspectives Old and New on Paul: The 'Lutheran' Paul and His Critics*, Grand Rapids: Eerdmans.

Westermann, Claus (1969), *Isaiah 40–66*, tr. David M. G. Stalker, OTL, Philadelphia: Westminster.

——— (1995), *Genesis 12–36*, CC, Minneapolis: Fortress.

Williams, Demetrius K. (2002), *Enemies of the Cross of Christ: The Terminology of the Cross and Conflict in Philippians*, JSNTSup 223, London: Sheffield Academic.

Williams, Sam K. (1987), 'Justification and the Spirit in Galatians', *JSNT* 29: 91–100.

—— (1988), 'Promise in Galatians: A Reading of Paul's Reading of Scripture', *JBL* 107: 709–720.

Williamson, Paul R. (2000), *Abraham, Israel and the Nations: The Patriarchal Promise and Its Covenantal Development in Genesis*, JSOTSup 315, Sheffield: Sheffield Academic.

—— (2003), 'Covenant', in *DOTP*, 139–155.

—— (2007), *Sealed with an Oath: Covenant in God's Unfolding Purpose*, NSBT 23, Nottingham: Apollos; Downers Grove: InterVarsity Press.

Wilson, Lindsay (2015), *Job*, THOTC, Grand Rapids: Eerdmans.

Woudstra, Marten H. (1970), 'Toledot of the Book of Genesis and Their Redemptive-Historical Significance', *CTJ* 5: 184–189.

—— (1981), *The Book of Joshua*, NICOT, Grand Rapids: Eerdmans.

Wright, N. T. (1993), *The Climax of the Covenant: Christ and the Law in Pauline Theology*, 1991, repr., Minneapolis: Fortress.

—— (1996), *Jesus and the Victory of God*, Christian Origins and the Question of God 2, London: SPCK.

—— (2001), 'The Law in Romans 2', in James D. G. Dunn (ed.), *Paul and the Mosaic Law*, WUNT 89, Grand Rapids: Eerdmans, 131–150.

—— (2002), 'The Letter to the Romans: Introduction, Commentary, and Reflections', *The New Interpreter's Bible*, vol. 10, Nashville: Abingdon.

—— (2009), *Justification: God's Plan and Paul's Vision*, London: SPCK.

—— (2013), *Paul and the Faithfulness of God*, 2 vols., Christian Origins and the Question of God 4, Minneapolis: Fortress.

Ziesler, J. A. (2004), *The Meaning of Righteousness in Paul: A Linguistic and Theological Enquiry*, SNTSMS 20, 1972, repr., Cambridge: Cambridge University Press.

Zimmerli, Walther (1983), *Ezekiel 2: A Commentary on the Book of the Prophet Ezekiel, Chapters 25–48*, tr. James D. Martin, Hermeneia, Philadelphia: Fortress.

Index of authors

Index of Scripture references

Note: Primary discussions of a passage are often indicated in **bold**.

238

Index of ancient sources

Titles in this series:

An index of Scripture references for all the volumes may be found at
http://www.thegospelcoalition.org/resources/nsbt